Hispanic Young People
and the
Church's Pastoral Response

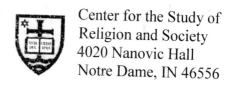

Center for the Study of
Religion and Society
4020 Nanovic Hall
Notre Dame, IN 46556

Prophets of Hope
> Volume 1
>> *Hispanic Young People and the Church's Pastoral Response*
> Volume 2
>> *Evangelization of Hispanic Young People*

Profetas de Esperanza
> Volumen 1
>> *La Juventud Hispana y la Respuesta Pastoral de la Iglesia*
> Volumen 2
>> *Evangelización de la Juventud Hispana*

❧ Prophets of Hope ❧

Volume 1

Hispanic Young People and the Church's Pastoral Response

Prophets of Hope Editorial Team

Saint Mary's Press
Christian Brothers Publications
Winona, Minnesota

OF HOPE

WITNESSES

The publishing team for this volume included Pedro Castex, Yvette Nelson, and Charles Capek, development editors; Charles Capek and Rebecca Fairbank, copy editors; Amy Schlumpf Manion, production editor and typesetter; María Alicia Sánchez, illustrator; Jayne L. Stokke of Romance Valley Graphics, cover designer; Francine Cronshaw, indexer; pre-press, printing, and binding by the graphics division of Saint Mary's Press.

Saint Mary's Press wishes to give special acknowledgment to the ACTA Foundation, for funding that helped to subsidize this publication.

The permissions are on page 291.

Printed in the United States of America

Printing: 9 8 7 6 5 4 3 2 1

Year: 2002 01 00 99 98 97 96 95 94

ISBN 0-88489-325-1

Library of Congress card catalog number: 94-066203

Prophets of Hope Editorial Team

General Editor: Carmen María Cervantes, EdD

Writers: Alejandro Aguilera-Titus
Carlos Carrillo
Pedro Castex
Carmen María Cervantes, EdD
Juan Díaz-Vilar, SJ
Juan Huitrado, MCCJ

Consultants: José Ahumada, CSC
María de la Cruz Aymes, SH, PhD
Rigoberto Caloca-Rivas, OFM, PhD
Rev. Ricardo Chávez
Juan Cruz, PhD
William McDonald
Gelasia Márquez
Isabel Ordoñez, STJ
Angeles Pla-Farmer
Elisa Rodríguez, SL
William Sousae
Carmencita Villafañe
Isabel Vinent

Translator into English: Richard Wood

Secretaries: Aurora M. Dewhirst
María Teresa Macías

❧ Contents ❧

To young leaders, youth ministers, and pastoral agents
who are giving their lives to carry Christ to Hispanic young people
in the United States.

❦ Preface ❦

1   Every year, the Catholic church in the United States includes more Hispanic (or Latino) members, nearly half of whom are less than twenty-five years old. These young people and young adults represent both a challenge and a hope for us, our church, and our society. They provide us with a challenge because millions of them are not receiving adequate pastoral attention. They give us hope because by incarnating the Gospel in their lives, these young people can help renew our church, transform cultural values, and build the Reign of God. To confront this challenge and make this hope a reality, we need Hispanics—both young people and adults—who fulfill their mission as Christians in the world.

2   In 1987, Saint Mary's Press in Winona, Minnesota, joined the effort to provide foundation and direction for Hispanic youth ministry by developing materials for publication. To identify the most urgent program needs, Saint Mary's Press representatives consulted with Hispanic pastoral leaders throughout the United States. This research led to the development of a bilingual series for the evangelization of youth and young adults and to the hiring of Dr. Carmen María Cervantes as director of the publishing program for Hispanic materials.

3   The need to have a pastoral-theological framework that would provide consistency and direction for these publications gave rise to the first draft of this book. In August of 1988, Saint Mary's Press hosted a discernment meeting about this framework and about related Hispanic publications. Twenty-four pastoral agents, representing eleven different Hispanic groups and their diverse ministries, attended that meeting. These pastoral agents established the foundation of the project, planned the materials to be published, and revised the first draft of the framework. A month later, participants of the discernment meeting and Saint Mary's Press representatives developed an editorial board that has played a crucial role in planning and revising publications and in identifying appropriate people to write materials.

4   Thirty people from around the country, whose careful analyses and suggestions proved invaluable, reviewed the second draft of the framework. The third draft was translated into English and refined through bilingual consultation. The final manuscript emerged from this consultation.

5   Developing and writing the pastoral-theological framework was complex and exciting. The broad pastoral-theological vision shared by the editorial team took root in the reality of Hispanic young people and became a source of direction for their evangelization, but only after many hours of reflection, prayer, and sharing of experiences. Seven persons wrote significant pieces of the manuscript, and several others contributed with their advice and editing skills, making a truly collaborative work of what came to be the Prophets of Hope Editorial Team.

6   Consultations in Spanish and English with experts in different fields, pastoralists, pastoral agents, young leaders—Hispanics and non-Hispanics—provided the comprehensive perspective needed in a publication that was dealing with the reality of Hispanic young people in the United States and attempting to provide a pastoral-theological framework for their evangelization. Two surveys were conducted in areas of key importance for the evangelization of Hispanic young people. The first one identified the reality of Hispanic youth ministry in the country. The second one provided insight on who Jesus is, what the process of evangelization is, and what the church means for Hispanic young people.

7   The reflections and input by the translator and the editors in English were extremely valuable. The translation was bicultural, meaning that several concepts, theories, and philosophical and theological approaches identified as hard to understand or easy to misunderstand by a non-Hispanic reader were clarified. The respectful, sensible, and careful reactions of Yvette Nelson and Charles Capek, who were not familiar with Hispanic culture and religious life, helped the editorial team tremendously in two ways: to see and value the many points of unity between the mainstream and the Hispanic pastoral approaches and to further clarify the differences between them. This crosscultural dialog gave origin to new sections in the framework that reinforce the identity and pastoral-theological vision of Hispanics in the United States who are faced with honest questions and the desire to learn from American pastoral agents of non-Hispanic background.

8   The complexity of the reality of Hispanic young people and the need to provide a pastoral-theological framework for their evangelization led Saint Mary's Press to publish two volumes of Prophets of Hope. This first volume focuses on Hispanic young people and the church's pastoral response. The second volume focuses on evangelization of Hispanic young people.

9   In a very special way, the editorial team wants to express our deep gratitude to Saint Mary's Press for making the publication of these two books possible; to Stephan Nagel, for his constant support and direction as editor-in-chief; and to Br. Damian Steger, FSC, president of Saint Mary's Press, for his patience and encouragement. We also want to thank those persons who helped to shape the manuscript with their valuable insights and all the other people who made the books in the Prophets of Hope series possible.

❧ Introduction ❧

Jeremiah: Prophet of Hope

1   Many years ago, a young man named Jeremiah lived among a people lost to their own egoism and idolatry and threatened by war. God made Jeremiah a prophet and gave him the mission of calling people to conversion—away from the greed, infidelity, and injustice that characterized their society. But the people would not listen, because, as has often been the case, the truth wounded and threatened them.

2   Perhaps some people thought of simply shutting Jeremiah up, of putting him back in his place, silent and obedient, until he learned to speak sensibly. Very likely, some well-meaning people tried to convince Jeremiah to be a "good" Jewish young person, to respect the laws and customs of his day and not rock the boat. After all, what could a young man possibly have to say to the adults, the wise, and the powerful?

3   It has always been difficult for people to hear the word of God when that word calls for change. When the word arises on the lips of youth, the difficulty is greater still. The words that Jeremiah spoke, however, were not exactly his own. They were the words of God, who called Jeremiah to cry out the hope that comes from conversion. Thus, Jeremiah spoke not only words of protest and denunciation but cries of hope to political and religious leaders and to other young people like himself—his sisters and brothers. His was a message of hope for all those who heard him, turned their hearts back to God, and straightened their life paths.

4   In facing God's call, Jeremiah felt afraid and insecure, felt his own inexperience and lack of qualifications:

> "Ah, Lord GOD! Truly I do not know how to speak, for I am only a boy." But the LORD said to [Jeremiah],
> > "Do not say, 'I am only a boy';
> > for you shall go to all to whom I send you,
> > and you shall speak whatever I command you."
>
> (Jer. 1:6–7)

Once he was convinced, Jeremiah fulfilled his mission with God's help, in spite of being misunderstood, scorned, and persecuted by most of his people.

5   Could God today be calling us through our young people? Do we hear them? Do the challenges and hopes presented by our young people call us to conversion? If we fail to hear the words of young Hispanics, if we fail to consider their actions, we once again fall deaf to God's prophetic cries. Today in the United States, Hispanic young people, like the prophet Jeremiah centuries ago, bring hope to a society often beset by greed, egoism, and idolatry.

Prophets of Hope

6   Prophets of Hope is a two-volume series that proposes a pastoral and theological vision for ministry with young and young adult Hispanics in the United States. This work brings together the social analysis, pastoral priorities, vision, and spirit of Hispanic youth ministry inspired by the three Encuentros Nacionales Hispanos de Pastoral, the *National Pastoral Plan for Hispanic Ministry,* and the call to a New Evangelization for America made by Pope John Paul II and ratified in 1992 at the Fourth General Conference of the Latin American Bishops in Santo Domingo.

7   The analysis of reality, reflection, guidance, and concrete suggestions for action that give substance to the pastoral and theological vision of Prophets of Hope is divided into the two volumes as follows:
- **Volume 1,** *Hispanic Young People and the Church's Pastoral Response,* is divided into eight chapters dealing with the personal, relational, cultural, sociological, and religious realities of Hispanic young people, and the response of the church to the pastoral needs of Hispanic young people.
- **Volume 2,** *Evangelization of Hispanic Young People,* is divided into eight chapters dealing with the evangelization of Hispanic young people, the evangelization process, a model of evangelization for small communities, and the role of Mary in these evangelizing efforts.

8   These two volumes are intended as *guides* for pastoral work and the formation of pastoral agents and young leaders. Volume 1's presentation of the reality of Hispanic young people and young adults is only a beginning and will continue to develop as this real-

ity is further studied and analyzed. The pastoral-theological vision is evolving and crystallizing through praxis and will be renewed as young Hispanics and those who minister with them put it into practice and reflect on that practice. Thus, to take full advantage of these books, readers must use their own creativity, experience, and reflection in adapting the material to their concrete reality. They must also avoid using the books as if they were textbooks or how-to manuals of techniques.

9　　　In using this volume, it is important to remember that the English concepts of *youth* and *young people* do not correspond to the Spanish concepts of *juventud* and *jóvenes,* although these are the correct equivalents in translation. References in this book to Hispanic youth or young people include Hispanic single young adults as well as Hispanic adolescents.

10　　　Special terms like *animation* and *mestizo* are boldfaced at their first occurrence in the book. A definition for all the boldfaced terms can be found in the glossary at the end of the book. Before beginning to read the chapters, we suggest that you scan the glossary to acquaint yourself with any terms that may be unfamiliar to you. Also note that the paragraphs in the book are numbered in the margin to make it easier for leaders to use both the English and Spanish volumes together in a bilingual setting.

11　　　We wrote this book for youth ministers, young leaders, pastoral agents, and adult advisers of young people. Prophets of Hope can also be useful to anyone who wants to understand more deeply the reality of young and young adult Latinos and improve their human and Christian formation. We share our hope that these books will stimulate dialog, reflection, and *pastoral de conjunto,* not only among Latinos but within the entire church.

12　　　We especially ask Mary to bless our young people and all those who minister to them. We pray that the Holy Spirit may fill us with enthusiasm and hope, so that our work will continue the work begun by Jesus, our brother and prophet of the Reign of God. In that way, we will fulfill with him his dream and his mission: to inaugurate the Reign of God among us.

Hispanic Young People and
Their Process of Maturation

Hispanic Young People and Their Process of Maturation

❧

$\mathcal{E}$ach one of you, young friends, is a favorite in God's creation. Therefore, you have been gifted by God so that you can flood the earth with God's glory, love, justice, life, and truth.

—John Paul II,
"Santa Misa con los jóvenes"

1   The clamor of young people can be heard daily, in innumerable cities and towns throughout the United States. In **Hispanic** settings, the clamor is especially strong, for Hispanics are a very young people: almost half of their population is under the age of twenty-five. The clamor itself rises in tones of hope and anguish, encouragement and reproach, challenge and promise. In this chapter, we introduce the challenges and hopes that Hispanic young people and young adults bring to the church, review the journey of Hispanic youth **ministry,** and reflect on the principles guiding Hispanic youth ministry and **evangelization** efforts today.

Challenges and Hopes

2   It is moving and inspiring to see groups of young Hispanics who struggle daily to grow and mature as human beings, to be faithful disciples of Jesus, to participate actively in the church, and to construct a better world. It is encouraging to see that many of these young people have the support of their families or youth ministers. It is heartening, though painful, to see that others persevere even without adequate support. These young people are a gift of God to our church and our world. How can we fail to perceive God's presence through them? How can we fail to hear them, hear their collective cry, as they ask for direction and support in their pilgrimage of faith?

3   What are we to think of the clamor of young people whose lives have been damaged by broken relationships, discrimination,

violence, drugs, **consumerism,** and promiscuity? What is the message sent to us by those young people who are stagnated in their personal development, who are indifferent to God, who do not know God, or who have a mistaken idea of God? The lives and unrest of these young people frequently produce lamentable situations. But these same lives are cries of challenge. We must listen to these young people and lift them up to Jesus so that their lamentations and cries of challenge may become cries of hope.

Bringing Jesus to All Walks of Life

4   The voices of many young **Latinos** are prophetic voices that speak out about human alienation and isolation from God. They cry out for a community of love and salvation in Jesus Christ. We need to challenge this alienation with a living, alternative **reality.** We need **pastoral agents** and committed young people and young adults who demonstrate the love and power of their faith, so that young and troubled Latinos experience God and are encouraged to follow Jesus. Above all, we need young and young adult Latinos giving witness to the hope that surges in them, shouting out the Gospel with their values and ways of life, and making Jesus present in the streets, schools, homes, work sites, and places of recreation.

5   Evangelization and **pastoral action** cannot be reduced to include only those young people and young adults who participate in youth movements or parish groups. Evangelization must begin with involved young people, but it also must go out and reach those young people who have forgotten or never received the Good News. This mission is the responsibility of the whole church, but above all, it is the mission of the young people. They are the prophetic voices that will be heard. They are the messengers of the Good News to their own people. Like missionaries they are sent by God to invite brothers and sisters of their generation to enjoy liberation in Jesus Christ, to participate in a community of disciples, and to construct a culture led by the values of the **Reign of God.** Young people who are alive in their faith shout hope with their very lives. And they can fill with faith the lives of others who, without realizing it, are looking for God.

Uniting to Transform

6   Pastoral action must make it possible for young people and young adults to find the God they are looking for, even when they do not

realize they are searching. It must allow their emptiness and desperation to be converted into life and hope. And although the success of making God present to many young people often depends mostly on the evangelizing zeal of Christian youth, adults are a necessary source of hope and support for both involved and alienated young people.

7   The quality of pastoral care provided by adults is vital for the Christian development of young and young adult Latinos. Therefore, adults wishing to participate in ministry to Latino young people must be aware of and live certain realities.

- They must understand deeply young Latinos' ways of being, cultural conflicts, questions, and religious longings.
- They must direct young people with a Christian style of leadership.
- They must identify and empower young leaders.
- They must plan activities that correspond to young people's reality, in order to make possible the incarnation of the Gospel in young people's lives and encourage them in their formation and mission as Christians.
- They must support young people in moments of crisis, counsel young people appropriately, share their joy, and celebrate life and faith together with them.

8   Young people and adults together must confront the challenges that today's youth bring to the church. Young people and young adults, when encouraged and supported by more experienced adults, will be able to fulfill their dynamic role and renewing function in the church, as Pope Paul VI indicated:

> We think that we have every reason to have confidence in Christian youth: youth will not fail the Church if within the Church there are enough older people able to understand it, love it, guide it and to open up to it a future by passing on to it with complete fidelity the truth which endures.[1]

Building a New Society

9   Although many young prophets today are not heard, just as the prophet Jeremiah in his time was not heard, their voices ring out nonetheless, giving testimony to the Risen Jesus, Savior of All Humanity. Sooner or later, the lives of these young people, like the life of Jeremiah, will bear fruit. The challenge of constructing a different society, once given to Jeremiah, now falls to young Latinos:

Then the LORD put out his hand and touched my mouth; and
the LORD said to me,
"Now I have put my words in your mouth.
See, today I appoint you over nations and over kingdoms,
to pluck up and to pull down,
to destroy and to overthrow,
to build and to plant."

(Jer. 1:9–10)

10   Building a new society requires creativity and rebelliousness.
This rebelliousness does not mean violence or hatred, but rather
nonconformity in the face of sin and the destructive values of society. Jesus was a rebel and a nonconformist. He protested against
Pharisaism, the behavior of a religious sect that put more importance in the law than in the **person.** He also rejected the elitism that
marginalized the poor, the machismo that alienated women, the
ritualism that killed the spirit. He opposed hypocrisy, **materialism,**
egoism, and violence. Jesus' protests, however, like Jeremiah's, were
not simple denunciations; they were cries of hope that became reality in announcing the Reign of God to the world.

11   Hispanic young people, in union with Christian youth of other cultures and all people of goodwill, must protest against the sins
and false idols of current society. We need the young people of our
church to proclaim the Gospel that inspires them and to denounce
everything that oppresses youth and the rest of humanity. As with
other Christian prophets past and present, the mission of young
people today is not basically or exclusively to protest, but to announce the Good News and create a new way of living, a way that
makes hope a reality. The young adults gathered in the Tercer Encuentro Nacional Hispano de Pastoral publicly recognized this mission:

As Hispanic young people, as members of the Catholic
Church, we wish to raise our prophetic voice in order to announce the values of the Gospel, to denounce sin, to invite all
youth to struggle for the Kingdom of God.[2]

Who Are Hispanic Young People?

12   In this book, when we refer to young people, we are generally
speaking about adolescents between fifteen and eighteen years of

age and single young adults between eighteen and twenty-nine years old; these are the ones who participate in Hispanic youth ministry. However, in this chapter, dedicated to the process of young people's maturation, we cover youth development from age twelve, which is about the time that adolescence begins.

13   Adolescence and young adulthood are stages of transition from childhood to adulthood, characterized by emotional and intellectual changes as well as by physical and biological changes. Identity formation is a particularly significant and almost universal part of growth during adolescence and young adulthood.

14   Probably the most fundamental question about identity that every human being asks is this: Who am I? This question is often asked intently by young people, because to some extent, *every* young person is a "living unknown"—a horizon open to the world, asking questions that are profound and difficult to answer: Why do I exist? What is important in life? Why do pain, illness, and the problems of life exist? What will become of me as I grow? What will become of me when I die? Young people respond to these questions as they come to know themselves, identify their needs, and discover their identity as Christians and as valuable members of creation.

Children of God

15   In their search for identity and for answers to the profound questions of life, young people need to be made aware of a basic religious truth: Human beings are by nature beings of great dignity. Every human being is created in the image of God, as the Bible reveals:

> Then God said, "Let us make humankind in our image, according to our likeness; and let them have dominion over the fish of the sea, and over the birds of the air, and over the cattle, and over all the wild animals of the earth, and over every creeping thing that creeps upon the earth."
> So God created humankind in [the divine] image; male and female, [God] created them. (Gen. 1:26–27)

16   Young people need to see themselves in relationship with God, other people, and their own inner self. In seeing themselves as children of God, young people can become aware that as persons they belong both to this world and to God. Their existence is rooted in God, for whom they live, die, and rise to eternal life. In seeing

all people as children of God, young people can understand that being human means caring for one's own well-being and for the good of others. In seeing their own self as an image of God, young people can find greater self-respect, shape their internal attitudes according to Gospel values, and day by day live closer to Jesus.

17   The formation of each young person's identity is vital. Young people need to know themselves, to be able to identify their feelings and talents, their limitations and weaknesses, their ideals and aspirations. By discovering these features, young people can internalize and order their values, clarify their ideals, and forge the discipline necessary for acting freely and responsibly. This process of discovery does not occur by itself or suddenly. It occurs gradually through reflection and the influence of others. Thus, life shared with a Christian youth group and the support of adults are both key in this growth stage.

18   Youth ministers, pastoral agents, young leaders, and Christian adults should encourage young people to reflect on the mystery of human existence and on the sacred character and value of every human being. Without such reflection, young people can easily fall into the trap of materialism and self-centeredness, of valuing persons according to what they possess and produce and not for who they are. Without a faith that recognizes the sacredness of all human beings, young Hispanics are left without a basis for finding dignity or meaning in life. They are left vulnerable to manipulation and domination by the destructive values present in society. Given the necessary support, however, young people can take advantage of their characteristic idealism and energy by responding positively and creatively to such destructive challenges—by becoming visible signs of the Reign of God.

Signs of Hope

19   The bishops who met in 1979 at the Third General Latin American Episcopal Conference, held in Puebla, Mexico, drew the following picture of young people:

> They are characterized by a non-conformity that calls everything into question; a spirit of risk that leads to radical commitments and situations; a creative capacity with new responses to a changing world, which they hope to keep on improving as a sign of hope. Their strongest and most person-

al aspiration is freedom, emancipated from all outside tute-
lage. They are a sign of joy and happiness. They are very sensitive to social problems. They demand authenticity and
simplicity, and they rebelliously reject a society invaded by all
sorts of hypocrisy and anti-values.

This dynamism makes them capable of renewing cultures
that otherwise would grow decrepit.[3]

20 We live in a period of time marked by profound and rapid cultural changes that frequently alter the points of reference by which
values are formed. These changes are so dramatic that among
young people separated by six or even four years of age, differences
in values and experiences can be so great as to be almost genera-
tional differences. Such differing realities broaden the already-
present generation gap and aggravate problems in communication
and understanding between Hispanic young people and their parents or other adults.

21 Further obstacles to communication and understanding are
present in the many contradictory messages our society offers:
• We claim to value people and the environments in which they live
  and work, but we place technology and profit above them all.
• We speak of human dignity, but we only show regard for people
  with power, high social status, academic education, and money.
• We speak of love, but we promote egoism, sexual aggressiveness,
  and marketable, short-term pleasures.
• We proclaim the value of the Hispanic family, but we live
  through severe family crises and ruptures.
• We mention the vitality and potential of youth, but we ignore
  young people, stifle them, or put them down.
• We develop vast technologies for communication, but we live in a
  vacuum of dialog or personal relations.
• We portray society as a community where everyone can participate and be responsible, but social discrimination and racism
  marginalize many people.
• We speak of multicultural awareness, but we fail to respect the legitimate rights and desires of each culture.
• We publicly promote freedom of thought and expression, but we
  privately manipulate, falsify, and suppress information and ideas.
• We generate an evangelism through the mass media and many diverse religious groups, but we often experience absence from
  God.

22   As the Latin American bishops pointed out, however, young people possess valuable qualities for confronting society's confusion and hypocrisy. Young people's critical spirit, nonconformity, and desire to be responsible for their own decisions help them to articulate ideals, discover new paths, and respond creatively to problematic situations. Their authenticity, sincerity, and search for meaning help them to struggle against social conventionalism and to be the protagonists of history. Their friendship, joy, and solidarity with their *compañeros* help them form Christian communities. Their willingness to work hard and make sacrifices in reaching goals; their courage and daring in the face of challenges; and their energy, hope, and open spirit carry them to great and noble projects. These characteristics, which define young people in their stages of growth, make Hispanic young people productive and transformative members of society.

Stages of Development in Hispanic Young People

23   Latino young people, like young people in any culture, pass through the normal stages of adolescence and young adulthood. They also exhibit the physical and emotional characteristics typical of most young people in these stages. In addition, however, Latino young people and young adults exhibit particular characteristics due to their culture and environment. These characteristics, as well as the factors that cause them, need to be considered in ministry to Latino young people and young adults. In this chapter, we reflect on the nature of young people in general and analyze the psychology, philosophy of life, social relations, modes of expression, and process of maturation typical of Latino youth and young adults.

24   Young people's personality formation and their productive integration into society require continuous development throughout their various stages of growth. These stages themselves vary according to culture and social environment. For instance, in the dominant U.S. culture young people are primarily defined by their level of schooling, whereas Latinos define young people according to their family role, responsibilities, and age. That is, Latinos often consider their sons and daughters as "youth" in a broad sense, un-

til the young people get married, leave their parents' home, or assume significant responsibility for themselves or their family.

25   The concept of adolescence also varies between cultures. Some people in the dominant U.S. culture define adolescence as extending to twenty-five years of age. Adolescence itself is then divided into three substages: early adolescence (ages thirteen through fifteen), middle adolescence (ages sixteen through nineteen), and late adolescence (ages twenty through twenty-five). In the Latino world, adolescence is seen as a shorter stage and is defined according to the accelerated physical and psychological maturation that occurs between the ages of thirteen and eighteen. After age eighteen, young people are considered young adults or adults, according to their roles and responsibilities in their family and society.

26   The age-groups ministered to in youth ministry also differ between Hispanics and non-Hispanics. Hispanic youth ministry includes young people from twelve or thirteen years old to unmarried young people in their middle or late twenties. In the dominant U.S. culture, youth ministry involves young people only from grades seven through twelve, and young adult ministry serves young people from ages eighteen to thirty-five, whether the young people are single or married.

27   Although Latino youth are much like other youth, Latino young people do exhibit particular characteristics due to their cultural and social environment. Not all young people pass through the same stages at the same age, nor do they exhibit the typical characteristics of a given stage with equal intensity. In general, Latino young people pass through adolescence more rapidly than do American young people of European descent. Many Latino youth cannot even identify the various stages in their own lives, because they move quickly from childhood to young adulthood as they confront responsibilities early in life.

Hispanic Adolescents

28   As understood by Hispanics, adolescence entails deep changes in both physiology and psychology, changes that occur between the ages of twelve and eighteen. Regarding psychological changes, adolescence is a time of idealism, emotional instability, social adjustment, and an increased awareness of problems in the world. Physiological changes primarily involve sexual maturation and

physical growth. Because of the importance that the process of sexual maturation has in young people's lives, the next major section of this chapter is dedicated to the process of sexual integration throughout life.

29   Adolescence can be divided into three substages: the beginning of adolescence (ages twelve to fourteen), the heart of adolescence (ages fourteen to sixteen), and the end of adolescence (ages sixteen to eighteen). Certain characteristics stand out in each substage.

The Beginning of Adolescence

30   Between the ages of twelve and fourteen, young Hispanics generally exhibit the following characteristics:

31   **They begin to be concerned about their own personality.** Young people who do not yet know themselves often feel confused or uncomfortable as they begin to look inward, examine their own personality, and discover themselves. They tend to be reserved, to focus upon themselves, and to think that their parents and teachers do not love or understand them. Thus, they feel insecure. To compensate for feelings of insecurity, young people place great emphasis on fashion, try to behave like adults, and look for friends with whom to identify and feel comfortable. They limit themselves to few friendships, generally with people of the same sex. Those friends become the mirrors in which young people see themselves.

32   **They show greater personal and social sensitivity.** Young people in general easily fall into moods and can quickly swing from feeling sentimental, happy, and optimistic to feeling sad, moody, or pessimistic. Young women generally overcome these emotional mood swings earlier than young men do and are able to establish more stable romantic relationships that are oriented toward marriage.

33   **They become more independent from adults.** Young people entering adolescence begin to show a greater capacity to take initiative and responsibility. They do not easily accept rules imposed by adults; instead, they ask for good reasons for accepting those rules. They reject paternalism and maternalism and demand recognition that they are no longer children. Because they are often insecure, however, young people are vulnerable to ridicule and prefer to be corrected privately by adults, rather than publicly.

34   **They are dynamic and restless.** Especially during their growth spurts, young people are easily bored and become anxious and restless when there is too much quiet. They need to be occupied, and they need to experience success in finishing their projects so that they feel good about themselves. In reading, listening, or conversing, they like new and varied themes that help them understand the meaning of their experiences.

35   **They show signs that their moral character is taking shape.** Younger adolescents still see the world and the society they live in as somewhat distant and mysterious. Because their analytic abilities are still developing, they are strongly influenced by the world but hesitate to make firm judgments about it. They become quicker to recognize injustice toward humans, however, and they broaden their vision of human rights by reflecting on their intuitions and specific experiences.

36   **In favorable conditions, they tend to develop a very personal relationship with God.** Young people who participate in religious youth groups or family environments seek out God for help and understanding. They tend to reject or question moral norms that are meaningless to them, and they consider the religious practices of most adults very boring. Those young people who are distant from God simply ignore religion or remember God only in times of extreme need.

37   **Physiologically and psychologically, girls develop more rapidly than boys.** Girls tend to mature earlier than boys both in their physiology and in their attitudes toward the other sex. Because the changes they undergo are not only dramatic but rapid, girls also tend to experience greater emotional instability than boys in the beginning stage of adolescence.

The Heart of Adolescence

38   From about fourteen to sixteen years of age, young Hispanics show these traits and developments:

39   **They fully enter into their own identity formation.** Young people become protagonists in the process of forming their own identity, attracting attention to themselves and looking for affirmation of what they discover about themselves. They tend to be

self-centered, to observe their own behavior and physical appearance constantly, and to spend much time enjoying or worrying
about what they see in themselves. Young people in the heart of
adolescence are especially vulnerable to peer pressure and thus always try to be on good terms with their peers.

40   **They develop their capacity for logical thinking.** Young people demand explanations and reasons for the behavior, ideas, and
rules of their parents and society. If the young people do not see
these things as logical, they tend to reject them. Although they demand this logic from adults, adolescents are not yet capable of be-
having entirely in accord with what they themselves believe and
think. However, they are able to recognize their own inconsistent
behavior.

41   **They need a group of *compañeros*.** Young people need a special group of peers, a group in which they are affirmed and can
freely express their rebellion and criticism against the adult world.
Young people's increasing sense of loyalty and fidelity is oftentimes
first applied toward their *grupo de compañeros*.

42   **They begin to seek out members of the other sex.** Young people spend a considerable amount of their time talking about their
peers of the other sex. They enjoy having a boyfriend or a girlfriend
but experience difficulty in maintaining stable relationships and
commitments. A heightened awareness of sexual orientation often
arises at this stage of development.

43   **Their relationships with other people and with God grow
more intense.** Young people broaden their interests to include environmental and social issues, and they begin to commit themselves
to the values they accept as their own. They continue relating to a
God who is centered around themselves and who gives them security or relieves their problems and anxieties. Young people become
more aware of the impact of religion on human life, and they begin
to personalize their faith by idealizing and internalizing religion—
or by rejecting certain religious beliefs and practices.

The End of Adolescence
44   By age eighteen, Hispanic young people are for the most part
done with the major physiological changes of adolescence, but have

not achieved maturity. Among the principal characteristics of young people at the end of adolescence are the following:

45   **They live out their desire for independence more intensely.** Older adolescents often try to affirm their own personality by opposing others, being unique, or seeking the admiration of other people. They increase their independence from and criticism of their parents. They reject the structures and discipline imposed by adults, even though they fail to find others that are satisfying. They argue in order to test their ideas, and they sometimes stay set in their points of view in order to affirm themselves as adults. Young people's attitudes toward friends, family members, and other people are often inconsistent.

46   **They explore the communal dimension in themselves and others.** Young people can see more clearly their relationship to the rest of society and begin to understand other people and other people's points of view. Older adolescents worry more about problems ranging from social justice to ecology, and they begin to take an interest in psychology, economics, and politics. They fluctuate between a revolutionary idealism and a defeatist pessimism. On their own, they do not easily take on social responsibilities, but they can do so successfully in groups.

47   **They develop their capacity for abstract thinking.** Young people at the end of adolescence can identify and reflect on the causes and effects of their actions. They can also *anticipate* the consequences that various personal and social actions may have. They begin to discern and specify their values, ideals, and goals more successfully. This ability for abstract reflection represents a key stage in learning to analyze life objectively.

48   **They frequently experience a strong religious crisis.** Young people proceed to voice doubts about their childhood faith and about the validity of religious practices. They tend to reject the church as an institution and try to build a religion to their own liking. They continue personalizing their experience of God. Older adolescents think that God understands their rejection of traditional religion, but at times they feel guilty about their religious doubt and their abandonment of religious practices. They understand Jesus as a model and friend of those who suffer, and they

become more aware of God's presence in the world. Despite the negative values and pressures peddled by a materialistic, egocentric world, young people can find support for resisting those pressures in Jesus and the Christian community.

Hispanic Young Adults

49   After they have passed through adolescence, young people enter a stage of greater emotional and physical stability. Their capacity for maintaining stable personal and professional relationships increases, as does their capacity for responsible reflection and action. Thus, young people entering adulthood can become *agentes de cambio*—significant, positive forces for change within their society and their church. In this stage, young people usually exhibit the following developmental characteristics:

50   **They focus on and search for their ideals.** Young adults have greater knowledge, understanding, and acceptance of themselves and others than they had as adolescents. Young adults are more aware of their struggle for a personal identity, and that struggle has a stronger sense of direction. They usually have more stable relationships with other young adults of both sexes. Their desire for intimacy and complementarity with a partner intensifies. They can make decisions and take on responsibilities without depending on a group of friends.

51   **They begin to order their values.** Young adults hold clearly defined ideals and can order their values, recognizing some as more important than others. They try to define their professional occupation and explore their religious vocation in life as a layperson, religious, or ordained minister. They are capable of objective critical analysis and can view their world with broader perspectives, relating human social problems to political and economic realities.

52   **They intensify their appropriation of faith.** Young people entering adulthood react less negatively to the religious beliefs and practices of their parents, reflect more on their own faith, and may take an interest in the Scriptures and in the history of the church. They relate better to God, primarily through Jesus—whom they can see not only in other persons but in social, cultural, economic, political, and religious systems as well. Because young adults no

longer need their social group to revolve around themselves, they are more capable of forming Christian communities.

Diversity in the "Young Adult" Concept

53   Because of the influence of the dominant U.S. culture, Hispanic ministry has begun using the phrase "young adults" to refer to youth over the age of eighteen. In the Hispanic context, the young adult concept embraces many diverse attitudes, situations, and life experiences of young people, all of which must be considered when ministering to them.

- First, we need to consider as young adults those adolescents who, often at age fourteen or fifteen, have immigrated without their family and now confront adult responsibilities. Many of these young people confront life by themselves and seek support from young adults barely older than themselves. Some of these young immigrants are received into the home of their extended family but have to earn their own living and send money to their families abroad. Others become migrant farmworkers, sharing their life with groups of older men and women.

- Second, we need to recognize those adolescents or young adults who have assumed financial responsibility for their family and totally or partially support their parents or younger siblings. Similarly, we must acknowledge adolescents or young adults who have assumed parental responsibility for their younger siblings.

- Third, we must emphasize and encourage the potential of those young adults—eighteen or older—who have acquired the rights and obligations inherent to their legal age and have taken on the civic responsibility of adulthood.

54   All of these realities deserve special attention because their implications at the personal and social levels are very different. It is extremely important to support and provide formation for those adolescents who do not count on their parents' support and who carry on their shoulders the weight of responsibility for their family. It is also necessary to recognize and emphasize the radical change that occurs when these young people make decisions and take on responsibilities that previously belonged to their parents.

55   Especially with older adolescents and young adults, youth ministry must avoid prolonging adolescent attitudes that retard young people's process of maturation. We must make clear to young

people their ability as adults to shape the society around them. Failing to emphasize the potential of young adults denies them their strength to become effective *agentes de cambio* for renewal in the church and for change in society. We must remember as well, though, that significant differences exist between eighteen-year-olds, who are just beginning to try out their freedom as adults, and twenty-five-year-olds, who have greater experience and responsibility in life.

The Process of Sexual Integration

56   Due to the importance of sexuality in human life, it seems necessary to discuss the process of sexual integration. Human sexuality includes four essential dimensions: the *relational,* which focuses on companionship and relationships between people of the same or different genders; the *reproductive,* which focuses on the biological aspect and its capacity to procreate; the *erotic,* which relates to sensual pleasure; and the *religious,* which links men and women with their Creator. Sexual integration refers to the interweaving of these four dimensions of human sexuality. Sexual integration is influenced by the other aspects of human development and impacts the total integration of the person.

57   Human sexuality begins at conception. As soon as a child is conceived, the process toward sexual integration becomes a dimension of the child's integral development. This process evolves continually throughout the child's life and presents specific characteristics at different stages. When this evolution does not follow a healthy path, the young person is at risk of having sexual fixations or regressions that may hamper his or her **holistic** development as a person and hinder his or her relationships with other people, specifically with those of the other sex. Christian formation in sexuality, especially in the adolescent and young adult years, should focus on facilitating the process of sexual integration.

58   The normal developmental process of sexual integration consists of the following five phases: the beginning of life, childhood, adolescence, single young adulthood, and the marriage option.

First Phase: The Beginning of Life

59   The first phase prepares the person for her or his sexual integration. This phase is marked by the combination of the sex chromosomes that determine the gender of the child. Each human being carries two sex chromosomes. In females, both sex chromosomes are female. In males, one sex chromosome is male and the other is female. When a man and a woman conceive a child, the child receives one sex chromosome from the mother and one from the father. Because the mother always contributes a female sex chromosome and the father can contribute *either* a female or a male sex chromosome, it is the father's chromosome that determines the gender of the child.

60   The process of sexual differentiation occurs in the fetus under the genetic influence of either two female chromosomes or one female and one male chromosome. About eight weeks after conception, the genital system of the fetus can already be identified as male or female. Before the child is born, the genital system has been completely formed.

Second Phase: Childhood

61   As soon as the child is born, he or she starts a second phase of sexual integration. This phase consists of integrating his or her sexuality into his or her emotional, intellectual, and behavioral life. As the child grows, the parents have an important role in assisting the child in his or her process of sexual integration. By talking openly about the differences between the sexes and about the process of creating life, parents set the tone for deeper dialog during the adolescent years. As families share their ideas about God's gifts of life and about the beauty and functions of the male and female bodies, they start a process of Christian formation about sexuality.

62   Major factors that can hinder sexual integration during childhood and adolescence are sexual molestation, rape, and incest. Young people who have suffered these types of violations to their human dignity require special attention, because the violations have strong physical, psychological, emotional, moral, and social effects. Parents and pastoral agents have a responsibility to identify these cases and to offer appropriate counseling to young victims. Such intervention is of paramount importance to the young victims' personal and social development.

Third Phase: Adolescence

63   In adolescence, issues related to sexual expression become very important and may excite young people more than anything else in their life. Young people need to befriend their sexuality and their sexual feelings gradually. They do so by learning to appreciate the power of their feelings, to think positively about their sexuality, and to make decisions about sexual activity that are consistent with their Christian values.

64   During adolescence, the reproductive system matures, making young people capable of procreation. The process of sexual integration undergoes a period of adjustment and thus requires special attention from parents and pastoral agents. The fact that adolescents are physically able to have children does not mean that they are psychologically and spiritually mature enough to have the kind of sexual relationships that are appropriate for married couples.

65   Fascinated by sexual pleasure, eager to grow up and mature, or fearful of being rejected by the person to whom they are attracted, young people become more aware of their sexuality during adolescence. Adolescents are so easily aroused by physical touch that they frequently equate every touch with genital arousal. In some cases, they become frightened by this arousal and may avoid all expressions of affection.

66   When adolescents have learned to differentiate between signs of affection and actions that lead to genital arousal, they can begin to express appropriately their femininity or masculinity in all their personal relationships, especially their relationships with friends of the other sex. Signs of affection such as embracing and kissing somebody in order to express care, compassion, and friendship should be differentiated from caressing and kissing that lead to sexual arousal.

67   Regardless of each young person's specific situation, adolescents need compelling reasons for not going "too far" or "all the way." They look for clear guidance, powerful motives, and forceful arguments to help them with their struggle. Moral norms that restrict sexual activity only to marriage are not enough. To overcome peer pressure and the influence of the media, young people need a Christian environment in which chastity is valued and virginity is not ridiculed.

68   By presenting adolescents and young adults with strong moral ideals and values regarding sexuality—ideals and values based on

Christian faith and Catholic Tradition—they are led to the conviction that sexual intercourse is sacred and should be reserved for marriage. On the contrary, imposing meaningless rules or generating false feelings of guilt usually assure rebelliousness, shame, and an unhealthy attitude toward sexuality.

69   Some powerful reasons to remain chaste during adolescence are the following:

- the need to foster self-identity, self-esteem, and self-assurance; to build self-respect; to develop communication skills; and to grow in freedom—all necessary qualities for any worthwhile human relationship
- the value of love for all people, and the reservation of sexual intercourse as an expression of love in marriage
- the need to learn as a couple how to sustain a relationship based on communication, respect, trust, and kept promises
- the development of will as a means of self-control that enables one to pursue other noble goals and to live according to personal values
- the interference an active sexual life may have on the education needed to succeed in one's career or vocation
- the need to avoid pregnancy and the responsibility it requires of each partner
- the avoidance of sexually transmitted diseases, especially AIDS

Fourth Phase: Single Young Adulthood

70   Young adulthood is the stage in which sexual integration, as well as other dimensions of personal and social development, should achieve maturity. Mature sexual integration can be achieved by single young adults and is not exclusively reserved to married couples.

71   People always relate to one another as sexual beings, therefore *all* their relationships have a sexual connotation. However, not all relationships between men and women imply or lead to sexual intercourse. Close friendships between men and women are more common in young adulthood, and as these relationships develop, other-sex friends may become confidants and sources of support for each other. Sometimes friendship leads to romance and then to marriage. Most of the time, however, it remains as friendship.

72   By integrating their sexuality into their emotional life, young adults become aware that love has the capacity to generate physical and spiritual life. By acquiring sufficient sexual maturity and

understanding of the physiology and responsibility of sexuality, young adults become capable of relating well with persons of the other sex and, when or if the time comes, of confronting the challenges of marriage.

73   In the Catholic Tradition, single people are called to live their sexuality by integrating it with the project of extending the Reign of God, giving life to people in ways other than procreation, which is reserved for marriage. It is in this context that celibacy makes sense. The relationships of a celibate person have all the dimensions of human sexuality except for genital expression. As Jesus did, so may single young adults bear fruit and build lives filled with love and commitment. Christians have seen in this type of life a sign of Jesus' radical commitment to his Father and to the mission entrusted to him.

74   Young adulthood is marked by the quest for intimacy and the strong desire for a loving sexual union. These natural yearnings make the practice of chastity a true challenge. At this age, and even during adolescence, some young people engage in "necking" or physical sexual stimulation that may lead to orgasm but that does not include penetration. These practices present serious problems not only from the Christian perspective but also from the psychosocial perspective, in that they encourage the use of sexuality for pleasure and consumption. In addition, this type of sexual activity can distract young people from the difficult task of developing good communication skills and can hinder the significant and profound dialog that leads to intimacy.

Fifth Phase: The Marriage Option

75   During the young adult years, most people identify their vocation and choose their marital status. To do so, young adults need to have self-confidence and the ability to discern the type of life that is right for them.

76   Although many people in today's world are getting married later in life or are deciding to live together as a couple without marrying, matrimony is still the most common goal among young people and the ideal for all Christian couples. Yet some young people choose to remain single, and some commit themselves to the priesthood or religious life. Each of these options implies a particular way to integrate sexuality into one's life.

77   Regardless of one's decision concerning marital status, the Christian ideal is to mature in the virtue of chastity. Chastity cultivates a spirituality that values the gift of sexuality and enhances respect of oneself and others. Chastity is an attitude directly connected to the integrity of the person and to her or his life of love. It helps young people to give themselves to others, to love and be loved, and to relate to many people in healthy ways, without having sexual intercourse outside of marriage.

78   Chastity supports the love among husband and wife and reinforces the exclusivity of sexual intercourse in marriage. The most perfect sign of sexual integration is the sexual relationship between husband and wife, usually known as conjugal love. The fulfillment of marital or conjugal love requires that both persons have a level of maturity sufficient to integrate their personal sexuality in the new reality of marriage without compromising their own identity. In addition, it implies an attitude of openness to procreation.

79   Sexual intercourse achieves its highest meaning in matrimony, where it becomes a key means for interpersonal communication. Sexual intimacy nurtures the spouses' love, intensifies and complements the encounter of the *I* with the *you*, has the potential to create a family and thus make fruitful the love between wife and husband, and provides a satisfaction that compensates the hardships of parenthood. In lovemaking, couples learn to both give and receive pleasure. This interchange of pleasure is rooted in the gift of sexuality given by God to both partners and linked to the responsibility, generosity, and fruitfulness of love.

80   Consecrated virginity also finds its meaning in a similar context of love, fidelity, commitment, generosity, fruitfulness, and chastity. Celibacy may be chosen as the best way for particular persons to work for the Reign of God and to deepen their relationship with Jesus, because they have received a call to the priesthood or religious life, or because they have the conviction that celibacy is the only way to fulfill their vocation to minister.

Masturbation and Homosexuality

81   Masturbation consists of seeking sexual pleasure by self-stimulation; it may arise from sexual impulses that are intentionally or unintentionally provoked in a person. In some cases, masturbation may be a psychological reaction to a sexual disorder resulting from

negative sexual experiences, such as incest or rape. Because masturbation may have numerous causes, it is important to help young
people identify these causes.

82   Generally, masturbation causes no damage on the biological
level. But on the psychological and social levels, it may contribute to
self-centeredness, **hedonism,** and difficulty in heterosexual relationships. However, masturbation has no direct relationship to homosexuality. Masturbation is more common among males and
among young people who lack healthy friendships or have a domi-
neering mother or father. In summary, masturbation may be destructive and may seriously compromise young people's process of
development and maturation.

83   Homosexuality is also an issue that parents and pastoral agents
must deal with openly and sensitively by doing the following:
- educating young people to relate to their homosexual peers with
a Christian attitude of respect
- helping to eradicate prejudices that label homosexuals as sick,
sinful, or criminal people and working to create a society that
does not oppress homosexuals
- helping young people who may feel confused about their sexuality to identify and accept their sexual orientation
- supporting homosexual young people in their inner struggles,
helping them to heal the psychological, emotional, spiritual, and
even physical violence they may have suffered

84   Homosexuality is not principally a sexual phenomenon. Rather, it is a personal condition of a human being. Homosexuality includes all aspects of the person and is marked by exclusive
attraction to people of the same sex. Science has not achieved clear
and complete knowledge of homosexuality, but it is generally accepted that homosexuality is not a disease or a deviant form of sexuality. Although the relative incidence of homosexuality arising
from genetic, psychological, or social causes is unknown, it is
known that there are genetic types of homosexuality and other
types that result from psychological problems or environmental influence.

85   The Christian vision of the dignity of all persons applies to
homosexual persons as well. They are sons and daughters of God,
just as heterosexual persons are. Thus, homosexual persons should
be treated with the same respect and love and should have the same

human and social rights as heterosexual persons. The church does not consider homosexuality a sin. However, it does see homosexual activity as a sin. Therefore, as with all unmarried people, homosexual people are called to exercise the virtue of chastity and abstain from sexual intercourse.

86   For cultural reasons, open homosexual behavior—as expressed in some parts of the U.S. dominant culture—is not common or acceptable among Hispanics. Therefore, Hispanic young people may generate a high level of anxiety when they discover feelings of sexual attraction to their own sex. Also, young Hispanics who are homosexual may suffer severe rejection, mockery, misunderstandings, and marginalization in their families and peer groups. These experiences generate a low self-esteem, a great deal of pain, and a sense of guilt that can threaten to destroy them. Ministering to young Hispanics who are homosexual requires a special formation in pastoral counseling and a special ministry to their families as well.

Challenges Faced by Young Hispanics

87   Although Latino youth in general face challenges similar to those faced by youth from other cultures, specific challenges and their degree of significance vary widely among Latinos. This variation results largely from the different environments experienced by each of the following Hispanic groups:
- recent immigrants
- citizens who have been in the United States for generations
- students in secondary schools
- students in colleges and universities
- persons in the military
- gang members and youth living in neighborhoods with gangs
- blue-collar workers
- migrant farmworkers
- professionals, or white-collar workers

88   To be effective, Hispanic youth ministry needs to evangelize from within the realities experienced by different groups of Latinos. Within these groups, however, certain principal challenges confront *all* Latino young people in their development as whole persons.

Positive Challenges

89 Among the most important positive challenges faced by young Hispanics are the following:

90 **Identity formation:** The formation of young people's identity tends to be very difficult emotionally for young people, because different aspects of their culture and environment often pull them in opposing directions and cause them much confusion.

91 **Maturation:** Young people mature as they confront life's realities and take advantage of their personal gifts and the opportunities offered to them by society. But this process is frequently subverted by social or economic discrimination, hedonistic and materialistic values, escapist tendencies, or the young person's own psychosocial problems.

Negative Challenges

92 Among the most important negative challenges young Hispanics must overcome are the following:

93 **Parents' traditionalist views about women:** Parents who were raised with traditional, conservative views about the role of women often forbid their daughters to leave home in order to continue studies of higher education. Such parents frequently oppose their daughters' desires to attend youth meetings at which both sexes are present and seldom allow their daughters to take leadership roles.

94 **The exploitation of women in the home and at work:** In the home, exploitation of young women commonly occurs when parents demand that their daughters give their full salary (from jobs outside the home) to the family, so that the sons of the family can continue their studies. At work, especially in domestic service, young women lack freedom and tend to work long hours for low salaries. In addition, many young women in domestic service are sexually molested by their employers. In extreme cases, young women feel they must become prostitutes in order to generate income for their family.

95 **An overall lack of security:** A general feeling of insecurity can be caused both by conditions in the family and by conditions in society. Within the family, parents too often lack the resources needed to give their children education and support. In society, factors

such as an environment of poverty, a lack of medical services, unemployment, and the prevalence of drugs and gangs cause great insecurity.

96 **Family disintegration:** The same factors that cause an overall lack of security can also lead to broken families. In a vicious cycle, broken families in turn can worsen young people's alienation in relationships and lead young people to drugs and gangs.

97 **Marginalization and discrimination:** In discriminating against and marginalizing Hispanics, society diminishes Hispanic young people's self-esteem, increases their frustration, and reduces their personal expectations and vocational opportunities. The gravest situations of marginalization occur in the poor barrios—Hispanic neighborhoods—of cities, among migrant farmworkers, and among young people schooled in Latin America who can only find work below their aspirations, training, and potential.

98 **Conflicts with parents' religiosity:** The parents of many Hispanic young people were raised within the **popular Catholicism** of Latin America, prior to the Second Vatican Council, with a limited catechetical formation and vision of faith—far away from the experiences of young people today.

A Challenge for Hispanic Youth Ministry

99 Human development and Christian formation are so intimately related that there cannot be Christian maturity without human maturity. Only within the process of their overall human development can Hispanic young people experience the Good News as a source of life that liberates them from oppression, reconciles them in their personal relationships, heals their interior woundedness, and encourages them to develop to their potential.

100 We in Hispanic youth ministry want to call Hispanic young people to a maturity that requires pastoral attention focused on the following:
- achieving the harmonious integration of young people's identity with their own unique personality
- promoting the development and utilization of young people's personal talents
- facilitating a continuous process of conversion and faith formation focused on a willingness to serve others

- providing appropriate spaces and opportunities for young people to express their feelings, articulate their experiences, and share their creativity
- maintaining hope by encouraging young people's human growth through moments of crisis, experiences of conflict, and struggles with the challenges that life presents

Volume 2 of Prophets of Hope, *Evangelization of Hispanic Young People,* focuses on the impact of evangelization in different aspects of young Hispanics' process of maturation.

101 Echoing the Latin American bishops who, at the Fourth General Latin American Episcopal Conference in Santo Domingo in 1992, stated the following, we also

> reaffirm the "preferential option" for young people announced at Puebla [and in the *National Pastoral Plan for Hispanic Ministry*] not merely in feelings but practically.

In order to make that option we propose that there be pastoral activity:

> —That meets the needs for emotional maturing and the need to accompany adolescents and young people throughout the process of human formation and the growth of faith.[4]

Human Relationships and Hispanic Young People

❖ 2 ❖

Human Relationships and
Hispanic Young People

❖

The Church offers itself to young people as a place to meet Christ the friend, who looks toward them and calls them; as a place to meet their sisters and brothers, particularly other young people; and as the path on which to encounter God.

—Consejo Episcopal Latinoamericano,
Yes to the Civilization of Love

1   Hispanic young people and young adults strongly value their human relationships and the companionship, friendly *convivencia*, understanding, dialog, mutual support, and *cariño* they find in their relationships. Young Hispanics show their natural willingness and great capacity to form relationships when they open themselves up to other people and establish friendships and youth groups. Unfortunately, many Hispanic young people live in environments where they experience tensions, frustrations, and misunderstandings that contradict their positive values and tendencies toward relationships. In this chapter, we speak about the **communitarian** spirit of Hispanic young people and about how to use that spirit to improve their relationships as family members, friends, and *novios*.

The Hispanic Communitarian Spirit

2   Human beings are by nature social, and young people are by nature curious and "searching." Thus, young people experience a special yearning to enter into contact with different people, social environments, and cultures. Young people and young adults alike yearn to meet, communicate with, and know other people; to understand and identify with other people's experiences; and to express welcome, friendship, and care for other people. At the same time, young people are eager for other people to notice them, value them, need them, and show them care.

3   In addition to experiencing these feelings, which are common in all youth, Hispanic young people and young adults also experience the movings of the Hispanic communitarian spirit. Hispanic people in general express a communitarian, cooperative spirit toward others in nearly all aspects of their lives, particularly in the following actions and attitudes:

- supporting their family, collaborating with *compañeros,* being loyal toward friends
- spontaneous socializing (*convivencia*) with, approaching, and welcoming of other people—even strangers
- acknowledging the need to both give and receive support, help, and hospitality
- showing a strong empathy for other people—being able to weep with those who are weeping and laugh with those who are laughing
- preferring open, inclusive, and friendly groups and bringing that openness to meetings, parties, and other celebrations
- displaying solidarity, companionship, and fraternal feelings toward other people that lead them to defend the rights of other people, organize *cooperaciones,* and make sacrifices for family, friends, and ideals

4   The communitarian spirit may be the greatest gift that God has given to Latinos to help them build a more human world in the midst of their tension, pain, and poverty. When this gift is valued, nourished, and well directed, it gives birth to a Christian solidarity that has great potential to revitalize the church and society.

5   When young Latinos face settings that inhibit or discourage a communitarian spirit, they try to bring into those settings the warmth, informality, joy, and openness that allow people to form a community. If the obstacles to forming a community are too great (due to individualism, legalism, or the presence of **cliques** in schools, work, or the church), young Latinos tend to marginalize themselves, close themselves off within exclusively Latino groups, or become bitter or vengeful.

6   Youth ministry should take advantage of the communitarian tendencies of Hispanics. By drawing on a communitarian spirit, youth ministers can initiate and reinforce the participation of Hispanic young people in the church, encourage young people's civic and Christian commitments, and improve their intercultural and

interracial ties. *Conviviencias* at the parish and diocesan levels are valuable opportunities for improving contact between young people and other generations, for countering individualism, and for promoting a healthy interdependence between young people, their families, and their community.

Hispanic Young People and the Family

The Latino Concept of Family

7   Generally, Latinos highly value the family as the source of *cariño* and support, the carrier of traditions, and the center of evangelization. The Latino concept of family includes both the nuclear family (made up of parents and children) and the extended family (made up of grandparents, aunts, uncles, and cousins—even of the second, third, and fourth degree; *compadres* and *comadres;* and intimate friends). In fact, the extended family includes many nuclear families that provide Latinos with a rich experience regarding the meaning of family. The Latino family emphasizes the inclusion of family members who live far away from one another as well as those who live close to one another. Normally, the family as a whole is more important than single members and more important than any other social institution. As a result, family obligations often have priority over other commitments and personal aspirations.

8   The family is a complex system in which people interact with and influence one another constantly, at many different levels and in many different ways. Family relationships evolve and change over time. Any change in the family or in a family member affects the life and vitality of the family and each of its members. As a rule, the family fulfills certain functions and has certain roles for all members:

- It defines and gives meaning to individual members' experiences.
- It establishes the possibility of living with joy, peace, and optimism.
- It consolidates the personality of its members.
- It is the most efficient support system for facing life.
- It is the most favorable environment for human formation and the development of children and young people.

- It is the natural means to introduce a person into the human family (society) and into God's family (the church).

9   Ideally, the family should be the center where young people develop, mature, and prepare themselves to form their own families. For the family as a place of formation, three of the most important elements are love, harmony, and unity. Without love, there can be no shared life, growth, or mutual improvement. Without a certain level of harmony, family members seldom feel secure enough to truly share their lives with one another. Without unity, significant shared life, which is vital for growth, is not possible.

10   Family unity and strong commitments to the family have traditionally been a part of Hispanic culture. However, as the National Conference of Catholic Bishops pointed out in their pastoral letter *The Hispanic Presence,* social pressures in the United States can weaken even that traditional unity:

> The unity of the Hispanic family is threatened in particular by the uprooting caused by mobility, especially from a rural to an urban life style and from Latin American countries to our own; by poverty, which a high proportion of Hispanic families endure; and by pressures engendered by the process of assimilation, which often leads to generation gaps within the family and identity crises in young people.[1]

Different Types of Families

11   In their ability to provide members with some basic resources for living, Hispanic families are usually at a disadvantage compared with most families in the dominant U.S. culture. Hispanic families have fewer opportunities for good health-care programs, their babies are less likely to survive the first year of life, and their elderly members are less able to live comfortably. Their level of education tends to be lower both in quantity and in quality, and they face greater difficulties in helping their children prepare for a professional career. Among Hispanics, chances are slim that one parent could remain at home to care for the children, that both parents together could pay for infant day care, or even that the family could afford to live in a neighborhood free of violence and drug trafficking. The income of Hispanic families tends to be lower than that of families from the dominant culture, even when the wage earners' level of schooling is comparable.[2]

12 Many Hispanic families find themselves making superhuman efforts to survive in the midst of these problems and to contend with the added effects of culture shock and social discrimination. Nuclear, extended, single-parent, and blended families alike try tenaciously to preserve an environment of warmth and security and to maintain with great sacrifice a sense of community and hospitality. But the discouraging fact remains that efforts and goodwill are not always sufficient and that many Hispanic young people do not experience the environment they need for favorable human development and Christian formation.

Nuclear Families

13 The Catholic church strongly values the nuclear family as a natural cell of the larger social body, emphasizing the sacramentality of marriage and the responsibility of parents for the procreation, nurturance, and education of children. Young Hispanics who are raised in nuclear families where harmony and *cariño* reign have beautiful and enriching experiences. Less fortunate young Hispanics, who live in homes with severe problems resulting from poverty, divorce, infidelity, physical abuse, addiction to alcohol or other drugs, or sexual abuse, usually suffer from emotional instability, low self-esteem, a lack of confidence, anxiety, hopelessness, and crises of faith.

14 Socioeconomic factors in the United States often push parents to work long hours to better their family or simply to survive. This decreases the amount of time parents spend with their children, their interest in hearing their children's problems and achievements, and their ability to support their children's studies. In addition, the resulting absence of parental involvement in the young people's lives produces an emptiness in the young people that neither economic advancement nor occasional luxuries (which many parents use to express their love and concern) can fill.

15 In U.S. society, the acceleration of cultural change, the excessive pace at which people live, the availability of drugs, and the easy access of sex bring devastating consequences to nuclear families. Many parents feel that when their children arrive at adolescence, peer influence becomes more powerful than parental influence. Usually, parents consider their own influence as formative and stabilizing but unappealing to young people. Parents perceive peer influence as more attractive to their children, but they also see peer

influence as causing rebelliousness and risky behaviors. In addition to these perceptions, parents have feelings of insecurity due to their personal limitations in raising their children in an environment foreign to them. Because of this, parents sometimes abandon their responsibility to their children—which in turn leaves their adolescent children in the hands of the youth environment.

16   Family unity can only be maintained with sacrifice, because unity demands from all members a good deal of generosity, understanding, openness to dialog, tolerance, and reconciliation. This unity is more difficult in families where young Hispanics consider their parents ignorant, traditionalistic, or out of place in the United States. In these cases, young people need strong support to shed the attitudes of superiority and rebellion that they feel toward their parents. Parents need equally strong support to talk to their children, to understand and trust them, to avoid misinterpreting their behavior, and to offer them adequate support and advice. The behaviors and attitudes of parents *are* decisive influences on their children's lives. Therefore, it is imperative that ministry to Hispanic young people involve the young people's parents, and that it collaborate with **small ecclesial communities,** the PTA, and other support groups for parents.

Extended Families

17   Extended families are more likely to train young people about living in society than exclusively nuclear families are. Extended families offer young people opportunities to have more and broader emotional ties—with family members, friends, godparents, and individuals with or without similar character traits, interests, and ideals as the young people themselves. Young people who have an extended family are highly fortunate, especially given the communitarian functions that extended families serve:

- They offer housing, counsel, food, or financial support when necessary, sometimes for lengthy or indefinite periods of time.
- They care for parents, grandchildren, or children of family members.
- They give moral, material, and spiritual support to widows and widowers, to divorced people, to women who have been abandoned, to orphans, and to ill family members.
- They take the place of the nuclear family during times of crisis.

- They help family members obtain work or education, often through an exchange of favors among extended family members, friends, acquaintances, and fellow immigrants.
- They provide an intergenerational setting in which the social and religious dimensions of life are celebrated.

18   Many young Hispanics who arrive in this country alone are taken in or supported by their extended family until they can strike out on their own. Young people taken in by their extended family need to be careful not to cause tension by abusing the extended family's hospitality or by being an economic burden. On the other hand, these young people should not allow themselves to be exploited or manipulated by unscrupulous family members. Young people in the latter situation need support to confront the situation or search out other alternatives.

19   The social environment of the United States does not foster thriving, extended families. First, simply by coming into the United States, immigrant families leave the extended family they knew in their place of origin. This fact causes parents in these immigrant families to experience a discontinuity that affects their good habits, customs, and values, which in turn has negative consequences for their children. Second, the majority of young Hispanics in the United States experience a world that is more limited in social relations than Latin America. This limitation weakens the Hispanic communitarian spirit, a weakening that in turn increases young people's vulnerability and diminishes their willingness to seek healthy support when facing conflict.

20   The formation of intentional small communities is a way to consciously reinforce extended families, wherever they exist, and to replace the loss of extended families for those who do not have them. Small church communities add the faith dimension to the richness of the family-type networking that is created in them, providing young people with an environment that is very valuable for their lives.

Single-Parent and Blended Families

21   Nearly a fourth of all Hispanic families are supported by only one parent, in most cases, the mother.[3] Divorce rates remain high in general in the United States, and a growing number of families are simply being abandoned by the father. Among Hispanic families,

the phenomenon of a father supporting one family in his country of origin and another here is becoming common. These situations cause heavy psychological and economic pressures that complicate the education and development of young people.

22 Nearly a third of all first marriages and *more* than a third of all second marriages in the United States end in divorce.[4] Children experience particular difficulty during divorce, because they often feel responsible for causing it. In many cases, before and after a separation, family dialog becomes extremely difficult, misunderstandings multiply, discipline diminishes, family time together decreases, and economic tensions intensify. When divorced parents remarry, they create homes with stepparents, half brothers, and half sisters. These blended families demand new psychological, social, and economic adjustments from young people.

23 Youth ministry should be a reliable source of support for young people who confront these family situations, because the resulting conflicts are too overwhelming for the majority of them to manage on their own. In stressful circumstances, which include the changing family structures mentioned here, a lack of understanding or emotional sustenance may lead adolescents to alcohol or other drug abuse, gang membership, sexual relations, or running away from home.

Families with Severe Problems

24 Normally, all families experience different crises, which sometimes are foreseeable and other times are unexpected. These crises can drastically affect the way a family functions—in the long or short term. Support to the family as a whole and to each member is key so that problems can be overcome before they seriously damage family members—especially the children and young people, who tend to be the most vulnerable.

25 Problems such as alcoholism and other drug addiction, poverty and unemployment, and sexual abuse and other acts of violence cause internal difficulties and unbalance the usual roles within families. In addition, young people frequently believe that they can solve their family's problems, so they take on more and greater responsibilities than they can manage. Failing to resolve their family's problems typically leaves young people feeling guilty and worthless. On the other hand, parents often evade their responsibility and

blame their children for conflicts caused by the parents themselves. The seriousness of all these difficulties makes it vital that young people have access to strong, reliable sources of support outside the family.

26 **Alcoholism and other drug addictions:** The abuse of alcohol and other drugs considerably worsens existing problems in the family. Many studies agree that parental use of substances is a major factor in young people's attitude toward and use of substances.[5] That is, when parents are addicted, young people often follow their example. And when young people become addicted to alcohol or other drugs, their parents frequently reject them and shut them out of their hearts and homes; or, on the contrary, they cover their child's addiction with excuses and unfounded hopes that it is only a temporary situation. Both attitudes make rehabilitation of the young people more difficult and increase the likelihood of their turning to crime or suicide.

27 **Poverty and unemployment:** It would be difficult to overemphasize the impact that poverty and unemployment can have on the health of families, especially the health of young people. Food, shelter, medical care, and even education are all-too-dependent on income. But poverty and unemployment may affect far more than just these basic needs. Emotional and economic instability in the parents oftentimes cause problems of physical and emotional safety in the home:

> Perhaps the most common social-structural explanation of child abuse is that it results from stress caused by economic hardships associated with inequality, poverty, and unemployment. . . .
>
> . . . 48 percent of the fathers in [a] U.S. sample of child abusers had experienced unemployment during the year preceding the abuse.[6]

28 **Sexual abuse and other violence:** Although the family can be a paradise offering love, security, shelter, clothing, sustenance, and mutual support, it is also the most common setting for violence. According to FBI statistics, about 20 percent of all murders in the United States are committed between family members, and nearly 33 percent of all female homicide victims are killed by their

husbands or boyfriends.[7] Regarding sexual abuse, one examination of adolescents in the United States had this to say:

> The AMA White Paper reports an estimate that 6 percent of boys and 15 percent of girls have been sexually abused prior to their sixteenth birthdays. . . . Incest is a serious problem among teenagers; 60 to 70 percent of foster children, runaways, and serious drug abusers report experiencing incest in their lives.[8]

Machismo and Hispanic Families

29   Much has been said about machismo as a cause of problems in Hispanic families. Because Hispanic men are so easily stereotyped as *machistas,* it is important to distinguish between a *machista* attitude and the strong, vigorous attitude a male has toward his family and the world. The strong, healthy attitude of a well-adjusted male includes positive characteristics such as courage, honor, respect for others, a sense of responsibility for the well-being of the family and for maintaining good family relationships, and an ability to defend oneself and one's family members. The *machista* attitude, which causes many problems, includes negative characteristics such as a sense of superiority and absolute authority over women, highly aggressive behavior, an irrational insistence on achieving a particular goal—whether that goal is important or not—and a stubborn resistance to personal change.

30   Machismo exists in all cultures and displays certain characteristics in each one. The display of machismo by men in Latino families in the United States frequently becomes exaggerated because of the many strong tensions that Latino men confront—the unequal education they receive, their lack of economic means to provide for their family, and their limited ability to dialog with their children, support them in an unfamiliar or alien school system, or educate them in the midst of contradictory cultural values and traditions. In struggling with these tensions, some Latino men may lose their self-esteem and their status or authority at home. Thus, they may try to compensate for these losses by exaggerating the attitudes and behaviors identified with their role as a "man." The families most affected by *machista* attitudes are those in the lower socioeconomic levels, where men usually lack the support and formation necessary to overcome the hostile and challenging environments in which they live.

31   *Machista* attitudes have a powerful effect on the freedom of women and the personal and social development of both men and women. In many marriages, the husband forces his wife and frequently his daughters to take on all the household labor as well as the care of the children. These demands prevent the women from continuing their education, making their own decisions, or engaging in social activities or responsibilities outside the home. When machismo is exercised at its peak, women suffer degradation, psychological and emotional manipulation, and sexual or physical abuse. Such situations can create unhealthy **codependent** relationships that require special attention to be repaired.

32   A *machista* father frequently detaches himself from truly helping to raise his children and settles instead for giving orders and dictating rules. He thus fails to enrich his capacity for dialog and understanding. At the same time, he thinks that he is "king of his castle" and has already achieved his goal in life, when in fact he has only succeeded in stalling his personal development.

33   Youth ministry needs to help young people deal with machismo at home when it is hurting them. It should also strive to abolish machismo among young people by promoting a change of attitude among young men and women. Men must recognize the natural equality and dignity of both sexes, learn to relate to women as *companions* in life's journey rather than as servants, and stop seeing the promotion of women as a threat to their "male supremacy." Women must demand their rights, which include an equal sharing of responsibilities by men in the home. All couples must prepare to educate their children with a focus on equality, in keeping with the Christian spirit.

34   In view of this, youth ministers, pastoral agents, and young leaders should question their own attitudes regarding machismo. How were they raised? What is their attitude toward the other sex? What do they need to do in order to have healthier relationships as men and women?

Youth Ministry and Family Life

35   The development of young people depends greatly on the quality of their family life and on their relationships with their parents and their siblings. In and through the family, young people can be educated, come to know Jesus, learn to pray, and discover the Christian

life. When love, recognition of personal dignity, unselfish service to others, and profound solidarity inspire the life of the family, young people experience intensely the value of community. Thus, the family is the most effective promoter of authentic communion and maturity, the earliest and most irreplaceable shaper of society, and the example and motivator for all community relations lived out in a climate of respect, justice, dialog, and love.

36   To promote healthy family environments for young people, and to encourage a spirit of community, youth ministry should do the following:

- offer an environment of welcome, *cariño*, accompaniment, and security—an environment that shapes young people with a spirit of unselfish generosity, self-discipline, sacrifice, service, and hospitality
- have a strong family dimension that emphasizes the value of the sacrament of marriage and offers courses to prepare young people for family life
- promote access to professional counseling services that are sensitive to Hispanic culture and to young people's stages of development
- develop counseling abilities among young people and young adults so that they can support their friends who are experiencing family conflicts
- facilitate dialog between young men and women in order to improve their understanding of the other sex and to cultivate the experiences of equality and reciprocity that are necessary for overcoming *machista* attitudes

Friendship Among Hispanic Young People

37   Friendship is a fundamental and vital element in life for all young people. To experience friendship with other people is to know the joy of a warm relationship, to be generous toward and receptive to the generosity of others, to share one another's interior life and individuality, and to strive for a material and spiritual unity. Friends are willing to share what they own and what they are and to find greater happiness in giving than in receiving.

38   Hispanic young people and young adults have a great capacity to establish enduring and profound friendships that constantly pro-

vide them with warmth, generosity, and loyalty. The Hispanic spirit of family includes friends and *novios*. This spirit is expressed in the willingness of young people to put a friend's well-being ahead of their own and oftentimes to marry motivated by a desire to help their boyfriend or girlfriend. Young people frequently consider their friends as brothers and sisters and thus may bring them to their parents' home as family members—living out the popular sayings *"de pared a pared, todo es colchón"* ("from wall to wall, all is a big mattress") and *"donde comen cinco, comen seis"* ("where five eat, six can eat").

39   When young people are truly friends, they make friendship an extension of themselves and may carry this attitude into the world around them. The friend of a friend is considered a friend of oneself, an attitude that continually opens families and social groups to new members. Young Latinos demonstrate their warmth and friendship by taking an interest in what happens to their friends, creatively seeking out ways to contribute to their friends' happiness, expressing solidarity with their friends' pain, and offering their friends help and support. This type of friendship establishes roots for an authentic and lasting love.

40   When it is founded on love, friendship safeguards, encourages, and exalts personal authenticity; it becomes the base for young people's pursuits in life, philosophy of life, and struggles for a better world. Spending time, sharing, and struggling together all highlight the communitarian aspect of love. Friends watch out for one another and orient this mutual care toward intimacy, confidence, and sacrifice.

41   Like every aspect of life, however, friendship confronts certain dangers and is vulnerable to certain abuses. When young people seek friends out of self-interest or egoism, friendship becomes corrupted. When adults demand respect from young people but do not give young people respect in turn, true friendship is not established. Youth ministers in particular need to appreciate and respect young people's genuine emotions and expressions and avoid legalistic or moralistic attitudes in relating to young people. Such attitudes can only alienate and repel young people, who look on youth ministers as friends.

42   Similarly, the creation of groups or small communities of young people should be considered a fundamental aspect of youth ministry. Within small communities or groups, young people can

develop in themselves an attitude of service to others, and can share their affection in a Christian setting. Young people learn about the way the other sex thinks and acts, so that communication and mutual understanding between young women and men improve. Warm, communitarian environments nurture and encourage young people's solidarity and missionary spirit, motivate young people to celebrate their faith, and favor group reflection and dialog.

Human Sexuality and Hispanic Young People

43   In spite of the general impression that most young people in the United States are experts on sex, it is clear that the majority of them do not receive adequate education about sex or sexuality. For Hispanic young people in particular, this incomplete understanding about sexuality has its origin in three major limitations of their human formation. First, the concept of human sexuality is commonly misunderstood and frequently limited to sexual intercourse. Second, the differences between the two sexes have been traditionally seen from a patriarchal perspective. Third, the cultural and religious traditions of Hispanics have strong taboos against speaking openly about sexuality—a restraint that has strong negative consequences.

44   Hispanic families usually address sexuality only within moralistic perspectives that regard the topic with shame, prohibition, and punishment. These taboos and moralistic perspectives cause feelings of confusion and guilt among young people, who are naturally curious about sex. Sex thus becomes the subject of "sinful" curiosity and "dirty" jokes among young people and their friends, a result that contradicts biblical perspectives on sexuality and reduces its beauty and dignity.

A Holistic Perspective on Human Sexuality

45   As an integral part of human nature, sexuality is expressed in nearly all aspects of human beings' lives—in their relationships with themselves, with others, with God, and with the world. A person's sexuality has three major dimensions, all of which are intimately related and cannot be separated from one another:
• The *biological dimension* consists of the morphological (physical),

genetic, and hormonal characteristics that help define the sex of a person. The combination of these three biological factors determines the sexual physiology of a person and influences his or her behavior.

- The *sociocultural dimension* refers to the way people live out their sexuality, projecting it into the outward, "social" part of their life. The sociocultural dimension of people's sexuality results from the type of education about sexuality that they receive at home and the way they are socialized by society.
- The *personal dimension* consists of the particular way people combine their biological sexual characteristics, education about sexuality, **socialization,** and individual psychological traits as a source of strength for their personal development and as a reality out of which they live their values. People's attitudes toward life and their means of communicating with others result in large part from the personal dimension of their sexuality.

46   Our identity as female or male persons is an essential part of what God intended in creating human beings. In being created, we receive sexuality as a gift of God, and from the Bible, we learn of the natural dignity that God intended for sexuality: "The man and his wife were both naked, and were not ashamed" (Gen. 2:25). The Bible also indicates that both men and women, in equal measure, reveal themselves as images of God:

> Then God said, "Let us make humankind in our image, according to our likeness. . . .
> So God created humankind in [the divine] image; male and female, [God] created them. (Gen. 1:26–28)

Remembering this basic equality and keeping in mind the three major dimensions of human sexuality can help us arrive at a holistic perspective on human sexuality.

The Relationship Between the Sexes

A History of Patriarchy

47   Although the roots of Christian tradition clearly state that God created men and women with the same nature, to reveal through themselves the same God, even "Christian" societies have rarely recognized or lived out this equality. For the last two thousand years, in fact, most societies have been patriarchal in both

outlook and operation. In patriarchal systems, men and masculine qualities are considered superior to women and feminine qualities, a situation that almost by definition oppresses women. The Catholic church, as part of a patriarchal historical tradition, still maintains structures and philosophies that marginalize women, though to a certain extent these are being overcome by society.

Unhealthy Behaviors and Attitudes

48   Many Hispanics, including pastoral agents, youth ministers, parents, and young people, have been raised with unhealthy attitudes about both their own sex and the other sex. In order for people to achieve healthy attitudes toward their own sex, the other sex, and sexuality in general, society will have to re-educate people about and struggle against the following behaviors and mind-sets:

49   **An attitude of male superiority:** The attitude of "male superiority" comes from the patriarchal structure of our Western culture, in which men have been considered naturally superior to women. Qualities traditionally associated with men, such as physical strength, aggressiveness, competitiveness, and the ability for analytical thinking, have thus been valued more than qualities traditionally associated with women, such as caring, accommodation, cooperativeness, and the ability for intuitive thinking. **Fundamentalist** readings of the Bible have often been used to justify or reinforce "male superiority"; chapters 2 and 3 of Genesis, in which the woman is said to be made from the rib of the man and in which the woman leads the man to sin, are frequently used to rationalize men's oppression of women in the family and in society.

50   **The repression of "feminine" qualities in men:** In general, Hispanic men are raised with the idea that they should not show or express feelings of affection, such as tenderness, caring, and concern. Likewise, Hispanic men are also taught not to show feelings of "weakness," such as anguish, sadness, and worry, because these feelings supposedly belong only to women. The repression of these feelings, which begins early in childhood, restrains boys and young men from speaking freely about their inner self, makes dialog about interpersonal conflicts difficult for them, forces boys and young men to wear "masks" of false strength, and promotes authoritarianism as a **defense mechanism.**

51   **A disregard for the value of women to society:** Although women are gaining more respect for their contributions and value to society, the fact remains that most women's contributions are either unrecognized or devalued. In general, in Hispanic families, a woman's work at home is considered without socioeconomic value. A husband controls his wife's time outside of the house, and women are allowed to work outside the home only in situations of economic need—not for their own development or for the good of society. These problems are common among immigrant families, and they create strong conflicts for Hispanic young women who, influenced by the greater equality and respect given to women in the United States, want to continue their own development and be active in church ministries or community services.

52   **The glorification of women:** A way of compensating for the low value assigned to women is by exalting some of their "traditional" qualities and placing them on a pedestal. This attitude, which may be unintentional, is a form of not accepting women as equals. When women are glorified, they are removed from reality and considered above their basic needs as human beings. In addition, they are expected to have strong virtues and moral strength in all circumstances, and they are supposed to ignore or sublimate their feelings of anger because of these situations. As a result, many women increase their sacrifice and self-denial, which in turn tends to place them on an even higher pedestal. Oftentimes, this glorification helps to disguise the way women are exploited in the home and in society.

53   **An attitude of contempt for men by women:** For a variety of reasons (economic, social, psychological), many Hispanic men abandon their wife and children. Other men try to escape from the hard realities of life through alcohol. Still others, unable to cope with their daily struggles and the cultural changes and challenges they face, may just give up trying to cope with them. As a result, many Hispanic women have sustained and raised their families by themselves. The frequency of these situations among Hispanic families has provoked women's contempt for men, a contempt that boils down to the attitude "Men are good for nothing." Obviously, both sexes lose when such a negative attitude is generalized to all men.

Approaches to Male-Female Interactions

54   In order to overcome the unhealthy behaviors and attitudes just mentioned, the two sexes need to approach the interactions with each other with an awareness that characteristics traditionally thought of as either masculine or feminine are found in *both* sexes. This approach is known as the *reciprocity* approach. Previous approaches to male-female interactions have considered the differences between the sexes from *superior-inferior, parallel,* or *complementary* perspectives:

55   **The superior-inferior approach:** The superior-inferior approach corresponds to a patriarchal position and simply maintains that men are, as a group, superior to women. Throughout history, men have created "scientific" studies, psychological theories, philosophical ideologies, and social systems to "prove" the validity of this approach, which has thus become institutionalized in patriarchal social structures. Transforming these structures is taking considerable efforts from conscientious women and men.

56   **The parallel approach:** The parallel approach assigns one particular set of qualities to women (such as caring, tenderness, emotionality, subjectivity, intuitive thinking, and a spirit of acceptance, preservation, endurance, and abnegation) and another set of qualities to men (such as self-control, objectivity, analytical thinking, assertiveness, and creativity) without acknowledging that such qualities are shared by both sexes. This approach leads to a lack of understanding and dialog between the sexes as well as to tensions and destructive competition. Moreover, in the parallel approach, women's qualities are still considered inferior to men's qualities.

57   **The complementary approach:** The complementary approach views each sex as having different characteristics that the other sex needs; that is, men and women are viewed as having to interact with each other to complement or "complete" each other. From the psychological perspective, this approach considers both men and women incomplete human beings. From the physiological perspective, the sexes are complementary in order to procreate new human beings. If these two different dimensions of complementarity are confused, the acceptance of celibacy, even for the sake of a full commitment to the priesthood or religious life, is made difficult.

58   Like the two previous approaches, the complementary approach tends to reinforce an attitude of male superiority. Men are

considered to complement women with the valuable traits that women lack, but women's qualities are put "at the service of" men.

59   **The reciprocity approach:** Unlike the superior-inferior, parallel, and complementary approaches, the reciprocity approach recognizes that although men are primarily "masculine" in their psychological characteristics, they also have traits traditionally considered feminine. Likewise, this approach recognizes that women are primarily "feminine" in their psychological characteristics, but they have traits traditionally considered masculine. In reality, the traits themselves are neither masculine nor feminine; they simply tend to be exhibited more strongly and with greater frequency in the members of one sex rather than in the members of the other sex.

60   Under the reciprocity approach, women and men come to know themselves and each other through dialog about the reciprocal relationship between them. Both sexes recognize the fullness of their own sex and the other sex. Also, both acknowledge the tremendous potential for mutual enrichment that exists when they share experiences, live, think, and act together, in communion. Differences between the sexes are recognized, accepted, and valued as constructive parts of a growing, diverse community. In the perspective of the reciprocity approach, people's ability to accept and deal with one another, and to form community with one another, despite their differences, constitutes the strength of their human identity and personality.

61   Youth ministers need to pay special attention to how they deal with the sexual development and interaction of Hispanic young people and young adults. The impact that a particular approach has on young people today may also have effects that reach far into the future, because today's young people have in their hands the formation of future Hispanic generations.

The Impact of Social Change on Sexual Attitudes

62   The way a society is structured and carries out its socioeconomic functions has considerable influence on the sexual attitudes and behaviors of its people. For example, agricultural societies rely on large families to cultivate the soil and thus tend to have many children, while industrial societies try to control the birth rate. Societies that foster equality between the sexes allow for more social

and political participation of women, a fact that influences the relationship between the sexes.

63   The radical changes that have occurred over the last three
decades in the way our culture treats sexuality have had both positive and negative consequences. Among its positive fruits are the
following: an increased knowledge and understanding of sexuality,
a better balance between the feminine and the masculine aspects of
sexuality, and a reduction of social prejudices and sexual taboos.
These changes have encouraged a healthier and more integrated approach to sexuality, made feelings of guilt attached to sexuality less
intense and less common, and fostered a sexual ethic that in some
ways better corresponds to the human condition and to Christian
values.

64   On the negative side, changes in sexual attitudes have made
sexual intercourse seem commonplace, favored the use of sex as a
narcotic in the face of life's anguishes, and encouraged multiple sexual relations as compensation for a lack of personal maturity. In addition, by emphasizing individual judgment rather than collective
wisdom, and an egocentric self-understanding rather than a communitarian self-understanding, sexual attitudes common nowadays
have undermined marriage and the family as regulators of sexual
relations. In the process, unsatisfying and poor-quality sexual relationships have become widespread among young people and adults,
and sexual intercourse has become dissociated from marital fidelity. All these changes have had devastating personal and social consequences for humans, especially for young people.

65   Today, many young people see themselves fundamentally as
human beings in search of sexual pleasure. They view sexual intercourse as a biological *need* to be fulfilled, as an act that has little or
no connection to marital commitment. They dissociate sexuality
from procreation and value sexual pleasure as a success in itself.
They become anguished when they cannot achieve this "success."
Young people thus become slaves to sexual activity, because they do
not understand its expression in the personalized, committed, and
loving context of a marriage relationship. Oftentimes young people
think that premarital sexual activity is fine because it is so common. Many involve themselves in sex with a consumer attitude;
others think that "the important thing is to enjoy without risk."
These attitudes allow young people to avoid making the commitment required to mature fully as human persons in a sexual rela-

tionship. In addition, they put young people at risk of sexually transmitted diseases or unwanted pregnancies.

Stresses in Sexual Maturation

66 Sexuality is an essential component of the human personality. To a large extent, a person's sexuality influences the way that person feels, understands, and expresses reality, as well as the way that person establishes relationships, experiences love, and solves problems. Sexual consciousness emerges slowly throughout a person's life, but due to hormonal changes, it becomes more intense during puberty, adolescence, and young adulthood. This process of sexual maturation is characterized by a heightened interest in sexual issues and the physical appearance of the other sex, and by sexual attraction and arousal. These increased sexual tensions in young people need to be acknowledged (by both young people and adults) and dealt with in a way that provides young people with a healthy self-knowledge and self-respect, as well as with appropriate releases for these tensions.

67 Changes in young people's reproductive system and in their interests, attitudes, and behaviors make up a large part of young people's development during adolescence and young adulthood. Strong preoccupations with issues of sexuality are generally temporary, as are the psychological crises and sudden mood swings common in adolescence. However, when these crises are not resolved during adolescence, serious problems may arise. These problems tend to occur when young people's expression of sexuality is isolated from the rest of their human experience, limited to seeking genital pleasure, or tainted with taboos that make them think sexuality is sinful or undignified.

68 Young people in the United States live in an eroticized society that offers an overabundance of available, commercialized, and cheap sexual activity. Humans are reduced to objects, and both humans and objects are eroticized in order to generate profits. These circumstances reduce human sexuality to its genital expression and do not consider sexuality an integral part of the human personality, thereby devaluing the integrity or "completeness" of the human person.

69 Viewing sexuality simply as genital sexual expression subverts young people in a number of ways:

- The severing of sexual relations from their intended expression in a marriage relationship severs a committed, caring covenant of love.
- It leaves young people empty and unsatisfied by removing the emotional dimension and the transcendence of love.
- It degrades young people's dignity as persons, making them easy prey for prostitution and sexual commercialization.
- It promotes the exploitation of women and men as sexual objects and accords women and men value *only* as sexual objects.
- It emphasizes and encourages superficial, loveless relationships.
- It leads to the procreation of unwanted children, for whom young people are generally unprepared to care for as parents.
- It prompts young people to engage in sexual relations with multiple partners and increases the risk of contracting AIDS and venereal diseases, which young people typically suffer in secret, foregoing medical attention and moral support.

70   More than 50 percent of young people in the United States have had sexual intercourse by the time they are seventeen. More than a million teenage girls in the United States become pregnant each year. About half a million of these pregnancies end in abortion. Of those who give birth, nearly half are not yet eighteen. Pregnancy, abortion, and childbirth not only stress the physical, mental, and economic well-being of adolescents and their parents, but they also contribute to the continuous formation of weaker family structures.[9]

71   Young women in particular are affected by a limited vision of sexuality and by the consequences of that limited vision. Young women confront more physical, psychological, and moral traumas related to pregnancy or abortion than their male partners do, and young women usually end up with the responsibility of raising any children. Many young women suffer emotionally, morally, and socially in losing their virginity; others feel marginalized because virginity is no longer valued by those around them.

72   If these problems are to be avoided, it is absolutely essential that adults provide young people with a good sex education as an integral part of young people's human formation. Any *truly* good sex education program emphasizes mutual self-giving, faithfulness, and transforming, creative love—all traditional elements in the Christian vision of a marriage relationship.

Hispanic Young People, *Noviazgo,* and Marriage

73 *Noviazgo* refers to a particular stage during which a man and a woman who are in love prepare for marriage. Couples in this stage are called *novios.* However, couples who are going out together and dating are not necessarily *novios.* It is important for young people to be able to identify the distinct purposes of and differences among their various relationships, and it is especially important for young people to know the difference between a dating relationship and a relationship in *noviazgo.* These awarenesses help young people become involved in different healthy and enriching relationships with members of the other sex.

74 In *noviazgo,* couples discover what they have in common and dedicate themselves to strengthening and deepening their relationship. Young people develop more fully their potential to love and be loved during *noviazgo.* They also get to know and understand themselves and their partner better, increase their ability for dialog, and become aware of the lifestyle and responsibilities that await them in marriage, from a reciprocity perspective (see "Approaches to Male-Female Interactions," earlier in this chapter).

75 It is essential that *novios* strive for dialog, mutual respect, and understanding; give the best of themselves to aid the development of their partner; be loyal and sincere to each other; and try to nurture a Christian spirit in all their relationships. These are the foundations that young couples need in order to create a home in which love, respect, and dialog prevail. Young couples who have shared a healthy *noviazgo* and are well prepared for family life tend to have better marriages than those who lack these foundations.

76 Parents play an important role in helping to sustain their children's Christian values when their children date or enter *noviazgo.* Parents do so by raising their children with an open attitude and by expressing confidence in them. Young people today insist on having freedom and responsibility. Oftentimes when parents are too strict, young women tend to date secretly, make no mention of having a *novio,* or even flee their family home with their boyfriend.

Marriage Preparation

77 When young people have a sound Christian formation, they do not settle for casual romantic experiences. They realize that any

worthwhile venture demands preparation, training, and formation. Unfortunately, Hispanic young people are rarely offered any solid preparation for marriage or family life. As a result, few Hispanic young people are aware of the responsibilities, challenges, difficulties, joys, and sadness they will experience in a marriage relationship. Many flee or become disillusioned in the face of the crises that inevitably confront them.

78   Youth ministry and family ministry must offer adequate formation programs for *noviazgo* and marriage. This formation process should be gradual but continuous, and it should include two phases—the *remote* phase and the *immediate* phase. The remote phase should enable couples entering *noviazgo* to do the following:

- prepare themselves for living as a married couple in an interpersonal and dynamic relationship of communion, responsibility, respect, knowledge, and growth
- face possible faith crises and overcome cultural pressures to discard Christian and Catholic values regarding marriage and family life
- make conscientious decisions based on clear criteria regarding their partner

79   The immediate phase should further prepare couples for marriage and should be at least three months long. This preparation needs to include the following:

- a profound effort at communication and dialog that leads partners into a more complete knowledge of each other and a more sincere love for each other
- a reflection about the meaning and responsibilities of marital love, which places a couple's sexuality at the service of love
- a review of the biological processes involved in marital life—not only in terms of procreation but in terms of maturation and aging
- a reflection on Christ's relationship with the church as a model for the sacrament of marriage
- a continuous spiritual growth as a couple
- an awareness of Christian and Catholic concepts of, and teachings on, birth control and paternal and maternal responsibilities
- an analysis of key elements needed for an effective management of their home

80   Special efforts should be made to provide an intensive pre-marital formation program for those couples who did not have an appropriate remote preparation. A couple's formation during *noviazgo* affects not only the quality of life of the couple but also the quality of life of their children.

81   Couples already living a married Christian life can offer effective support to unmarried couples who are going through a period of formation. These married Christian couples can share their own experiences with young people, help them discover the value of sacramental marriage, and dialog with them about the normal problems and pleasures of marriage and family life. The most valuable contribution married Christian couples make, however, may well be their witness of love, life, understanding, pardon, good communication, plans for responsible parenthood, and willingness to support a family. If such witness is important for young people in general, it is vital for those who come from broken or problematic families and who have not had examples of healthy marriages and family life.

82   When young people receive sound preparation for marriage and approach marriage as a consecration of their love to God, they find in God's love the foundation for their marriage and the strength to live out their marriage. God's love becomes the spring from which a couple's love for their family, community, and society generously flows. The papal encyclical *On the Family* (*Familiaris Consortio*) emphasizes this in saying:

> The very preparation for Christian marriage is itself a journey of faith. It is a special opportunity for the engaged to rediscover and deepen the faith received in baptism and nourished by their Christian upbringing. In this way they come to recognize and freely accept their vocation to follow Christ and to serve the kingdom of God in the married state.[10]

Hispanic Young People
and Their Culture

❧ 3 ❧

Hispanic Young People
and Their Culture

❧

*T*he Kingdom which the Gospel proclaims is lived by men who are profoundly linked to a culture, and the building up of the Kingdom cannot avoid borrowing the elements of human culture or cultures.

—Paul VI, *Evangelii Nuntiandi*

1 Every human being lives, grows, and strives for fulfillment within a culture. Culture is to people what soil is to plants. In and through their culture, people establish roots, grow, nourish their customs and values, and develop to maturity. However, in addition to being shaped *by* their culture, people also *create* their culture. Thus, to speak of a people and their culture is to speak of a dynamic relationship: human life is a process of transformation and mutual influence between human beings and their culture. The cultural realities in which Hispanic young people live are very complex and have powerful influences on their lives.

2 This chapter describes the cultural context in which Hispanic young people live, examines the dynamics that exist in Hispanic young people because of their contact with the dominant cultural environment in the United States, and reflects on their evolving identification as a new Hispanic–North American people. In volume 2 of Prophets of Hope, chapter 7 is dedicated to the evangelization of Hispanic young people within their culture.

The Cultural Context of Hispanic Young People

3 "Culture," as a concept, is extremely broad and can be understood in various ways. In this book, we understand culture as the whole collection of meanings and values that define the way of life of a human group. Included in this understanding are certain functions performed by a culture:
 • providing the group with its own roots and unique character
 • integrating the ideals, interests, social institutions, traditions, and

customs into an overall group vision of life, shared by the members of the culture

- shaping the symbols with which people communicate, both in passing on old knowledge and in developing new knowledge
- creating the system of social norms (principles or standards considered to be representative of a group) that guide and give meaning to life
- limiting the incorporation of elements that are foreign to the culture

4   All cultures are transmitted from one generation to another, although the particular cultural elements that are passed on can vary from place to place and age to age. In order to understand the culture of Latino young people, we must see the world as they see it, interpret their experiences through their own system of meanings, and come to know their cultural world and the elements that make up that world—the dominant U.S. culture, Latino culture, youth culture, and **popular** (or **"pop") culture.** Only in this way can we identify the special possibilities and challenges faced by Latino young people and thus plan with them a ministry that meets their needs and ideals.

The Dominant U.S. Culture and Hispanic Culture

5   The dominant culture in the United States has a North European background with an American style of living, is English-speaking, and takes a technological and consumptive approach to life. This dominant U.S. culture has a powerful influence on other cultures, both nationally and internationally, partly because the United States is such a world power and partly because U.S. cultural products are aggressively marketed worldwide. The origins and *idiosincrasia* of the dominant U.S. culture are difficult to characterize, for they include elements from Western European cultures, Native American cultures, and immigrant cultures all over the world.

6   Many aspects of the dominant U.S. culture reflect a culture that is more modern than it is traditional. This modern outlook is also present, though less pervasive, in Latin America. Some aspects of **modern culture** provide important resources for the development of Latino young people. Modern ideas about human rights, democracy, the dignity of women, and the development of science and technology, for instance, are positive influences on young peo-

ple and their human formation. Other aspects of modern culture, such as ideologies of capitalism, materialism, consumerism, and individualism, can be negative influences on young people.

7   The contrast between a **traditional culture** and a modern culture is sharp, and a person's passage from one to another generally causes significant adjustment problems. The chart on pages 78–79 highlights some major differences between traditional Hispanic culture and the dominant, modern U.S. culture. These differences indicate the intense culture shock that Hispanic young people can experience in the United States, particularly when they come from traditional Latin American settings. We recognize that the chart does not fully do justice to either culture, for both cultures include traditional as well as modern elements.

Youth Culture and Popular Culture

8   Youth culture began to develop in the United States as a permanent subculture around thirty years ago, when society and young people started to create a unique set of images, symbols, meanings, rituals, and environments. The development of this youth culture is, at the same time, the cause and effect of young people doing the following:

- having an active sexual life at a younger age
- working part-time jobs to earn their own money
- spending more years in school

9   The delayed entrance of young people into a more mature, adult way of life in today's society provides the basis for their long exposure to youth culture. Industries and the entertainment and communications media take advantage of this long exposure time to promote "youth values" and to sell "youth products" at a great profit. These values include pleasure through fashionable clothes, jewelry, and music; rebellion against authority; the glorification of sex, drugs, and violence; the demand for immediate gratification; and the idea that "only what *I* experience exists."

10   Youth culture is closely related to the general culture in the United States known as popular or "pop" culture. Several characteristics sum up this popular culture:

- It often holds values that degrade the person.
- It tends to incorporate values when they are convenient and discard them when they are inconvenient.

Hispanic Culture and the Dominant U.S. Culture

Cultural Elements	Seen in Traditional Hispanic Culture	Seen in U.S. Dominant Culture
1. Personal image of members	• based on personal relations	• based on personal success
2. Tradition	• important for both the present and the future	• without much importance or influence
3. Cultural force	• persons and community seen as coprotagonists of history with God	• individual protagonism in making history
4. Language	• concrete and rich in stories, symbols, and myths	• abstract, technical, and concise
5. Social organization	• centered on the extended family and the community	• centered on the nuclear family
	• based on interchange and cooperation	• individualistic, functional, and contractual
	• strong influence of rural culture and the culture of poverty	• strong influence of industrial culture and electronic communication
6. Land and home	• seen as part of self and personal history	• seen as economic entities
	• emotional ties lend stability	• transitory and functional
7. Time	• focused on persons and events	• functional
		• focused on chronological time as a means to economic gain
		• punctuality is important

Cultural Elements	Seen in Traditional Hispanic Culture	Seen in U.S. Dominant Culture
8. Religion	• expanded and connected to other aspects of life	• compartmentalized and severed from other aspects of life
	• fluctuates between fatalistic determinism and hopeful dependence on God	• can be intellectualized and controlled by science
	• relationship with God experienced and expressed in a community setting	• relationship with God seen as individualistic and expressed in a privatized setting
	• strong Catholic influence	• strong Protestant influence
	• sense of life as God-given	• sense of personal control over life
9. Authority, order, and loyalty among members	• group loyalty and strong social conventions	• participation by voting and respect for individual rights
	• male dominance	• greater equality between the sexes
	• submission seen as important	• freedom seen as important

- It encourages an attitude toward others that is materialistic, superficial, and changeable.
- It is created for people's consumption rather than as expressions of people's lives.

11   Popular culture's messages are transmitted through programming and advertising in the mass media. Popular culture intentionally offers an educational agenda that influences the minds and feelings of youth to the extent that many young people make pop culture the reality of their lives. In doing so, young people invert their values and convert themselves into objects to be manipulated by economic interests and social myths. On the one hand, young people relate to other persons as if others were simply objects to be used for obtaining pleasure and to be discarded when no longer useful. On the other hand, young people treat objects as if they were persons, attributing to objects the capacity to give life and fulfillment.

12   Youth ministry has a crucial educational role to play in the face of these negative influences, which are directly proportional to a person's lack of both positive values and community spirit. Youth ministers should be familiar with popular culture, help young people reflect on its present and future implications, and provide a supportive environment of human formation so that young people free themselves from popular culture's negative impacts. The words of the First Letter of John illuminate this situation when they say:

> Little children, you are from God, and have conquered [the false prophets]; for the one who is in you is greater than the one who is in the world. [The false prophets] are from the world; therefore what they say is from the world, and the world listens to them. We are from God. Whoever knows God listens to us, and whoever is not from God does not listen to us. From this we know the spirit of truth and the spirit of error. (4:4–6)

The Acquisition and Formation of Culture by Hispanic Young People

13   Every person is born within a culture, but no person is really born "with" a culture. Culture is acquired throughout life through a

process known as **enculturation.** Enculturation takes place primarily in two ways:

- In the home, culture is acquired principally through the values, behaviors, and actions communicated by the parents. This process is called **endoculturation.**
- In society, culture is acquired principally through the values, behaviors, and actions communicated by the mass media and by institutions and social groups such as schools, churches, and peer groups. This process is called *socialization.*

14   In previous generations, these two processes complemented and reinforced each other. The home played an important role in the transmission of faith, values, and traditions, while society promoted scientific, religious, and cultural development. Today, these two processes support each other less, due to the accelerated pace of cultural change and the disproportionate influence of pop culture. Among Latinos, the divergence between endoculturation and socialization is greater still, because of the conflicts between Latino cultures and the U.S. dominant culture.

The Process of Acculturation

15   When two or more cultures enter into direct contact, both the people involved and the cultures themselves are transformed, usually by adapting to or borrowing traits from one another. This process is known as **acculturation.** When acculturation occurs in an environment of dialog and respectful interchange, it can contribute to personal and cultural development as well as generate a pluralistic society in which it is possible to achieve unity in diversity. In contrast, when acculturation is marked by domination and conquest, the dominated persons and cultures are destroyed, and the dominators lose a large part of their humanity.

16   The effects of acculturation vary according to the power structures and the magnitude of differences among cultures. In the United States, four great processes of acculturation have occurred, and today we are experiencing a fifth one. Each of these has involved different circumstances and consequences:

17   1. The first European colonizers and their descendants invaded the lands inhabited by native peoples, killed thousands of them in conflicts, and generally reduced the rest to life on reservations.

There, native people were stripped of their own way of life and forced into a marginalized, scorned, and exploited existence.

18   2. Beginning in the seventeenth century and lasting until the mid-nineteenth century, Africans were forced to migrate to the Americas in the brutal context of slavery. Their life after arrival was marked by extreme human and economic exploitation. Recognition of their basic right to freedom came shamefully late and only after a civil war. And racial discrimination and political marginalization against African Americans continue today.

19   3. Diverse groups of European immigrants flocked to the United States from about the middle of the nineteenth century to the beginning of the twentieth century. These groups experienced fewer conflicts with the established population because they were mostly members of the white race. They intermarried with one another and with the established population, and their goal was to become "Americanized." In addition, Catholic immigrants had the support of national parishes and schools that cushioned the stress caused by cultural change.

20   4. The acculturation of Hispanic people began with Mexicans, as a result of the political annexation of Mexican territory to the United States in the mid-nineteenth century. Both the annexation of territory and the acculturation of Mexicans were marked by human and civil rights violations. One particular feature of the Mexican acculturation was that it was in their own territory that Mexicans had to acculturate to a foreign and invading culture. Since then, continuous new waves of Mexican immigrants have increased the presence of Mexicans in the United States.

21   The second period of Hispanic acculturation began with the political union between Puerto Rico and the United States at the end of the nineteenth century. This acculturation was a result of a population shift of Puerto Ricans to the United States and has been characterized by widespread conditions of poverty among Puerto Ricans in the United States. The strong dependency and economic exploitation of Puerto Ricans today is such that they have the most social and economic problems of any Hispanic group living in the United States.

22   The immigration of Cubans, as a result of political instability in Cuba during the first half of the twentieth century, signaled the

beginning of Cuban acculturation. This acculturation, which has been reinforced by the increased immigration of Cubans since the Cuban revolution of 1959, has two particular characteristics: Cuban immigrants, as a group, have a high level of academic education, and they have practically created a Cuban "city" in Miami. These two factors have furthered a more egalitarian acculturation with the dominant U.S. population in comparison with the two cases previously considered.

23   During the last two decades, the arrival of immigrants from all of Latin America, especially from Central America, has further diversified the process of Hispanic acculturation. The acculturation of these peoples has benefited from legislation open to racial and cultural diversity and a larger acceptance of cultural pluralism in the United States.

24   Nevertheless, the process of Hispanic acculturation has been characterized by economic exploitation, racial discrimination, and social marginalization. In the Catholic church, Hispanics have also experienced discrimination and marginalization in terms of decision-making processes and leadership opportunities. In addition, acculturation in the church is generally accomplished by the imposition of the Euro-American manner of living the faith.

25   5. Currently, given the presence of diverse ethnic and cultural groups in the same areas of the United States, the acculturation process is very complex. The multiracial, multiethnic, and multicultural composition of many cities presents additional challenges beyond the traditional problems of racism, discrimination, and exploitation of minority groups.

26   Young Hispanics are the fruit of a process of acculturation and *mestizaje* that began in the sixteenth century, when Spanish explorers first came into contact with the people and cultures in Latin America. This acculturation resulted in *mestizo* societies that were highly stratified by social class and that oppressed native people and African slaves. Currently, Latin American nations differ from one another in their racial, cultural, and ethnic compositions. For example, in Mexico the population is overwhelmingly *mestizo*. In Bolivia, the majority of the people are *indígenas*. In Cuba, where little *mestizaje* took place between the Spaniards and the African slaves, the population today is approximately two-thirds Spanish and one-third mulatto (of mixed European and African ancestry).

27   Today, the process of acculturation in the United States varies greatly among young Hispanics, depending on the level of acculturation of their parents, the economic status of their family, and the age at which they immigrated. In their acculturation, young Hispanics feel the impact of the dominant culture most strongly, but they also feel the influence of African American and Asian American cultures, due to their contact with people of these cultural groups at work, school, or in the community. This contact affects Hispanic young people's search for identity and frequently causes conflict and competition when young people from different cultural groups vie with one another for prestige, resources, and social services.

Reactions to Acculturation

28   People's reactions to the process of acculturation can be described broadly as "patterns of cultural adjustment." These patterns can be positive or negative, depending on the impacts that they have on the involved people and cultures. Here we focus only on the reactions of Hispanic young people to acculturation in the dominant U.S. culture.

Negative Patterns of Adjustment

29   When young Latinos react impulsively to culture shock, without later analyzing the reasons for their reactions or the consequences of their reactions, they usually fall into one of three negative patterns of cultural adjustment. These are as follows:

1. *Assimilation of the dominant culture:* Young people reject their culture of origin and try to acquire the dominant culture in order to integrate themselves into it. In assimilating the dominant culture, young Latinos lose their language, the roots of their identity, and the values of their culture of origin. To make matters worse, these losses often occur without young people's necessarily acquiring the positive values of the dominant culture or being accepted into it. Nevertheless, assimilation is oftentimes promoted by teachers, ministers, and other people who believe that Americanization is the only acceptable way for people of cultures different from the dominant U.S. culture. In addition, assimilation is almost universally encouraged by those industries that have youth products to promote and sell.

Assimilation is illustrated with the "melting pot" image, which encourages different cultural groups to lose their own flavor in order to create a better "stew." Assimilation does *not* benefit Latino young people, who are often left with the worst of both cultures and feel that they belong to neither.

2. *Rejection of the dominant culture:* In rejecting the dominant culture, young Latinos seek refuge in their culture of origin and form cultural niches or ethnic ghettos, isolated from the rest of society. In these niches, they seek the support of family members and compatriots. This pattern of adjustment is most commonly seen among adults, but it also occurs among young people who live in Latino barrios, among recent immigrants who do not speak English, and among young people who strive to maintain their own culture. Rejection of the dominant U.S. culture, however, neither eliminates the influence of popular culture nor lessens the impacts of racism, economic discrimination, and social and political marginalization.

3. *Adoption of functionalist attitudes toward both cultures:* To avoid being rejected by either culture, young people frequently accept those aspects of the dominant culture and their culture of origin that will allow them to function, at least superficially, in both cultures. This reaction is common among Latino young people, who have the need to adapt to their various cultural environments—family, school, church, peer group, and workplace.

Usually young people adopt functionalist attitudes without realizing how such adaptations affect their personal development. Adopting this type of attitude does not encourage young people's holistic human development, nor does it make young people active agents of their own history. On the contrary, functionalist attitudes make young people change their ways of thinking and acting, depending on the cultural groups they are with. This negatively affects young people's self-identity, values, emotional balance, and family harmony. It also erodes the coherency (connection between different aspects or dimensions) of young people's life and inhibits their acceptance of sociopolitical responsibility in their community.

Positive Patterns of Adjustment

30   Positive patterns of cultural adjustment are based on a careful analysis of the risks and opportunities of acculturation and the

possibility of consciously choosing a way of life that fosters personal, cultural, and social development. Latino young people show two positive patterns of adjustment that complement each other and can be considered two dimensions of the same process. These patterns are as follows:

1. *Integration without assimilation:* Without leaving their own culture, Latino young people integrate themselves into the dominant U.S. culture, seeking mutual respect and equal rights and responsibilities. This type of adaptation occurs among recently immigrated adolescents who speak English, as these adolescents come to know the dominant culture, and among young adults who were raised in the United States but who have strong roots in their culture of origin.

2. *Creation of a mestizo, Latino–North American culture:* Young people freely and consciously integrate elements of both cultures into a new cultural vision that is founded on a coherent system of values. The majority of Latino young people view this alternative enthusiastically, because it reinforces their identity even as it allows them to become integrated into society—*without* becoming assimilated into the dominant culture. It also allows them to be active agents of their own history and authors of a new culture. This culture keeps Latino values alive and generates a Latino–North American way of life that corresponds to the real world that young Latinos live in.

31   Hispanic youth ministry should promote positive patterns of cultural adjustment, encouraging in young people a clear cultural identity. Hispanic youth ministry should also help make young people aware of their role in the new *mestizo* culture, so that they incorporate into it the best elements of each culture, according to the criteria of the Gospel. For these things to occur, several elements are needed: special formation programs for Hispanic youth ministers, **conscientization** of the adult Hispanic community, collaboration on the part of non-Hispanic youth ministers, and profound dialog with young people from other cultures.

Identification as a Hispanic or Latino People

Language Use and Hispanic Young People

32   Language is crucial to the personal development, social relations, self-image, and faith formation of both individuals and groups. Language fluency and comprehension vary widely among Hispanic young people. Some young people are completely bilingual; others are monolingual in Spanish or English; and still others are semi-bilingual. Among young people who are semi-bilingual, some speak only one language but understand both; others can speak both languages but only read and write one; and still others speak hybrid languages, such as "spanglish," understandable only to those accustomed to them.

33   This diversity of language affects both the quality and quantity of dialog between Hispanic parents and children, especially when the parents do not speak English and the children do not speak Spanish. At times, parents fail to understand the seriousness of this situation, and the onset of their children's adolescence intensifies the usual problems of lack of communication, misunderstandings arising from the generation gap, cultural conflict, and the difficulty parents experience in educating their children. This linguistic complexity also affects pastoral ministry, because language and faith are intimately related, both for receiving the Good News and for expressing the faith. Thus, it is vital that youth ministers speak the language of the group and be sensitive to the language preferences of the young people.

"People" and "Population": Two Different Concepts

34   To speak of the U.S. Hispanic or Latino *population* is not the same as speaking of Hispanics or Latinos as a distinct *people* in the cultural mosaic of the United States. The term *Hispanic population* refers broadly to persons of Spanish or Latin American descent and slightly less broadly to persons who speak Spanish as their native language. The term *Hispanic people* implies a new, collective identity among persons from different Latin American groups and cultures in the United States, an identity that unites them while respecting their individuality.

35   The formation of Hispanic (or Latino) people in the United States is a slow process. It requires considerable dialog, mutual

respect, and understanding among all persons and groups involved in the formation process. In addition, people must have the explicit desire to give birth to a new, collective Latin American identity among people who live in the United States with people from Mexico, Central America, South America, Spain, and the Spanish-speaking countries of the Caribbean. This process is not always easy. Such union requires acknowledging and reconciling historical, cultural, political, and economic differences among all of these groups. It also demands a personal decision to identify oneself as Hispanic (or Latino) and an effort to integrate—without assimilation—the diverse traditions, customs, philosophies, artistic expressions, and manners of living out one's faith.

36   Pastoral work with this new Hispanic people means confronting many challenges:

- struggling for recognition of the civic festivals and liturgical celebrations of the many different cultures and groups involved
- eliminating stereotypes that persons of Latin American origin believe about one another
- using common or well-understood vocabulary in communications among different cultural groups
- being careful when using idioms or slang
- balancing the tendency to form closed circles of friendship among young people of the same cultural origin
- avoiding the continuation of the strong exploitative classism that predominates in Latin America

37   Meeting or even just working on these challenges helps young people and adults alike build the openness and unity with which Saint Paul characterized the Christian community:

> For just as the body is one and has many members, and all the members of the body, though many, are one body, so it is with Christ. For in the one Spirit we were all baptized into one body—Jews or Greeks, slaves or free—and we were all made to drink of one Spirit. (1 Cor. 12:12–13)

Concepts About the Terms *Hispanic* and *Latino*

38   Currently, some groups prefer to use the term *Hispanic,* and others prefer the term *Latino* to identify all people originating from areas where the Spanish language dominates. *Hispanic* also stresses the

importance of ministering in Spanish to millions of people who are monolingual and to bilingual people who prefer Spanish for their human and religious formation or who find that they use the Spanish language to maintain family unity and educate their children. An additional point in favor of the term *Hispanic* is that the official documents of the Catholic church refer to "Hispanic people" rather than "Latino people."

39   Those who prefer the term *Latino* point out that the term *Hispanic* was imposed by the U.S. Census Bureau and did not originate from the people the term was intended to describe. Many people feel that the identification with Spain (in *Hispanic*) disconnects them from the Latin American roots of the immense majority of Latinos in the United States.

40   Because both positions have value, the Prophets of Hope series uses the terms *Hispanic* and *Latino* interchangeably and trusts that the two perspectives complement each other and are a step in the continuous process of becoming, feeling, and acting like a "people." This sentiment was similarly expressed in the Tercer Encuentro Nacional Hispano de Pastoral:

> We have faith in our people because we know that God, who abides in a special manner and forever among us, has raised it up. We believe that the waters of the Rio Grande and the Caribbean Sea are a unifying source, for as we cross over them to come here, they allow us to become instruments of God for fertilizing and enriching the land that received us.[1]

41   Although certain preferences and disagreements exist regarding the terms *Hispanic* and *Latino,* their common concept includes young people at all different levels of acculturation and integration—those who have recently immigrated to the United States and those whose families have lived here for generations; U.S. citizens, legal residents, and undocumented immigrants; English-speakers and Spanish-speakers. With this much diversity to deal with in ministry to Hispanic young people, resolving disputes over the terms is not nearly as important as helping young people understand and be a part of the terms' common concept (that of a new Latino–North American people with a collective identity).

42   Among the confusions and tensions caused by this complexity and diversity important in youth ministry, the following stand out:

- Immigrant young people usually identify themselves with their country of origin and do not yet even have a self-identity as "Hispanics" or "Latinos." Thus, they do not feel part of this new people still being formed.
- Young people who have been assimilated into the dominant U.S. culture, and those who desire to become assimilated, usually reject being identified as Hispanics or Latinos. Young people who favor assimilation and Americanization will even oppose other young people who identify themselves as Hispanics or Latinos.
- Some young people who have been assimilated into the dominant U.S. culture find themselves struggling to recover their Latino identity, roots, and values.

43   An increasing number of young people are consciously and intentionally trying to contribute to the formation of the new Latino–North American people. In the past, the process of the three **Encuentros Nacionales Hispanos de Pastoral** contributed strongly to the formation of a Hispanic identity and to the integration of Hispanics into the Catholic church in the United States. However, the young people who participated in the Tercer Encuentro in 1985 are now adults, and the majority of present-day Hispanic young people have not had this kind of valuable experience. It would be appropriate for leaders in Hispanic youth ministry to organize periodic youth meetings at the regional and national levels to help young people become integrated into the regional and national church community and into their identity as part of a new Latino–North American people.

Concepts About Biculturalism and Multiculturalism

44   The ways in which the terms *bicultural* and *multicultural* are used and understood have different consequences for the development of young people. If young people identify themselves as bicultural because they know and can adapt freely and consciously to both cultures without losing their own cultural identity, their concept of being bicultural is healthy. If they believe that being bicultural is a matter of possessing two cultures or of belonging alternately to each culture according to convenience, their understanding of being bicultural is inaccurate and likely damaging. A person can only have one culture, even if he or she is experiencing transition due to acculturation. Youth ministry must provide healthy understandings

of biculturalism and multiculturalism to avoid promoting a cultural schizophrenia that would damage young people's emotional stability and coherence in their life.

45   Society is bicultural when two different cultures coexist; it is multicultural when three or more cultures live together in the same social environment. This shared life of diverse cultures can be a source of enrichment for young people, but it can also cause tensions that need to be examined and resolved with a Christian spirit and understanding.

46   Lastly, youth ministry must guard against interpretations of multiculturalism that might lead to a generalized, formless youth ministry. That is, when a youth ministry tries to achieve "equality" toward ethnic groups by simply ignoring differences and focusing only on shared characteristics, that ministry fails to meet the needs of *any* group. Differences in special abilities and character are to be accepted and welcomed as part of a larger whole of the church community and in order to achieve a greater unity. In this view, it becomes important not to separate young people from the dominant culture or from other ethnic and cultural groups, because being a multicultural church means that all young people belong equally to the church and should relate to one another as brothers and sisters.

47   In his 1987 papal tour of the United States, Pope John Paul II referred clearly to the unity of all people and to the importance of preserving each culture's identity and particular gifts:

> It is time to think of the present and of the future. Today, people are realizing more and more clearly that we all belong to the one human family, and are meant to walk and work together in mutual respect, understanding, trust and love. Within this family each people preserves and expresses its own identity and enriches others with its gifts of culture, tradition, customs, stories, song, dance, art and skills.[2]

The Role of Hispanic Young People in Social Transformation

The Role of Hispanic Young People in Social Transformation

♥

*I*t is our personal witness through action that will dramatically offer hope to a world that seems hopeless.

—Secretariat for Hispanic Affairs,
Proceedings of the
II Encuentro Nacional Hispano de Pastoral

1   As members of a new Latino–North American people, and as a substantial and growing part of the U.S. population, Hispanic young people have a primary role in determining the future of Hispanics and other ethnic groups in the United States. Through their potential to enter into and change political, economic, and social worlds, Hispanic young people may have an influence that extends to the United States' relations with the countries of Latin America. In this chapter, we reflect on the potential of Hispanic young people to transform society, analyze the strong challenges they confront, and suggest ways of promoting their effective participation in society.

Effective Participation of Hispanic Young People in U.S. Society

Three Systems that Shape All Societies

2   Every society is shaped by forces that are complex and often rapidly changing. Chief among these forces are three intimately related systems: the political system, which controls and regulates power among both individuals and groups; the economic system, which is based on ownership and exchange of goods; and the social system, which organizes the way people participate in society. Whether these systems promote the common good, human rights, and social justice depends on how the systems are structured and how they function.

3   Ideally, a *political system* allows persons and social groups to exercise effective influence over the decisions and structures that affect their lives. Concentration of power under one person or group, or under a very few persons or groups, creates dictatorial, oligarchical, or *caciquistas* systems. Dictatorships and oligarchies (systems of government that are controlled by one person or a few select people) are typically characterized by legal systems that protect the interests of the ruling persons, legitimize their control and power, and oppress the people under their power. The *caciquistas* systems base their oppression by maintaining power through moral or physical coercion.

4   Ideally, an *economic system* allows employable individuals to find jobs that provide sufficient wages for living a dignified life. Further, an ideal economic system allows natural resources and produced goods to be distributed equitably among all economic sectors. The concentration of riches in a few hands unbalances the labor market and stifles the possibilities for exchanges of goods among members of society. This imbalance allows certain groups to control the economy while subjecting the rest of society to bare subsistence living or to workplace exploitation.

5   Ideally, a *social system* fosters a society in which all people relate to one another as persons with equal rights and duties. An ideal social system also considers each person as an integral part of society and advances each individual's good as well as the common good of the whole society. Unjust political and economic systems foster segregated and unjust societies: those who hold power and wealth generally relate to exploited and marginalized persons only through the legal system and the labor market, and not through informal acquaintanceships, close friendships, family or community bonds, neighborhood relations, and social organizations that seek common goals.

6   Hispanic young people as a group face serious disadvantages in all three systems. They have no political power in society, nor do they have the appropriate organization for acquiring it. They lack goods that they could exchange in the marketplace, and they have few opportunities, and little money, for acquiring goods anyway. They are also excluded from the social "powers that be"—that is, from the groups that make decisions and influence society. Recognizing this situation is the first step toward addressing it, because

recognition can give rise to a serious commitment to transformative action on the part of young people themselves and society as a whole.

The Church's Role in Shaping Society

7 Official recognition of the church's role in shaping society started more than a hundred years ago with the papal encyclical *Rerum Novarum*. Dramatic new perspectives on that role came with the Second Vatican Council and the ongoing renewal it brought to the church. Both the church as an institution and individual persons as members of the Christian community were challenged to do the following:

- move from a Christian faith that concentrated on the person in isolation from the world to a Christian faith grounded in collective human and social reality
- foster collaboration among all persons of goodwill rather than accept the isolation of such persons among themselves or the "enclosure" of Catholics in their own institutions
- strive to find reconciliation between Christian faith and advances in science and technology, in order to direct all toward the construction of a society based upon the values of the Gospel
- include the reflections of the people of God on their life in light of their faith as a way of doing theology, in order to avoid reducing theology to a philosophical speculation and clarification of religious concepts by specialists

In short, the Second Vatican Council challenged Catholics to transform the systems that shape society in a just way.

8 It remains the task of all Christians today, especially young people, to integrate into their world Christian thought, being, and action, keeping in mind these three principles:

1. Faith is not a private matter for each individual, but rather a communal matter that should influence all levels of life, from interpersonal relations to society as a whole.
2. People's faith affects and is affected by the sociopolitical and socioeconomic relationships they forge and within which they live as a community.
3. To achieve a communitarian faith capable of transforming the social order, Christians must critically analyze their reality and

commit themselves to building a society based on the values of God's Reign.

9   All pastoral work motivated by these principles is a source of hope for transforming society. Similarly, young people whose formation springs from these principles represent the same hope and transformative potential—not only for the present church and society but for the future as well. And perhaps no other group within the Catholic church represents a greater untapped source of life, hope, and transformation than Hispanic young people.

The Transformative Potential of Latino Young People

10   Due to a variety of experiential, cultural, and personal characteristics, Latino young people possess a remarkable potential to transform the systems and systemic injustices that surround them. Among the characteristics particularly valuable to Latino young people are their openness and welcoming attitude toward others; their consideration of friends as part of their extended family; their cooperative, communitarian spirit; and their firsthand experience of marginalization and discrimination. These characteristics help Latino young people, as individuals and as groups, transform society through their contact with others—simply by being themselves.

11   Individually, Hispanic young people can take advantage of their own opportunities for personal formation. Communally, they can establish informal groups and official organizations to improve or transform the systems that make their development difficult; they can also create new systems—organizational alternatives—to encourage that development. Politically, Hispanic young people can commit themselves to good causes, join with one another in pressuring politicians for improvement, and support people who promote the common good.

12   Ministry to Hispanic young people can and must contribute to changing the political, economic, and social systems of the United States by promoting the commitment of young Hispanics in this task. This ministry is urgent because the challenges confronting Hispanic young people (and youth from other ethnic groups) are too great to be overcome without organized support. A by-product of this action will be a much needed revitalization of the Catholic church's mission in the world.

Promoting a Prejudice-Free Society

Underlying Factors in Discrimination Against Hispanics

13 Hispanics are generally excluded from the economic, political, educational, and religious decisions that affect their lives, largely because they face discrimination in trying to enter positions of decision-making responsibility. This discrimination occurs in two ways: *inclusive* discrimination occurs when acceptance into positions of responsibility requires characteristics that Hispanics do not fulfill; *exclusive* discrimination occurs when Hispanics are excluded simply because they are Hispanic. Young people can overcome inclusive discrimination through great effort to acquire the academic training and skills necessary for entrance into certain sectors of society. However, only with great difficulty can they overcome exclusive discrimination, which is usually based on racism or ethnocentrism.

14 Defined broadly, *racism* is the belief that, for genetic reasons, one's own race is superior to others. *Ethnocentrism* is the belief that one's own ethnic group has more positive characteristics than other ethnic groups. In the United States, both racism and ethnocentrism run together and are rooted in the dominant culture. Both attitudes also have serious consequences in the lives of young Hispanics, who tend to react to racism and ethnocentrism with either passive resignation or destructive opposition. These reactions make it urgent that ministry to young Hispanics help them channel their emotions and behavior toward liberating, creative action.

15 Racism and ethnocentrism are built on prejudices and stereotypes that characterize people according to preconceived images. As defense mechanisms, stereotyping and prejudging avoid or manipulate reality and excuse people from changing their attitudes, even though their attitudes injure others. In general, prejudices have a limited basis in reality and often arise out of self-interest or out of an experience that neither takes into account all the facts nor analyzes the situation from other perspectives. Many prejudices exist and must be eradicated for the sake of promoting the development of young Hispanics, building a fraternal society, and creating a culture of sharing and peace.

Prejudices Confronting Hispanic Young People

16   **Cultural or ethnocentric prejudices:** Cultural prejudice involves assuming that one's own lifestyle or way of thinking, feeling, relating, writing, or speaking is the best or the most valid one. This type of prejudice is common among many Euro-Americans, who consider Hispanics inferior because of certain Hispanic "ways of being"—facing life emotionally rather than analytically, using their time and resources to maintain family relationships and friendships rather than to "get ahead" professionally, and speaking and writing indirectly and in long phrases rather than to the point and briefly. Although they are less obvious, cultural prejudices also exist between young Hispanics from different countries and between Hispanic, African American, and Asian American young people.

17   All cultural groups need a certain level of ethnocentrism to give them identity and coherence, so ethnocentrism isn't necessarily bad; in fact, it often maintains a healthy diversity. Problems arise, however, when ethnocentrism leads persons of one cultural group to demean, injure, and discriminate against persons from other cultural groups. For example, ethnocentrism becomes prejudice when Hispanic young people are considered incapable of serious academic study, are classified across the board as gang members, or are seen as lacking motivation to improve their economic well-being or social status. Other, subtler examples of ethnocentric prejudice include accepting only those Hispanic young people who unquestioningly accommodate themselves to the dominant U.S. culture, or helping Hispanic young people paternalistically without appreciating their gifts and potential.

18   **Racial prejudices:** Racial prejudices are behaviors and attitudes founded on racism—the belief that one's own race has greater intelligence, physical or mental ability, or other positive qualities than other races. Racial prejudices toward African Americans and other people of color have always been strong and extensive in the dominant U.S. culture. In fact, racial prejudices have been so strong that laws ensuring freedom, promoting affirmative action, and forcing the desegregation of schools were necessary in order to recognize the rights of ethnic groups of color and to provide opportunities for their self-development. These laws have provided greater academic and professional opportunities for some Hispanics, but

the "spirit" of these laws has not yet been equitably integrated into society.

19   Nor is the Catholic church free of racism. One of the three themes of the First National Youth Congress held in Indianapolis, Indiana in November 1991 was racism—its evolution, its frequent incidence in the Catholic church, and its destructive consequences for people of color.

20   Racial prejudice causes great frustration among Hispanic young people, for they cannot change their skin color or their physical appearance. The stresses from racial prejudice are especially grave during adolescence, when young people examine their personality, forge their basic identity, and establish their self-worth and security. Eliminating racism may be the most difficult task that young people and the church jointly face. Personal goodwill and words of concern or disregard toward racism will not be enough for such a task, as the U.S. bishops have noted:

> Racism is not merely one sin among many; it is a radical evil that divides the human family and denies the new creation of a redeemed world. To struggle against it demands an equally radical transformation, in our minds and hearts as well as in the structure of society.[1]

21   **Class prejudices:** Class prejudices are born when a society is organized in a hierarchy, according to social status acquired through money, power, ancestry, academic training, or professional prestige. People in such classist societies come to believe that those who have more "riches" are worth more, know more, and are better persons. Thus, the upper classes refuse to interact socially with the lower classes, and they seize for themselves the power to determine how the lower classes should live. The majority of young immigrant Hispanics have experienced strong class discrimination in Latin America, causing them personal insecurity, inhibitions in interacting with people from higher classes, and low expectations for their personal development.

22   **Religious prejudices:** People who hold religious prejudices see their own religion or way of living their faith as the only valid one, thus disparaging or attacking other religions or faith expressions. Many young Hispanics feel that the Euro-American community disparages Hispanic Catholicism. Young Hispanics also constantly

experience open attacks on the Catholic church by certain **proselytizing sects** and fundamentalist groups who try to convert people to an alternative set of beliefs. These experiences can seriously undermine young people's self-affirmation and formation in their faith, both of which are crucial processes in adolescence.

23   **Institutional prejudices:** By taking concrete shape in the laws and structures of a society, the prejudices already mentioned become institutionalized and are made the general norm for that society. In this way, groups in power legitimize the economic exploitation and social, political, or religious marginalization of the lower classes and ethnic minorities. For example, in the United States, women were not given the right to vote until 1920.

24   Consciously or unconsciously, the Catholic church in the United States has contributed to institutionalizing the four types of prejudices mentioned previously. Unless all these prejudices are overcome, *with* church support, both in the church and in society, Hispanic young people will continue to suffer institutionalized discrimination from structures and systems that were created for Americans of European descent:

- *Discrimination in the schools* results when examinations, teaching techniques, language, and learning styles alien to the Hispanic culture are used to categorize Hispanic young people as slow learners or as incapable of professional studies.
- *Discrimination at work* follows from Hispanic young people's low level of schooling and from prejudices regarding their suitability for well-paying jobs or jobs carrying responsibility.
- *Socioeconomic discrimination* forces Hispanics in general, including Hispanic young people, to live in an environment of poverty and in housing that is unacceptable to the middle class—thus further removing Hispanic young people from access to better schools and jobs.
- *Discrimination in the church* leaves Hispanic young people beyond the reach of most pastoral services, offers them pastoral programs of low quality, and excludes them from leadership positions.

25   All types of discrimination, but in particular institutionalized discrimination and prejudices, lead young Hispanics to close themselves off within Hispanic groups. This isolation then becomes part of a vicious cycle, preventing the cross-cultural interaction that helps reduce prejudice.

26   Ending prejudice will never be easy. Prejudiced people usually find details and stories to reinforce their prejudices, and they tend to avoid situations that could lead to a change of attitude. Helping to enlighten prejudiced people takes patience and care. Likewise, helping people who are victims of discrimination and prejudice takes understanding, patience, and support so they will *not* respond destructively to prejudice.

Efforts Needed to Terminate Prejudice

27   To overcome prejudice, then, both personal conversion *and* the transformation of the systems and structures that have institutionalized prejudice are required. In Hispanic youth ministry and in the Catholic church, accomplishing both of these results becomes a less gigantic and outer-directed task with the realization that personal and communal conversion often leads to structural transformation. That is, transformation comes primarily from within. This realization leaves pastoral agents working in Hispanic youth ministry with a fourfold task:

1. to reinforce the self-worth of young people
2. to help young people forgive prejudicial attitudes in others and try to change those attitudes
3. to conscienticize young people so that they shed their own prejudices toward persons from other cultures
4. to seek understanding and cooperation on the part of non-Hispanic pastoral agents in working to end prejudice

28   Hispanic youth ministers and pastoral agents should be aware that young Hispanics often carry a series of prejudices against Euro-American youth and that strong prejudices and **antagonisms** also exist between young Hispanics and young African Americans in inner city areas. The lack of mutual understanding and unity among young people from different ethnic groups makes it difficult to form coalitions and collaborative efforts to address the common problems faced by all of them.

29   Hispanic youth ministry needs to promote pastoral projects that focus on ending the prejudices and hopeless cycles of poverty that so many ethnic groups suffer. Efforts toward social, political, and economic justice should be based on three principles:

1. Every human being, regardless of race, ethnicity, culture, national origin, religious belief, or sexual orientation, possesses an inherent and inalienable dignity.

2. Human persons do not exist for themselves alone but for others as well.

3. God created the human race with a fundamental unity, to live in solidarity and to use differences to strengthen human unity and not to divide members from one another.

30   Specific rights and responsibilities of Hispanic people, as members of the human family and as an ethnic group struggling for justice, arise from these principles. These rights and responsibilities, like the principles they are drawn from, need to be promoted by Hispanic youth ministry. The rights include the following:

- enjoyment of freedom and opportunity to develop their human potential
- preservation of the Hispanic way of life
- ongoing development of Hispanic culture
- involvement and sharing with groups of similar or different cultural and historic traditions
- freedom of religion and of expressing, celebrating, and educating in one's religious faith
- access to the support necessary to change unjust laws and structures
- creation and enforcement of just laws

Hispanic people's responsibilities, which are equally important, are as follows:

- contributing to the common good through the richness of Hispanic cultural diversity
- promoting the freedom and dignity of each ethnic group
- respecting the decisions of those who choose to assimilate to the dominant U.S. culture
- advocating and struggling for the rights of brothers and sisters from other countries who suffer injustice

31   Jesus confronted prejudice in his society: he accepted Samaritans, who were discriminated against and looked down on; he associated with sinners, who were religiously marginalized; and he recognized the value and calling of women, who were traditionally considered inferior to men. Jesus' disciples today should follow his example, reaching out to eliminate prejudice in the church and in society, struggling for the dignity of all people, overcoming poverty, and bringing about liberation, conversion, and transformation of the systems and structures that institutionalize sin.

Promoting Justice and Peace at All Levels

32   Many Hispanic young people experience violence in their countries of origin, their barrios, their schools, or their homes. Most are familiar with the oppressive and often violent consequences of poverty and economic injustice. And all suffer, directly or indirectly, the effects of vast public expenditures on armaments and armed conflicts. Therefore, recognizing injustice and promoting peace *at all levels* are essential steps in enabling young people to participate in and transform society.

Economic Injustice and Violence in Latin America

33   The disproportionate enrichment of the wealthy and the deepening impoverishment of the poor, both internationally and in the United States, represents one of the most dramatic "quiet" patterns of violence in the contemporary world. Every year, nearly twenty-five million dollars flows from Latin America to the United States, largely through commerce and interest on loans. Yet during the 1980s, the real income of poor Latin Americans dropped between 20 and 50 percent. The United States and the economic elite in Latin America have thus acquired a "social debt" to the poor, because the well-being and luxuries of the few elite classes have negatively influenced the employment, nutrition, health, hygiene, infant mortality, psychological state, and education of the majority poor.[2]

34   Institutionalized violence on the part of the great economic powers and the ruling elite in Latin America has forced poor people to urgently seek social change. This has generated armed revolutions and military counterreactions in many countries. The Latin American bishops have questioned this situation since the 1960s, as is shown in the documents of the Second General Latin American Episcopal Conference in Medellín:

> Although we as Christians believe in the fecundity of peace as a source for arriving at justice, we also believe that justice is a necessary condition for peace. In many parts of Latin America, a situation of injustice exists that can be called institutionalized violence. Because of inadequate industrial and agricultural structures, national and international economic structures, and cultural and political structures—"entire

populations lack what is necessary and live in a situation of dependency that impedes their initiative, responsibility, and any possibility of cultural advancement or participation in social and political life." . . . This situation demands global transformations that must be bold, pressing, and profoundly renovating. It should not surprise us that the situation in Latin America gives birth to the "temptation to violence"; we must not abuse the patience of a people who for years have put up with a condition that those with greater awareness of human rights would never accept.[3]

Poverty and Violence in the United States

35 Many Latino young people and their families arrive in the United States fleeing situations of injustice and violence, and the immigration of Latin Americans to the United States will remain a constant factor as long as it represents a chance to escape the poverty and violence caused by economic injustice. Upon arrival, however, many immigrants find their hopes, and their futures, dashed:

> Poverty is increasing in the United States, not decreasing. For a people who believe in "progress," this should be cause for alarm. These burdens fall most heavily on blacks, Hispanics, and Native Americans. Even more disturbing is the large increase in the number of women and children living in poverty. Today children are the largest single group among the poor. This tragic fact seriously threatens the nation's future. That so many people are poor in a nation as rich as ours is a social and moral scandal that we cannot ignore.[4]

36 The delegates to the Tercer Encuentro saw poverty as a strong challenge for young people. Many young Hispanics try to study to enter a professional career, but fail due to lack of adequate guidance and financial support. Others, simply to survive, must work from a young age. Many have parents who work far from home, a situation that weakens family life, leaves children without guidance, and sometimes causes broken families and even child abuse.[5] Concrete challenges include elimination of the following:

- the gap between rich people and poor people, owners and workers, and intellectuals and undereducated people—both in the United States and in Latin America

- the poverty that persists even as nations continue to produce weapons
- the state of isolation in which exiles, refugees, prisoners, immigrants, undocumented workers, elderly people, disabled people, and single-parent families continue to live
- the abuse of workers by immigration officials; the relocation and closure of factories in order to increase profits; and the payment of subminimum wages for work often done under inhuman conditions
- the poor quality and unjust distribution of public services, especially education, health care, and justice
- the oppression and injustice in Latin America resulting from cultural, economic, military, and political intervention by rich countries
- the weak commitment of the Catholic church, which preaches the Gospel and its social doctrine but fails to practice either sufficiently
- the discrimination against Hispanics in parishes, the lack of training programs for new Hispanic leaders, and the current Hispanic leadership's weak commitment to justice

37   Youth ministry should be a source of *cariño,* reconciliation, healing, and support for the young people who have suffered such unjust experiences and situations. At the same time, youth ministry and the evangelization of Hispanic young people should also be sources of energy for promoting justice. Young people, encouraged by the church and empowered by their spirit, enthusiasm, and willingness to struggle and sacrifice, can join forces. Together, they can use the media to denounce injustice and become involved in urgent works of social assistance and social justice, including legal assistance and defense, literacy training, and civic and political formation.

Hispanic Young People in a Gang Environment

38   Gangs, or *pandillas,* which are frequently tied to drug dealing, are among the realities that most dramatically confront young people today. The presence and violence of gangs are greatest in poor urban areas, where the majority of Latino young people live. The family, school, and neighborhood environments in these poor urban areas, rather than contributing to young people's development (of

identity, self-esteem, and sense of belonging), instead facilitate gang life. In a way, the church contributes to this situation whenever it fails to provide healthy, community-oriented groups where socialization, recreation, and contributions to the common good can occur.

39   Gangs vary according to their geographic setting and socioeconomic and racial environment. Any realistic analysis of gangs must avoid a superficiality and moralism that would blame their formation entirely on the inexperience, naivete, or amoralism of young people. The formation, organization, operations, and interests of gangs are both complex and diverse.

40   Gang membership no longer results just from racial prejudice or adaptation by immigrant minorities to the dominant society. Neither gang conflicts nor their territorial boundaries are based on race or culture alone. Multiracial gangs exist, and conflicts often occur between gangs of the same race and culture.

41   Drug traffickers forge, encourage, and manipulate many gangs as primary consumers and as part of their distribution network. Other gangs arise out of the need for self-defense amidst the sudden, explosive violence young people often face on the streets and in their schools. The increasing presence of razors, knives, and firearms in schools and streets heightens fear and insecurity in young people. This leads many young people to become gang members in order to find the gang's security and support. The gang phenomenon is desensitizing young people to violence and "legitimizing" the use of weapons.

42   Not all young people are gang members, and gang members are not all young people. Adults—whether single or married, middle-aged or older, men or women—generally constitute the upper leadership in gangs. These adults direct gang members and activities for their own self-interests and purposes.

43   People in ministry must clearly understand these complexities and dangers, in order to develop effective pastoral strategies to overcome them and to evangelize young people in these settings— and thus prevent the development of gangs. Youth ministers with experience in this area believe that it is necessary to work directly with the young people, their families, and the barrio communities and to dedicate substantial time, resources, and trained personnel to the task. That is, the task cannot become marginal to overall youth ministry, and the action must be direct.

Direct Action with Young People

44   Certain elements and directions are fundamental to all pastoral work with young people in gangs and in settings where gangs are common. Youth ministers, catechists, and pastoral agents involved in ministering to and evangelizing young people will find increased success if they do the following:

- Offer a stable, regularly gathering youth group where young people can establish their identity, feel a sense of belonging, and mature gradually. Short efforts and limited programs, which lack the ongoing presence and support of pastoral personnel, are not sufficient alternatives.
- Focus pastoral work on conscientization, liberation, support, and human development, in order to help young people reject peer pressure and to find creative alternatives for personal and community growth.
- Avoid moralistic positions that create youth cliques in the parish and that lead young gang members to reject the church. Also, avoid crusades against the gangs; in fact, avoid all kinds of moralistic "side-taking" that would encourage hatred or make young people enemies of one another.
- Pay special attention to the emotional and sexual relationships among young people, because sexual promiscuity is a severe problem in gang and poor urban environments.
- Shape the collective political conscience of young people so that they struggle for federal and state legislation that seriously penalizes drug traffickers, controls the use of firearms, strengthens education, encourages the productive use of free time, and promotes employment opportunities and rehabilitation programs for youth.
- Know the forms of organization and recruitment of gangs (such as colors, signals, fashions, and territory) in order to prevent pastoral action from becoming identified with gang activities by using certain colors or holding activities in violence-prone areas.

Joint Action with Parents and the Community

45   Even though pastoral work is directed toward young people, active involvement with the young people's parents and community is crucial. Pastoral efforts in this area should do the following:

- Promote a community coalition that triumphs over the dynamics that lead to gang recruitment and proliferation. This work should be based on an analysis of the processes by which gangs grow in each specific setting, and it should organize attractive alternative groups for socializing young people.

- Conscienticize parents about their children's needs for identity, belonging, *cariño*, and affirmation. Support them in their role as parents, involve them in youth ministry, and promote their participation in the schools in order to prevent gangs' recruitment of children, which begins at a very young age.
- Form small communities with several families to support one another in their role as parents and to establish their goal as a community: to take young people out of gangs and provide all the orientation and support young people need in order to return to school or succeed in the job market.
- Promote community organization involving cleaning up and being present on the streets and in parks, in order to prevent the complete takeover of these spaces by gangs and the division of barrios into conflicting territories.
- Encourage the participation of the community in efforts led by civil authorities against violence and drug dealing, while preventing the community from becoming a battleground between gangs and the police.
- Try to eliminate outbreaks of racism in the police force, such as the police tactic of using gang presence as an excuse for arresting Hispanic young people.

46   Pastoral work with gangs is urgent and requires the support of the entire church. We cannot treat gangs as a passing phenomenon, as a developmental fad that young people will eventually leave behind, because many young people die in gangs and many others are seriously damaged for the rest of their life. Our faith gives us optimism and confidence in facing this struggle. We cannot allow pessimism to carry the day, for pessimism flies in the face of our faith and in the face of God, who is concerned and merciful toward us and who gives us the ability to do good. Christian hope sustains our commitment to the profound evangelization of young people and the creation of a better society for future generations.

Violence in the Barrios

47   Many barrios are permeated by violence, the causes of which are many: drug trafficking, family instability, racial tensions, peer pres-

sure, gang activity, and an absence or ineffectiveness on the part of law enforcement and other social institutions in promoting people's civic spirit and responsibility. This violence physically threatens hundreds of thousands of young people, terrorizes them, produces defensive and aggressive attitudes, makes education difficult, and impedes their participation in healthy activities, especially healthy nighttime activities.

48   In barrios where violence is common, Latino young people are incarcerated disproportionately to young people of the dominant U.S. culture. This injustice is worsened by the nature of antidrug laws, police abuse of ethnic minorities, and the difficulty of paying bonds, hiring lawyers, and gaining access to rehabilitation programs. Many Latino young people end up being jailed for their first offense, thus initiating a prison record that is more likely to multiply than to disappear. The inhuman conditions of penal institutions and the lack of programs for rehabilitation and re-entry into society cause the social death of young people, leaving them without hope of a better life.

49   God is present in the lives of all young people and entrusts them with a promise of a flourishing life, with the ability to construct a society of solidarity and love. Hispanic youth ministry should be a physical sign of this promise, offering young people impassioned ideals, a healthy environment, and an opportunity to improve the settings in which they live. Hispanic youth ministry should also include direct pastoral action with jailed young people and put forth projects to reincorporate them into the church community and into society, through a ministry that facilitates their conversion and integral development. We must urgently form youth ministers capable of this work, and our church must support these youth ministers and their formation.

War, the Nuclear Threat, and Expenditures on Armaments

50   Thanks to nuclear weapons and other technological "advancements," we live in a time when armed violence can have devastating consequences both for present and future generations. The Catholic bishops have repeatedly denounced war and urgently called for citizens and governments to oppose potential nuclear conflict and to end the use of all arms of mass destruction that impose indefensible situations of terror or capitulation on those they are directed

against. Military intervention by the United States in other countries, either directly or indirectly through arms sales and training of military personnel, also calls all Christians to take a firm position in favor of peace.

51   Today, more resources are invested in weapons than in peace projects. This reality does the greatest harm to young people of various ethnic minority groups, because arms expenditures reduce the resources potentially available to health, education, and human development. In addition, minorities are overrepresented in the military, because the armed forces offer them opportunities for study and economic betterment that are otherwise beyond their reach. In times of war, then, Hispanic young people are called to duty in disproportionate numbers. It is not enough for us, or for young people, simply to oppose war; we must actively promote peace and solidarity among people and constantly seek justice and the end to conditions that foster violence.

Participating Positively in Society and in the World

The Mass Media and Social Communication

52   All of life challenges us to communicate better with one another and with God. By providing information and by shaping human beings' images, values, and culture, the mass media can contribute to building understanding and mutual support among persons and groups. The media can also facilitate the effective participation of all members in society. Music, visual technologies, and computerized information networks are powerful means of stimulating human growth and social conscience.

53   Unfortunately, for commercial and political reasons, the mass media frequently alienate and depersonalize young people, cutting them off from reality and relegating them to degrading self-images and sentiments by using the following:
- openly immoral programming, loaded with violence, cultural stereotypes, and false, hateful, or superficial human relationships
- bombardment with advertisements that promote materialism, consumerism, egocentrism, hedonism, and sexual promiscuity
- frequent interruption of programs and the use of short reports to package news and information—both of which contribute to re-

ducing people's attention span and ability to concentrate
- the addiction to television, especially to "soap operas" that present a world far removed from reality and Christian values
- manipulated and poorly analyzed information about news and social events

In particular, overexposure to television undermines people's abilities to reason creatively and critically, to dialog, and to analyze, and it reduces the time available for more beneficial activities.

54   Tape recordings, compact discs, music videos, radio, television, magazines, and popular newspapers strongly attract young people. Therefore, if evangelization is to touch the lives of the young, it should promote a critical analysis of the messages promoted by these media, reorienting their use toward projects of human and social development.

55   Music is a gift from God, a gift that possesses great power to express and evoke feelings of joy and peace, move young people to action, and reinforce youth culture with the values of the Reign of God. Secular and religious noncommercial music must be promoted so that their positive messages penetrate to the hearts of Hispanic young people. In this way, we will help dilute the effects of commercial music, which frequently promotes violence, sexual promiscuity, drug use as an acceptable way to solve problems, **occultism** and **satanism,** and suicide as an escape from reality.

56   Many young people spend up to seven or eight hours a day listening to music, and they spend a surprisingly high percentage of their money on music recordings, electronic goods, and concerts. We need to discourage young people from relying on music to escape reality and the responsibilities of life, to become shut up inside themselves, or to avoid contact with their family and wider society. By helping young people be selective in choosing what music they listen to, and by encouraging them to compose music that promotes or is compatible with the values of the Reign of God, we can recover music as a means of bringing peace and joy to life.

57   Computers and computerized communications systems, although they are very useful for science, technology, research, and providing services, also allow excessive "warehousing" and manipulation of information. In addition, the ownership of computers and the ability to use them may be creating a new kind of education and a new "educated elite" class to which few Hispanics have access.

Up to the present, computers have been little used for promoting the development of Hispanic young people. Hispanic youth ministry, if it aspires to form Christians committed to creating a more just and humane world, can no longer ignore the power of information technologies to have both positive and negative effects.

The Environmental Crisis and Hispanic Young People

58   Although the effects of human beings on the environment have been a concern for quite some time, the increasing rate of species' extinction; the pollution of air, soil, and water; and the desertification (the process by which mismanaged land becomes an arid desert) of many land areas have became so pronounced in the last decade as to require immediate attention. The earth and its atmosphere must be repaired, endangered animal species must be preserved, and nonrenewable natural resources must be used wisely. Efficient land-use planning is also urgent, so that human developments do not negatively alter a healthy equilibrium between human life and the rest of the natural world.

59   The biblical mandate of humans having dominion over all creation, which appears in the first chapter of Genesis, should be understood within the context of having responsibility for the entire creation. As human beings created "in the image of God," we must exercise dominion over nature in the manner of God. That means caring for all creation as a source of life for people. God's plan is for us to take care of resources given by God for the benefit of all humankind, using and transforming them without destroying them.

60   The rapid consumption of the earth's resources robs young people, who stand to inherit a deteriorated world—impoverished by erosion, reduced in number and diversity of species, and depleted of nonrenewable resources. If the devastating effects of uncontrolled industrialization and urbanization continue, pollution and other problems may well become negative controls on the human population. On a hopeful note, young people have in their hands the possibility of renewing creation by redirecting the same science and technology to foster human development and ecological balance.

61   The environmental crisis requires a new solidarity of people with nature, at the individual, national, and global levels. We will only solve this crisis if we seriously examine and revise our lifestyle,

its demand for immediate gratification and consumption, and its indifference to the damage these demands cause.

62   Hispanic young people can make valuable contributions to the environmental movement with elements of Hispanic tradition and spirituality. These elements include a focus on the importance of the individual, a focus on liberation from oppression, a communitarian spirit, a sense of the close relationship between human beings and nature, and a feeling of solidarity with poor people. For Hispanic young people to make valuable contributions, however, Hispanic youth ministers must help in young people's environmental conscientization by doing the following:

- promoting a critical awareness of ecological reality and the attitude that nature should be a source of life for all of humanity and not a source of luxuries for a privileged few
- developing a spirituality that contemplates and gives thanks for the work of God in nature and that leads young people to view themselves as part of nature and as cocreators with God
- avoiding the use of toxic and disposable objects, recycling industrial materials, and discarding garbage and waste in appropriate ways
- organizing environmental campaigns and projects at the national and international levels

Political Action and Latino Young People

63   Although promoting personal development and struggling for peace, social justice, and environmental causes are worthwhile undertakings, by themselves they are not sufficient for achieving a "culture of sharing and peace." Ideology, beautiful words, and isolated projects will rarely transform a society or produce a new reality. Young people and adults must participate effectively in politics by directing government and legislation to promote solidarity, mutual respect, and the common good.

64   In the United States, the proportion of eligible voters who actually vote in a major election tends to hover around 50 percent. This is ironic when so many people in other countries are struggling to achieve even basic democracy. We need to increase our participation in electoral politics, legislative efforts, the defense of human rights, and community organization. The right to vote may belong only to those at or over age eighteen, but participation in

the processes mentioned is within reach of all young people. Furthermore, early participation in such projects helps prepare young people for future political involvement. The political formation of Latino young people is a key element in working to bring about many changes—a more just economy, greater support for the family, quality education for all people, medical services within reach of all, international relations based on justice and peace, a clean environment, and the eradication of violence, racism, drug addiction, adolescent pregnancy, and **euthanasia** (bringing about a gentle and easy death for a person suffering from a painful, incurable disease).

65   The political formation of young people begins with their becoming aware of the negative, alienating influences of some approaches and ideologies that they receive in school and through the media and popular culture. Young people's political formation should also include strategies for facing the complexities and bureaucratic complications of governments and social service agencies.

66   In providing visible signs of the Christian commitment to justice and peace, all people involved in youth ministry and all the activities of the church have an important responsibility in the political formation of young people. It is imperative that the church end its passivity in promoting political action among young people. Young people have a vital role as the most dynamic element of the social body, an element able to reinterpret and renew the meaning of life and of culture. Young people can bring new perspectives and apply "Reign of God" values to their own historic circumstances. In order to turn their abilities into realities, though, young people need to have clear concepts and goals, solidarity with those who are poor, good organization, support from the adult community, and a continuous process of education in the midst of action.

67   Young people can participate politically at the local level by collaborating in community-organizing efforts; forming pressure groups that promote changes in schools, health institutions, and workplaces; exercising the right to vote; affiliating with or confronting a political party; and discerning their possible vocation in public service through politics. Pope John Paul II, in his apostolic exhortation *Christifideles Laici,* sums up Christians' responsibility in public life as follows:

The lay faithful *are never to relinquish their participation in "public life,"* that is, in the many different economic, social, legislative, administrative and cultural areas, which are intended to promote organically and institutionally the *common good.* The Synod Fathers have repeatedly affirmed that every person has a right and duty to participate in public life, albeit in a diversity and complementarity of forms, levels, tasks and responsibilities. Charges of careerism, idolatry of power, egoism and corruption that are oftentimes directed at persons in government, parliaments, the ruling classes, or political parties, as well as the common opinion that participating in politics is an absolute moral danger, does not in the least justify either skepticism or an absence on the part of the Christians in public life.[6]

The Religious Reality
of Hispanic Young People

The Religious Reality
of Hispanic Young People

❧

*D*esiring to be the light of the world and salt of the earth, many Hispanic young people dedicate their energies and talents to the mission of the Church. Their values are deeply Christian. Whatever their circumstances, they feel themselves members of a spiritual family led by their Mother Mary. This is evident in their art, poetry, and other forms of expression. Yet pressures on Hispanic youth to adapt and live by self-seeking values have led many away from the Church.

—National Conference of Catholic Bishops,
The Hispanic Presence

1   The majority of young Hispanics living in the United States are Catholics. Many of them have been born and raised in Latin American countries, in environments in which Hispanic **popular religiosity** influenced the earliest stages of their faith lives. As a result, this religiosity now provides the lens through which they perceive and express their faith. We cannot isolate young people from the popular religiosity and popular Catholicism they have grown up in, because young people approach God precisely through these religious expressions. Instead, we need to understand and respect them, and strengthen those aspects that help them experience and live out the Gospel message.

2   This chapter reflects on the main aspects of the religious reality of Hispanic young people. First of all, it presents some characteristics of Hispanic popular religiosity. Second, it deals with Hispanic popular Catholicism. Third, the chapter presents some features of the Christian faith among young Hispanics, according to their own opinions. Fourth, it presents a critical analysis of the challenges that **secularism** poses to young people.

Hispanic Popular Religiosity: An Expression of Faith

3   In every culture, a religiosity arises out of the innate human need to relate to God and to live out and express the mystery of the sacred. This religiosity includes the beliefs, experiences, and religious celebrations through which a people live and affirm their faith. In other words, popular religiosity
   • is the cultural form of a religion adopted by a specific people
   • embraces all aspects of life
   • is the intuitive manner by which people perceive, feel, and live the mystery of God in their life
   • constitutes the individual and collective conscience through which people live their relationship with God
   • is made of a set of beliefs about God, basic attitudes expressing these beliefs, and the way these beliefs and attitudes are celebrated

4   Hispanic people express their religiosity in various ways, embodying different kinds and degrees of **religious syncretism.** The most common form of Hispanic popular religiosity is the popular Catholicism that resulted from inculturating sixteenth-century Spanish Catholicism among native peoples and African slaves in Latin America. But Hispanic popular religiosity also includes forms centered on pre-Hispanic, native religious expressions with some Christian elements.

5   The popular religiosity of Hispanic young people is highly complex, for while many young people preserve their popular Catholicism, some are in a state of frank rebellion from the traditional religiosity of their parents; others have fallen prisoner to secularism; and others are incorporating elements of Pentecostal evangelism.

6   The popular religiosity of young Hispanics embodies the particular characteristics of Hispanic people as well as the individual psychology of each young person. Therefore, as these elements change over time, popular religiosity also evolves.

7   Throughout their history, Hispanic people have made choices in response to their life situations, counting on God's help in the process. Many times, Hispanic popular religiosity has been misinterpreted or manipulated by groups that wanted to keep Hispanics

oppressed. These groups worked by instilling in people a deterministic, fatalistic attitude or by promoting unconditional submission—either toward society or toward the church.

Popular Religiosity and Cultural Identity

8   Popular religiosity is an identity-forming and integrating force for Latino young people, because it expresses the worldview, feelings, and values of the Latino people. Popular religiosity also embodies the sacred in young people's daily lives—through beliefs and rituals.

9   Hispanic popular religiosity is closely related with the poverty and marginalization in which the majority of Latin American people have lived. Although popular religiosity is typical of poor sectors of the population, in many aspects it is also lived by people in other social strata. In this way, popular religiosity maintains some links between people of different social classes, political convictions, and nationalities. Thus, popular religiosity leads to the gathering of large multitudes, particularly in the celebration of religious feasts.

10   It is possible to appreciate cultural identity given by popular religiosity in a parish, barrio, or town. It is shown by the way people understand and celebrate life; organize the community; transmit religious traditions to the next generations; engage in art, dance, and music; celebrate feasts of the patron saints; and participate in local devotions. At regional and national levels, popular religiosity integrates people through common devotions and general perspectives about life.

11   Popular culture and popular religiosity are usually intimately joined, and together they embody the *idiosincrasia* of a people. For Latin American immigrants, the strong cultural and religious diversity found in the United States can cause familiar points of reference and sources of cultural support to disappear. The sheer variety of available choices disorients young people, complicates the educational task of parents, and pushes both young people and parents to replace their cultural and religious foundations with values rooted in materialism and hedonism.

12   Young people continually look for forms of religious expression connected with youth culture (such as T-shirts with religious messages, posters, popular music, and stickers) to reinforce their identity as a Christian youth community. In addition, young

people enjoy continuing Latino traditions such as *posadas, mañanitas,* dramas, *pastorelas* (pageants), musical competitions, and dramatizations of the way of the cross. All these expressions of popular religiosity reinforce Latino young people's religious and communitarian experience, inspire and revitalize the adult community, and attract children like charms. But it remains critical to encourage both the creativity of the young people in these activities and their inclusion in the total experience of the church community.

13   The relationship between faith and culture has traditionally been very strong for Latino people. The loss of their language and culture of origin has weakened or destroyed the religiosity of many Latinos in the United States. Similarly, the lack of frequent, popular, large-scale expressions of their religiosity has contributed to a lack of cohesiveness among Latino people, who need a certain cohesiveness to overcome the challenges they face in this country.

Popular Religiosity and Spirituality

14   Hispanic popular religiosity carries important attitudes and values, such as humility, human solidarity, tenderness, acceptance of suffering, recognition of human weakness, acceptance of God's will, confidence in divine providence, recognition of God's power, awareness of the triumph of good over evil, and assurance of life after death. These attitudes toward God and human life shape a spirituality that has allowed Hispanic people to sustain their faith in God, their charity toward their neighbor, and their hope in life, even in the midst of poverty, oppression, and marginalization.

15   Hispanic people's spirituality is often expressed through devotions connected to the need for affection and immediate protection, for obtaining favors, and for expressing confidence and thanksgiving to God. This devotional spirituality results in part from Hispanic people's feelings of vulnerability in facing life. The spirituality of Hispanic popular religiosity also includes a rich symbolism that facilitates the relationship of the people to God—without the philosophical speculation and theological rationalization that are common among groups whose approach to God is more intellectual.

16   Many Hispanic families live out traditional attitudes and values, successfully transmitting them from generation to generation. But the social environment in the United States seldom allows these

values to flourish; rather, it suffocates them and substitutes them with opposite values. Furthermore, the church frequently belittles or misinterprets these values, leading Hispanic young people to lose the foundations of their spirituality and become thirsty for God.

The Importance of Symbols and Miracles

17   Life's uncertainty and the unjust and dehumanizing conditions in which most Latino people live reinforce their need to feel close to God and to seek concrete ways of manifesting their trust in God. Consequently, vital elements of Latino people's religious life include religious signs, symbols, and rituals; sacred spaces, objects, and persons; miraculous events; and communal expressions of religious feeling. Even when young people cannot explain logically their meaning and importance, these elements often remain vital for them—as long as the elements connect with their personal experience and help them feel secure in the hands of God. However, if the signs or symbols are empty of religious meaning for them or are far removed from their experience, young people tend to discard them.

18   Hispanic young people's need to feel divine help in the face of serious difficulties in life predisposes them to believe in miracles. It is important to acknowledge this need and to recognize the religious experience behind Hispanic young people's belief in miracles, rather than just to label these young people as superstitious or lacking in religious formation. The promises, penances, and vows that young people offer (to God, the Virgin Mary, or the saints—in exchange for divine favors) symbolize their recognition that miracles result from God's power and occur only through God's will. Young people hold great faith in God's power to protect and save people in desperate situations. Sometimes, however, young people project God's power into control over all aspects of life, a view that diminishes young people's confidence in themselves and gives rise to a kind of religious determinism. To combat such determinism, concepts about miracles need to be clarified by interpreting them within the full context of the Gospel message.

The Importance of Belonging

19   Hispanic young people tend to create rituals that indicate their belonging to a group and that mark the various stages of their group participation. Usually they give greater importance to sacred rituals and objects than to sacred spaces and persons, because the

former are more likely to be within their reach. In fact, many young people tend to place a religious value on objects and rituals that are meaningful to them, whether or not they have a distinct religious nature.

20   Hispanic young people's search for identity, and the ease with which young people pledge their loyalty to a group, can make young people vulnerable to cults and **pseudoreligious groups** and rituals. These groups provide young people with sacred moments and experiences in which they hope to find security, protection, and affirmation. Unfortunately, these groups also tend to be extremely manipulative and out of touch with reality. They increase the likelihood of young people's turning to gangs, superstition, and even black magic or witchcraft as means to deal with their problems and to control the world around them.

Popular Religiosity's Risks: Oppression and Alienation

21   Although popular religiosity facilitates many people's experience of God and expresses their confidence in salvation and in God's protection, popular religiosity can also lead to oppression and serious alienation when it does the following:
- leads to superstition and manipulation of the sacred instead of affirming human values
- creates a false division in young people's experiences by disconnecting the sacred from their life in the world
- serves as an escape from reality, thus discouraging young people's personal development and their involvement in transformative social action
- leads to a fatalistic attitude in the face of unjust and inhuman situations
- favors a self-centered feeling or conduct in young people through their involvement in religious fringe groups and cults
- functions as a defense mechanism in the face of life's insecurities and conflicts
- encourages a fundamentalist interpretation of the Scriptures, thus taking as literal truth matters that are meant as religious truth
- reduces young people's relationship with God to a mere contract or interchange of favors

22   Every expression of popular religiosity faces these dangers, because these dangers are independent of religious tradition or church

affiliation. The dangers and negative aspects of popular religiosity represent a particularly strong risk for the following groups:

- profoundly religious young people who lack knowledge of alternative means of living out their faith
- young people who have had no significant religious experience and are emotionally sensitive
- young people who find in popular religiosity integrating forces that make them forget the social marginalization in which they live

23   Because expressions of religious experience can arise from so many different backgrounds and circumstances, it is not always easy to identify the positive and negative aspects of any given religious expression. Therefore, it is important not to indiscriminately attack or criticize popular religiosity; in doing so, one runs the risk of destroying the foundations of some young people's Christian faith. Effective evangelization must be carried out from a positive perspective that emphasizes young people's dignity and value as human persons, helps free young people from oppression, and leads young people to discover the Christian meaning of life. A strong theology integrated into a strong **catechesis** has great potential for purifying popular religiosity of its oppressive and alienating elements and for taking advantage of its positive qualities.

Hispanic Popular Catholicism: A Way of Being Church and Living the Faith

24   The popular Catholicism that exists today among Latino young people began with the evangelization and catechesis of the European missionaries, the popular religiosity of the colonizers, and the religiosity of indigenous and African peoples. This Catholicism—complex, **heterogeneous** (it embodies aspects from many different Latino cultural groups and peoples), and rich in expressions—is broadly consistent with official Catholicism.

25   Among Latino young people who belong to traditional Catholic families, pre–Vatican II Catholic elements predominate. Among those who come from marginalized rural areas, elements combining indigenous and European religiosity or African and European religiosity predominate. In the United States, a Latino

popular Catholicism incorporating some elements from Euro-American Catholicism and from other Christian influences is beginning to appear.

26   Popular Catholicism is dynamic, evolving over time through changing life circumstances and contact with other cultures. It includes a people's intuitive appropriation, adaptation, or rejection of certain elements of official Catholicism in order to make popular Catholicism fit better with the religious or cultural values that are important to them. Popular Catholicism also includes the creation of new ways of expressing certain beliefs. A given parish's attitude toward popular Catholicism determines whether popular Catholicism will live a harmonious and complementary coexistence with official Catholicism or face resistance and alienation from it. Therefore, every effort at evangelization should strive for a truly ecclesial spirit that values, supports, and orients the popular Catholicism of Latino people, while at the same time helping to purify it from those aspects opposed to the Gospel or Catholic doctrine.

27   For many Latino young people, popular Catholicism *is* their church experience. Through it, they relate to the ecclesial community and live their Christian faith. Because of this, it is important that young people as well as pastoral agents know, value, and judge this popular Catholicism in light of the Gospel. Doing so will enable them to strengthen and purify popular Catholicism in order to further Christian practice.

28   When evangelization and catechesis do not orient popular Catholicism, popular Catholicism faces the risk of not being centered on Jesus and his Gospel. When popular Catholicism is ignored or discriminated against by the institutional practices of the church, it may completely disappear, leaving young people with a religious vacuum. Or it may press young people toward fundamentalist sects that offer them a sense of belonging to a community.

The Importance of the Creed and of the Sacraments

29   Traditionally, the spirituality of Hispanic people has been fed by prayerful contemplation of God's greatness and the humbleness of humanity, trust in God's providence, petitional and thanksgiving prayer, and repentance for betraying God's love. Hispanic spirituality is expressed in a daily, conscious, and enriching prayer life; in routine practices that maintain one's closeness to God; and in sacra-

mental celebrations that bring God closer to the person in crucial moments in the person's life.

30 The basic beliefs of Hispanic popular Catholicism coincide with the fundamental mysteries of the Catholic Christian faith, although at times popular Catholicism carries limitations or distortions from inadequate pastoral instruction. The following beliefs stand out as most important to Hispanic Catholics: faith in a creative, provident, and saving God; veneration of Mary as a source of divine life and a model for women's formation; trust and devotion to the crucified Jesus, who shares human pain and accepts death in order to give people eternal life; and respect for the pope, priests, and other religious as representatives of God and authorities in the church.

31 Hispanics generally possess a strong sense of God, of transcendence, and of the sacramentality of life. They express this sense of the sacred primarily by celebrating significant junctures in human life through the sacraments of baptism, first Communion, and marriage. Hispanics also celebrate God's presence in their home and daily life through diverse sacramentals. (Sacramentals are sacred signs instituted by the church that bear a resemblance to the sacraments. They signify effects, particularly of a spiritual nature, obtained through the church's intercession. They prepare people to receive the sacraments and render holy various occasions in life.)

32 The sacramentals most widely practiced by Hispanics include using blessed water, receiving ashes on Ash Wednesday, saying the rosary, and carrying home palm fronds from the Palm Sunday liturgy. These and other devotional practices by which life can be rendered holy should not be belittled or eliminated, rather they should be valued as ways of relating to God and to the church.

33 In the Hispanic tradition, baptisms, first Communions, a daughter's fifteenth birthday, confirmations, marriages, and funerals are occasions for large celebrations that include as many relatives, friends, and colleagues from work as possible. Sunday Eucharist is also important to many Hispanic people. However, a large number of Hispanic people are unaccustomed to participating in the celebration of Sunday Mass, because rural towns and poor barrios in Latin America do not have a regular Sunday Mass. And Hispanics in the United States have not received sufficient pastoral attention to promote this practice.

The Importance of Symbols and Rites

34 In addition to the sacramentals, Hispanic Catholics use crosses, medallions, candles, incense, holy cards, and images for expressing their devotion to God, Mary, or the saints. They like to make offerings, vows, and processions; celebrate patron saints' feasts; hold rites of adoration of the cross; pray to the Blessed Sacrament; and re-enact biblical events, especially during Holy Week and the Christmas season. Also, Catholic Hispanics show appreciation for home altars, hermitages, local shrines, chapels, and temples. Venerating images and blessed objects and blessing people, houses, cars, and the fruits of people's labor are other signs by which Hispanics express God's presence at significant moments in their lives.

35 In the evangelization process, it is important not to approach or judge Hispanic religious expression from an outsider's perspective. Hispanic religious expressions offer opportunities to discover the presence of God and enflesh the Gospel in a person's personal and communitarian life.

The Importance of Identification with Jesus

36 Hispanic popular Catholicism is largely a Christ-centered spirituality, due to Hispanic people's identification with Jesus. Because of their own sufferings, Hispanic people tend to identify strongly with the crucified Jesus, who suffered mistreatment and persecution for them. As a result of this identification, Hispanic people have accepted much pain and persecution in the name of Jesus. They have suffered mistreatment and persecution for their solidarity with poor and oppressed people; they have accepted poverty and sacrifice; and they have kept hope alive even in circumstances beyond all hope.

37 Although Hispanic people in general do not openly verbalize their faith in the Risen Jesus, they daily live out the Easter mystery through their "way of being" and experiencing life's varied situations. Problems arise when other people take advantage of and subdue Hispanics through their disposition to accept suffering for the sake of those they love and for their love of God.

38 Because of the importance of Jesus in the life of young Hispanics, we surveyed several Hispanic youth groups regarding their ways of relating to Jesus and their opinions about the place of Jesus

in other young people's lives. The information we gathered is presented in the section of this chapter entitled "Hispanic Young People Speak Out."

The Importance of Marian Devotion

39 Another vital element of popular Catholicism is devotion to Mary. In her motherhood, compassion, tenderness, and closeness to God, Mary personifies the feminine role of divinity. In addition, Mary's image as mother reflects Hispanic people's view of and relationship to the land, which they consider sacred for its capacity to generate and nourish life. Given this context, Mary's appearances carry an authoritative weight for Hispanic people, legitimize their identity, reinforce their religiosity, and give them courage to confront difficult situations.

40 Veneration of Mary as the human being most able to bring one close to God arises out of Hispanic people's confidence in her. Devotions to Mary are profoundly evangelical experiences that when accompanied by a strong catechesis can bear fruit in a truly Christian way of life. In contrast, when Marian experiences are attacked, Hispanic people's whole faith is placed in doubt and can be destroyed.

41 Mary is the patron saint of all Latin American countries and lives in the heart of most Latino people. Her presence has played a key role in Latino faith and religious practices. Because of her importance, the initial reflection and chapter 8 in volume 2 focus on Mary. The initial reflection focuses on Mary in the Scriptures, and chapter 8 deals with Marian popular piety and presents Mary as a model for evangelizing action.

The Importance of Pilgrimages and Saints

42 The idea of making a pilgrimage in search of the divine presence and of going out to encounter God is very important in Hispanic spirituality. Pilgrimages bind together people's feelings of giving themselves to God, their experience of journeying toward salvation, the transitory character of life and their willingness to sacrifice, and the will to go further even when facing difficulties. Young people enjoy pilgrimages in which they can live out their adventurous and communitarian spirit, express their creativity, put to work their

organizational abilities, and recover or strengthen their cultural roots.

43   Also important in Hispanic spirituality are local celebrations of patron saints and personal commitment to the Virgin Mary and to certain saints as role models. Saints with whom young people strongly identify include Saint Francis of Assisi, Saint Martin de Porres, Saint Anthony, and Saint Joseph. The Virgin Mary has such an important place in Hispanic hearts that she is the ultimate feminine model.

The Importance of a Calendar of Religious Events

44   Just as Hispanic people emphasize certain beliefs in keeping with their vital needs, they also create a calendar of religious celebrations with which to feed their faith. This calendar, generally related to the liturgical year, plays important roles: it brings the community together in God's name, provides opportunities to proclaim the word of God, and generates strength for confronting daily life.

45   In the United States, new religious calendars for Hispanic celebrations are being developed. These calendars draw on elements and religious events from different Latin American peoples and cultures. While the process of creating new calendars can initially generate great conflict, it is an important part of coming to terms with a new, heterogeneous cultural setting.

Traditional Foci of Hispanic Spirituality

46   The religious elements and practices that have been presented in this section constitute foci of spirituality for Hispanic people. The creed, sacraments and sacramentals, symbols and rites, identification with Jesus, Marian devotion, pilgrimages, devotion to saints, and the religious calendar are foci from which the relationship between people and God spring out; the foci gather people together for the celebration of their faith. Hispanic youth ministry must use these traditional foci of Hispanic spirituality to nourish the faith of young people, to give them a broader sense of the ecclesial community, and to help them take advantage of all the means of spiritual growth that are available to them through the church.

47   Nowadays, Hispanic young people desire to know God's word and drink directly from it. This desire differs a bit from popular Catholicism, which transmits the Scriptures orally, making use of bib-

lical elements through proverbs or isolated stories of people and events, with additions and modifications coming from popular wisdom. The result is an urgent need to strengthen the biblical formation of young people—to help them know and correctly interpret the Scriptures, deepen their lives through the messages found in the Scriptures, and integrate the Scriptures into their daily lives.

48   Hispanic youth ministry also has a responsibility to remedy shortcomings in young people's spiritual formation in popular Catholicism. Oftentimes, the valuable experiences of popular Catholicism are offset by negative circumstances and happenings, such as having lived a faith handed out in a context of oppression and inferiority. In consequence, faith in God and devotion to Jesus may lead to fatalistic acceptance of oppression rather than struggle. In this context, Mary is used as a model for submissiveness to men rather than as a model of profound relatedness to God; devotion to the crucified Jesus stops at the cross and fails to remember the Resurrection; and respect for the exercise of church authority gives way to passivity and resignation.

Popular Catholicism's Risk: Ecclesial Marginalization

49   Although popular Catholicism frequently exists at the margins of church life, Hispanic young people who have developed within popular Catholicism rightly consider themselves part of the Catholic church. They were baptized into it, have been evangelized and catechized in the Catholic Tradition (albeit at only an initial level), and broadly and intuitively affirm the Catholic creed. Furthermore, they identify themselves as Catholics, seek out our parishes to meet their religious and social needs, and participate in Catholic liturgies.

50   For generations, Hispanic people in Latin America and the United States have sustained their faith through a religiosity that allowed them to be Catholic even without the pastoral ministry of the church. However, religious and cultural circumstances have changed for Hispanics in the United States, partly because of the activities of religious sects and partly because popular Catholicism is less intense in industrialized and urban cultures and less widespread in this country than in Latin America. At times, popular Catholicism is even rejected by the church itself.

51   As young Latinos become more aware of what it means to be a church, they refuse to continue being marginalized. Instead, they

seek a new synthesis between their popular religiosity and their active participation in the ecclesial community. But when the Catholic church does not give young people the pastoral attention they need, or when other churches or religious sects offer them that attention, young people may become part of another religious community as a way to abandon ecclesial marginalization. Sometimes young people take this action without much thought, and sometimes they seek another community after careful evaluation. But in either case, the outcome makes it crucial to give Latino young people their place in the Catholic church.

Hispanic Young People and Their Christian Faith

Levels of Evangelization Among Hispanic Young People

52   The quality of young Hispanics' faith-life depends partly on the kind of *religiosidad* and the level of Christian formation that shaped them at home, and partly on the pastoral and catechetical attention offered them by the church. Among Hispanic young people there is a broad spectrum of styles and levels of evangelization. Thus, we begin by identifying a segment of young people that is close to the Catholic church and another segment that is more distant from the church.

53   In the segment that is closest to the church, it is possible to distinguish the following categories:
1. *Young people with a popular Catholicism,* who nourish their experience of God and come into close contact with the church only at critical and significant moments in their life. It is necessary to recognize and use such moments to initiate a personal relationship with these young people in order to offer them a **new evangelization.**
2. *Young people engaged in sacramental practices,* who commonly attend Sunday Mass more out of custom, obligation, or family pressure than out of personal commitment or consciousness of their faith. These young people must be personally encouraged to participate in evangelizing experiences and to deepen their faith formation.
3. *Young people who live out their baptismal commitment,* promoting the values of Jesus and transmitting the Good News in their

daily life. These young people need to reflect on their faith and their mission in the world.

4. *Young people committed to ministry,* whether in youth pastoral work, catechesis, liturgy, or social action. These young people need theological and specialized pastoral ministry formation.

54   In the segment that is more distant from the church, it is possible to distinguish the following categories:

1. *Young people who are distanced from the church* because they live in homes with minimal religious spirit or practice, or simply because they have very limited contact with the church. These young people can best be reached by going through other young people and by addressing their daily concerns and interests as part of ministry among them.

2. *Young people who have abandoned the church* because religion was imposed on them, which they resented; because their lifestyle deviated from church teaching; or because they joined a religious sect. The first group needs *cariño* and patience to heal their wounds and clarify their confusion; the second group needs a process of reconciliation; and the last group needs to be treated with a fraternal and open spirit.

3. *Young people who have a non-Christian popular religiosity,* such as the superstitious belief in horoscopes or the practice of **santería, voodoo,** or witchcraft. Young people engage in such practices to seek contact with the supernatural, to find solutions to their personal concerns, and to gain self-affirmation. These young people need to discover God, purify their faith, and strengthen their cultural identity.

4. *Young people who have no religion* or awareness of the presence of God in their life. These young people need to discover and experience the greatness of God and of the human person, and they need to find life within the salvation offered through Jesus.

55   Thanks to God's abiding presence and to better pastoral attention, more Hispanic young people are becoming seriously committed in their faith and in the church. Many of these young people become missionaries who carry hope to other young people. This new evangelization is broadening many young Hispanics' horizons regarding God and their own mission in the world. Fresh fervor is making the Gospel message real through new methods of evangelization and new expressions of faith. Hispanic young people are already a force for renewal in our church; given official support and

resources from adults and from the Catholic church, they have the potential to help renew all of creation.

Hispanic Young People Speak Out

56 To understand who Jesus is for young Hispanics, we asked Hispanic young people from various youth groups and regions of the country to respond to the questions Jesus asks in this passage from Matthew:

> Now when Jesus came into the district of Caesarea Philippi, he asked his disciples, "Who do people say that the Son of Man is?" And they said, "Some say John the Baptist, but others Elijah, and still others Jeremiah or one of the prophets." He said to them, "But who do you say that I am?" (16:13–15)

These questions remain as important for us today as they were for the disciples in Jesus' time.

57 To better understand the image that Hispanic young people have about God, Jesus, and the church, the questions were formatted in the following way:

- Who do Hispanic young people—both those who are active members of the church and those who are not—say that Jesus is?
- Who do *you* say that Jesus is?
- Why do other young people not get excited about Jesus?
- What are the most common confusions and misconceptions that exist about God, Jesus, or the church?
- What are your concerns about young Hispanics' faith lives and about how young Hispanics relate to Jesus?

58 More than two hundred Hispanic young people responded to our questions. Their answers shed light on who Jesus is for Hispanic young people at various stages of their faith journey. In addition, their answers revealed their personal experiences with Jesus and with the church. The young people who responded to our questions presented two clearly distinguishable levels of knowledge about Jesus and relationship with him. The majority of the adolescents and young adults who had recently come to know the living Jesus held a very personal image of him. More mature adolescents and young adults—whose faith formation, like their personal formation, had grown beyond the initial stages—typically held an image of Jesus that was broader, more communitarian, and more challenging.

Images of Jesus from a Beginning Faith Perspective

59   Among adolescents and young adults whose faith has recently begun to grow, these images of Jesus generally stand out:

- *A personal friend:* Jesus listens and responds to young people and inspires confidence. Jesus is someone to whom they can speak intimately and give thanks for life and from whom they can ask forgiveness and help in being good, honest, diligent, and reliable.
- *A giver of life:* Jesus loves young people, pardons their sins, renews them, gives them life, and saves them. Jesus' joy, loyalty, and self-bestowal—even to the point of suffering and dying for others—attract young people and draw them to him.
- *A positive, challenging force:* Jesus challenges young people to goodness, gives them courage to confront their problems, provides clarity in the midst of doubt, and offers them alternatives and opportunities to begin anew after they have experienced setbacks.
- *A role model:* Jesus is a model of goodness, love, friendship, and humility. Young people accept him as a role model because of the good works he performed and the temptations he overcame in life.
- *An active presence:* Young people see Jesus as alive and active in the world, as someone they encounter in people who follow his example, in their parents' love, in the support of friends, in those who guide them toward goodness, and in their youth group. This Jesus reveals himself to people when they share his love with others.
- *A companion-guide:* Jesus accompanies young people throughout life and asks them to follow him both in spirit and in deed. Jesus asks young people to love, support, and forgive one another, to visit sick people, to be Jesus to those who are passing through difficult times, and to pray for people who are suffering, especially for those who get caught up in vice because they do not know him.

Images of Jesus from a More Mature Faith Perspective

60   Among adolescents and young adults who are more mature in their faith, the following images of Jesus stand out:

- *An exceptional human being:* Young people see Jesus as an exceptional human being, because of his mercifulness and understanding, his humbleness and fairness in dealing with others, his commitment to outcasts and sinners, and his love for and service to all, especially his love for and service to poor and oppressed people.

- *A marvelous person:* Young people see Jesus not only as an exceptional human being but also as a *marvelous* particular person; after all, only Jesus was truly both human and divine. Jesus also possessed great personality and **charisma,** was strong and firm in his mission, and showed patience and tenderness with people. He detested injustice, performed miracles, forgave and healed people, and promoted freedom and human development. He was an adventurous, hardworking person, untiring and full of energy, joy, optimism, peace, and hope.

- *An example to follow:* Jesus' life has meaning for young people, mainly for the coherence of his life; his loyalty to his Father; his generosity, sacrifice, and commitment; and his courage and zeal. Jesus teaches young people that they need not be rich in order to love and serve others.

- *A brother:* Jesus not only taught people to relate to God as Father, but he also invited all persons to share his faith, his Father, and his mission. Jesus is a person with whom young Hispanics can identify fully, because like many of them he knows poverty and suffering.

- *A teacher:* Jesus tells people that to be in right relationship with God, they must be in right relationship with other people; that is, their duty is to love one another as sisters and brothers.

- *A savior:* Jesus suffered and died to open people to a new life of hope and to give meaning to their existence. Young people see in Jesus a liberating savior who struggled untiringly for justice. Jesus also helps young people understand that they are not to wait until life after death for happiness, but that happiness, like the Reign of God, begins in this life.

- *A prophet:* Jesus challenges young people to fulfill their mission, regardless of the consequences—to create a world in which justice, love, and peace reign, and to work toward eliminating the evil that taints society.

- *One who calls people to partnership with him:* Jesus calls young people to proclaim the Good News, visit the sick, console the suffering, serve the community, help the poor and the sinners, and promote unity among people. In other words, Jesus calls them to become his partners in making his living presence known through words and deeds, thus helping people know God and live as Christians.

- *One who gives meaning to people's childhood faith:* Young people see Jesus as the embodiment of the faith that they learned and the religious practices that they experienced when they were children.

"Who Do Young People Who Are Not Active Members of the Church Say that Jesus Is?"

61   Young Hispanics in the youth groups also responded to the question: "Who do young people who are not active members of the church say that Jesus is?" Here are their opinions:

- Some young people simply do not know anything about God. Other young people, perhaps the majority, know that God exists, but they place no importance on God's existence because they don't know God well. These young people are not to be blamed for not knowing God or Jesus; these young people simply have not encountered Jesus in the love of a community. They know that Jesus lived a long time ago, performed miracles and died for us, but they do not know Jesus alive today.
- Many young people think that Jesus loves them, but their lives have not yet been changed by this knowledge.
- A certain number of young people do not believe in Jesus' power, because they have not experienced this power or because they do not really know Jesus and thus do not hope for anything from him.
- Other young people know stories from Jesus' life, but are unaware of his mission. Therefore, they have no enthusiasm for him.

62   As a whole, the adolescents and young adults who responded to the questionnaire think that a large percentage of young people lack enthusiasm for Jesus because they have not had the opportunity to encounter a living and attractive Christ. Their relationship with Jesus is often superficial: they know nothing of his mission—one in which every young person can collaborate—and do not realize that being Christian means actively promoting the good of humanity. They think that religion consists of listening to sermons and hearing other people talk about God. As a result, they get bored, and religion has no meaning for them.

Misconceptions and Lack of Clarity About Doctrinal Issues

63   The following are misconceptions that the survey respondents identified as preventing other young people from enthusiastically embracing Jesus:

- Young people experience that God is all-powerful and good, but they also experience God as one who punishes.
- Young people think that their own or others' misfortunes represent God's will and that Jesus' death was brought about by God. They conclude that God wants people to suffer.
- They believe that "heaven"—paradise and life with God—begins after death.
- Young people do not clearly understand the doctrine of the Trinity, the coexisting human *and* divine natures of Jesus.
- They think that Jesus was a miracle-working saint but do not know that he is God.
- Young people do not understand the fact that Jesus was both peaceful and revolutionary.
- They question themselves about what it means to follow Jesus' example today, and they are eager to know what Jesus was like as a young man.
- Young people do not always understand how their personal conversion relates to improving life for themselves and for others in society.

Some Concerns of Hispanic Youth Group Members

64   The adolescent and young adult survey respondents expressed various concerns about Hispanic pastoral ministry, among which the following stood out:

- Some parish groups and lay movements present only particular aspects of Jesus' life and personality, without helping young people to know deeply the real Jesus or to embrace his whole mission.
- Many young people stagnate at an individualistic "Jesus and me" relationship, unaware that Jesus is present in each person as a member of the church community.
- Evangelization efforts occasionally offer a sentimental vision of life that focuses on feeling good and being happy but fails to call young people to act in the world as Christians.
- The church lacks young people who are well trained, active, and enthusiastic enough to encourage others to join Jesus' cause and create a better world.

- Certain youth group leaders strive to be recognized rather than to serve.
- Frequently, service occurs only within the bounds of the church community or is seen by young people as just a requirement for confirmation.

Signs of Hope and Joy

65   Having in our hands these responses from Latino youth group members represents a sign of hope and joy. Knowing that Jesus is alive among Latino young people who are active members of the church, and realizing that many young people understand and are carrying out their evangelical mission, convinces us of the growing maturity and commitment of Latino youth. At the same time, recognizing the perceptions held by young people who do not participate in church life can greatly aid us in better focusing our pastoral ministry.

66   According to young evangelizers and missionaries, young people who are distant from God yearn to know that Jesus forgives them and desires good for them and for all people. Alienated young people begin to trust Jesus as they begin to know and trust the young evangelizers. These alienated young people then realize that through the evangelizers, they are receiving the power and mercy that they need to move forward or to find meaning in their life. Soon they want to know more about Jesus and try to imitate him by not doing harm to others. After a while, these young people try to imitate him by doing good. As a result, they get involved in church youth groups because they know that there they will find the support they need in their new life. Finally, when they become enthusiastic about their faith, they get involved in their church and later in their local community as a way to bring the Gospel to life in the society in which they live.

The Secularization Process Challenges Latino Youth

67   Two dramatic changes characterize today's society: the shift from an agricultural society to an urban, industrial society and the rise of science as a means of knowing the world. The first shift has changed people's religiosity and has generated a faith crisis among a large sector of the population. The second has led another sector of

the population to separate religious faith from the rest of life. Together, these two shifts have led to **secularization**—to separation of people's everyday world from the sacred or religious world and to the substitution of scientific, technological, or consumer values and symbols for religious values and symbols.

68   This secularization has caused a separation between God and persons as well as between faith and the elements of science, culture, and daily life. The rupture has generated internal conflict in people and led to inadequate and mistaken understandings of the human person, breakdown of valuable social structures, and visions of human life that are alienated from and even opposed to the Gospel. As a result, the Second Vatican Council and other church documents, such as *Evangelii Nuntiandi,* identify the separation as the greatest tragedy of modern culture.

69   In the following section, we analyze the principal challenges arising from the secularization process and discuss how these challenges confront young people with a series of pressing questions. We analyze the challenges generated by various visions of the human person, by current **cultural dynamics,** by science and technology, and by popular religiosity. Finally, we offer some guidelines for responding to the challenges in each of these areas.

Challenges Generated by Visions of the Human Person

70   God became incarnated in Jesus. In the mystery of Christ, God comes down to restore the dignity of human beings. Faith in Christ gives us the fundamental criteria for acquiring a holistic vision of the human being. However, even in Christian cultures, over the course of time, various theories and ideologies have introduced non-Christian outlooks on the human being. Such outlooks offer only a partial or distorted vision of the human being or even close themselves off from any such integral vision.

71   The following are the most common challenges to the Christian vision of the human person, based on the categories established by the Latin American bishops:[1]

72   **The view of determinism:** In the vision termed determinism, the human person is a prisoner of magical ways of seeing the world and acting on it. That is to say, people are not their own masters, but rather are victims of occult forces. When young people have

this view, their only suitable attitude is to collaborate with the occult forces. Young people often believe that the forces are good or bad luck, or that everything that happens has been determined and imposed by God.

73   A variant form of the deterministic view, which is more social and fatalistic, is based on the erroneous idea that human beings are not fundamentally equal. The supposed difference between persons gives rise to many forms of discrimination and marginalization that are incompatible with human dignity.

74   **The view of psychologism:** Psychologism is based on the idea that human persons are ultimately reducible to their psychic mechanisms. In its most radical form, this view presents the human person as the victim of a fundamental, erotic instinct or as a mere response mechanism to stimuli, devoid of freedom. These perspectives of the human person take young people away from personal responsibility and oftentimes lead them to be driven by their natural impulses and exposed to psychological manipulation.

75   **Economicist views:** Three distinct views of the human being have a common root in economics:
- The *consumptionist* view regards the human being as nothing more than an instrument of production and an object of consumption. This view is highly promoted by commercial enterprises, especially among teenagers and young adults.
- *Economic liberalism* and its *materialistic **praxis*** offer an individualistic view of the human being. This view leads young people to think that the dignity and value of human persons lie in their economic efficiency and in their use of their individual freedom.
- *Classical Marxism* replaces the individualistic view of the human being with a collectivist, almost messianic, view in which the goal of all human existence is the development of the material forces of production. In this view, individuals receive their norms of behavior from officials responsible for changing the social, political, and economic structures without recognizing people's interior conscience and religious freedom. Young people who accept Marxism place an absolute value on external structures, believe that human beings are constituted only by their social existence, and reduce the individual to an object manipulated by social systems.

76   **The view of statism:** Statism, grounded on the theory of national security, has been a common vision in Latin America. Statism enrolls the individual in unlimited service to the alleged total war against cultural, social, political, and economic strife—and thereby against the threat of communism. Young people who share this view maintain that in the face of permanent danger to the state, or in an emergency situation, individual freedoms should be restricted and the will of the state should become the will of the nation.

77   **The view of scientism:** Scientism, promoted by the scientific and technological organization of some countries, considers the vocation of the human person to be the conquest of the universe. Young people who assume this view reduce human beings to their scientific definition, recognize as truth only that which can be demonstrated by science, and justify, in the name of science, even those actions which are an affront to human dignity.

Christian Responses to the Visions of the Human Person

78   Young people and young adults can respond successfully to the challenges presented by the various visions of the human person:

1. Young people can reflect on the nature, process, and challenges of their development as persons, paying special attention to three pillars of Christian **anthropology:**
   - becoming conscious of and valuing their own dignity as sons and daughters of God; respecting the dignity of others in all their relationships; not allowing themselves to be treated, or treating others, as anonymous elements of an impersonal and individualistic society or as objects to be used or manipulated for one's own benefit or the benefit of the economic market or political system
   - recognizing that only Christ offers us freedom to love God and others, liberation from all of sin's oppression, and full realization as persons
   - establishing communion with God and with other persons on the basis of the dignity of all, the exercise of freedom, and the fulfillment of our communitarian vocation
2. Young people can accept God's invitation to collaborate in the liberating mission of Jesus, promoting a society that

- respects human life as a gift from God, from the moment of conception until the moment of death
- recognizes the place and dignity of the human being
- defends the rights of all persons, regardless of race, social class, religion, age, or gender
- promotes each person's acceptance of his or her personal and social responsibility
- appreciates, from the perspectives of faith and of the human sciences, the reality and greatness of being human
- seeks the common good and encourages shared human life based on love, service, justice, and peace

Challenges Generated by the Separation of Faith and Culture

79   The strongest challenges that young Latinos confront arise from the dynamic quality of modern culture, the process of secularization, the loss of intermediate social structures, and the appearance of new paradigms and cultural models.

80   **The dynamic quality of modern culture:** All cultures pass through periods of transition marked by their encounters with different cultures, the appearance of new cultural elements, or the development of new interpretations and expressions of human life. During these periods of change, society must create a new synthesis of the culture's vision of being human. As a result, traditional forms of social organization may change, decay, or die; old values may be challenged or rejected; and new systems of values to guide human life may be created.

81   **The process of secularization:** Secularization separates the human person from God and severs human life from its religious meaning. It leads people to see themselves in opposition to God; it considers the human being, the universe, and nature as exclusively the fruit of natural laws; it sees human beings as being exclusively responsible for constructing human destiny; and it considers persons only in their immanent or temporal dimension. Young people are vulnerable to the process of secularization, especially if they have been deprived of consumer goods or have suddenly experienced a dramatic increase in their income. In these cases, young

people are strongly attracted to new lifestyles. They tend to reject traditional religious values.

82   **The loss of intermediate social structures:** Individualistic materialism, the needs created by consumerism, and the accelerated rhythm of modern life have weakened or destroyed a series of intermediate social structures. These include the nuclear family, the extended family, and groups for support and collaboration, such as work groups, small church communities, and educational and social clubs. These fractured social structures have left young people without a sense of community and without settings that promote belonging, security, and rootedness.

83   **The appearance of new paradigms and cultural models:** The separation of faith and culture has changed our way of perceiving life. On the positive side, secularization has influenced our awareness of the dignity of persons and their rights and responsibilities, helped us understand the laws of nature, and purified religion of many superstitions. On the negative side, it has led to practical atheism; to evaluating persons, nature, and things strictly according to their functionality; to valuing things over people; and to treating persons as things.

Christian Responses to the Challenges of Modern Culture

84   Young people can respond to these cultural challenges by
- identifying in modern culture the seeds of God's word that exist in all cultures even before they are evangelized, for example, the presence of God and the values of the Reign of God
- understanding the process of secularization, critically analyzing it, and seeking concrete ways of living out Jesus' values within modern society
- promoting an evangelized and evangelizing youth culture that transforms modern culture from within by the authenticity of their Christian life
- creating bridges between personal life and social life, such as study circles, community organization groups, organizations for social action, and so on. These structures will serve as trampolines by helping young people launch themselves into social life and into projects through which they can benefit society and grow personally.

- creating and strengthening intermediate social structures that facilitate young people living the Gospel together; these include youth groups, clubs, apostolic movements, and small church communities
- articulating new paradigms for Hispanic youth ministry and creating new models of pastoral action in which young people can live, love, and act in the style of Jesus, thus laying the foundation for a better future
- celebrating, as an ecclesial community, the experiences of new life that do occur within modern culture

Challenges Due to Scientific and Technological Development

85   For a long time, scientific and technological developments brought religious beliefs and scientific beliefs into direct conflict. As a result, faith and science became mutually exclusive, leading to a separation between the intellectual and religious dimensions of life. Currently, humanism, the religious vision of life, and the materialist focus of science and technology are engaged in a more fruitful dialog. In this interaction we can begin to see a promise of a new complementarity and even harmony between scientific truth and the truth revealed by God.

86   Among the challenges that Latino youth face as a result of the developments of science and technology are the following: accepting the whole terrain of science as something belonging to them; recognizing the legitimate **autonomy** of science and religion; relating the applied sciences to Christian ethics; recognizing the appropriate roles of the human and social sciences to fostering human advancement; and using mass communication to create a society rooted in the values of the Reign of God.

87   **Accepting science as something belonging to Latino youth:** For many reasons, including the vicious cycles of poverty and racial discrimination, Latino youth in the United States generally have not viewed scientific endeavor as something appropriate for them. This represents a strong challenge, given that science and technology strongly influence nearly all efforts to improve the quality of human life and to create a better world. Thus, it is urgent for Latino young people to become trained in science and technology and to receive the formation necessary to take on the challenges of this realm of human endeavor from a Christian perspective.

88   **Recognizing the legitimate autonomy of science and religion:** In the field of human knowledge, two distinct orders exist: that of science and that of faith. Both kinds of knowledge respond to the desires and needs of humans, with their God-given intellectual and spiritual capacities for discovering the truth. Science and religion are two **autonomous** fields of human endeavor; they demand complementarity and not opposition. This relative autonomy can be noted in the following:

1. *The search for truth,* which in the sciences means searching for the laws that govern the natural order of creation, and in religion means discovering the meaning of human life and of the entire universe

2. *Knowledge of reality,* to which science contributes by describing the world and identifying its causal relations, and religion contributes by helping to discover the fundamental values and goals of creation

3. *Interpretation of reality,* which is carried out by science through causal and theoretical explanations, and by religion through discovering the presence of God in human life and in the universe

89   **Relating the sciences to Christian ethics:** The social function of both *pure science* (focused on discovering a scientific truth) and *applied science* (focused on using scientific knowledge for human activity) is to help improve human life. From a Christian point of view, obtaining scientific knowledge by sacrificing the well-being of persons or the environment, or using scientific and technological advances in projects that undermine human dignity is wrong. These ethical considerations demand critical analysis and continuous faith reflection by all laypeople committed to the task of building a better world. The critical reflection process should be aided by Christian theologians and scientists.

90   Some examples of the challenges presented by science and technology to Christian ethics are the following: in the *biological sciences,* the advances in genetic engineering that allow scientists to alter the genetic characteristics of human beings; in *chemistry and physics,* the creation of nuclear energy and substances that can be used for the development or destruction of human life; and in *medicine,* knowledge and technologies that can improve, extend, or destroy life.

91   **Recognizing the appropriate roles of the human and social sciences:** The human and social sciences include psychology, education, cultural anthropology, sociology, economics, and political science. Like the natural sciences, the human and social sciences involve pure knowledge and applied knowledge, both of which should be subjected to an ethical focus that assures respect for the dignity of persons and the use of knowledge for personal and social development. The involvement of Hispanics in these fields is especially relevant to promoting Hispanic development in the United States. Hispanic people must study Hispanic culture and psychology from their own perspective and engage in projects that promote Hispanic development by improving the economic, social, cultural, and political conditions in which Hispanics live.

92   **Using mass communication to promote the values of the Reign of God:** Mass communications, which have advanced dramatically with the rise of electronic technology and computing, present two main challenges to Hispanic youth: first, the new technologies demand that Hispanics become trained in using these means of communication, which are ever more needed at work and in daily life; second, Hispanics must become more involved in the communications industry to influence society by promoting the values of the Reign of God.

Christian Responses to the Challenges of Science and Technology

93   Young people can respond to the challenges of science and technology by doing the following:

1. Affirming the proper realm and autonomy of science and technology in relation to the realm of faith, through three complementary activities:
   - seeking coherence between the knowledge offered by science and their own faith experience
   - drawing on their scientific knowledge and faith experience to understand the reality of human life and the world
   - creating a culture that expresses and facilitates a synthesis between the world of science and technology and the world of faith, through family life, work, economic activity, art, reflection, education, and other human activities

2. Building a world based on the values of the Reign of God and a Christian anthropology that considers the human person as the principle and goal of all human striving, through two kinds of complementary actions:
   - using scientific knowledge and techniques to promote human and social development
   - illuminating scientific and technological enterprises with the fundamental principles of faith so that they serve human beings and always avoid abusing human persons

Challenges Arising from Popular Religiosity

94   The culture shock experienced by many Hispanics, especially those who have recently emigrated to the United States, often powerfully influences their faith. Among the factors that most strongly affect the faith of Hispanic young people are the conflict between popular religiosity and the process of secularization; the religious pluralism of the United States; and alienation, marginalization, and fatalism resulting from the limitations and deviations of Hispanic popular religiosity.

95   **The conflict between popular religiosity and the process of secularization:** Due to the strong relationship between religiosity and culture among Latin American peoples, contact with the secularized culture of the developed countries, including the United States, places into doubt their religious vision of life and the values and attitudes that are founded on that vision. In addition, the lack of popular religious expression among Hispanics in the United States weakens their Hispanic identity and reduces their cohesiveness as a people, making them vulnerable to the shower of new ideas originating in a culture that values materialism, consumerism, and hedonism.

96   The fact that Hispanics often do not have opportunities to express their beliefs and religious experiences in their own language and through their own traditions further weakens popular religiosity. This, too, increases their likelihood of succumbing to the influence of secularism and ultimately ignoring the presence of God in their life.

97   **The religious pluralism of the United States:** Religious diversity in the United States is extensive. This causes much confusion

among Hispanics, who for decades were accustomed to Catholicism as the only religion. In seeing the existence of many alternative religions and churches, Hispanics' religious paradigm (or the lens through which they focus their way of living in relationship to God) undergoes serious modification. The points of reference and support on which they counted disappear, the myriad of choices disorient them, and the confusion and traditionalism of their parents leave them without foundation.

98   **Alienation, marginalization, and religious fatalism:** Due to its close relationship to the poverty and religious marginalization in which the majority of Hispanic people have lived, Hispanic popular religiosity tends to contribute to their lack of consciousness of their situation of oppression and injustice, to their belief that God wills them to live this way, and to their not taking responsibility for their human development or for their role as God's coprotagonists of history. Furthermore, some practices of Hispanic popular religiosity, and of popular Catholicism in general, keep many young people from conscious participation and complete communion in the ecclesial community.

99   Because of the importance of belonging and identifying with a group, young people are very vulnerable to fundamentalist groups, occultist sects with esoteric rituals, personality cults, and magical or superstitious rituals. These kinds of groups alienate young people from their reality by overemphasizing ritual experiences and expressions. In these expressions, young people find false security, protection, and self-affirmation that help them evade the world and avoid taking responsibility for their life.

Christian Responses to the Challenges of Hispanic Popular Religiosity

100   Young people respond to the challenges arising from Hispanic popular religiosity by

- deepening their religious and communitarian experience through cultural traditions such as *posadas, mañanitas,* Mother's Day fiestas, musical events, *pastorelas,* and ways of the cross. These kinds of expressions, beyond fostering young people's creativity, encourage their involvement in the whole ecclesial community.
- taking their place in the church, both in receiving the pastoral care they need and in fulfilling their personal and communitarian missions as young Christians

- critically analyzing popular religiosity, thus discovering its values and its possibilities as a means of liberating evangelization
- accepting and adapting both traditional and new cultural expressions in order to create a religious environment that is meaningful for their current life and helps them share the faith
- participating in evangelizing catechesis that helps them know and mature in the faith, practice their Christianity, and purify their religiosity of anything that is contrary to the Gospel
- knowing about ecumenical relations with the other historic Christian traditions and distinguishing Christian churches from non-Christian religions and fundamentalist sects

Embracing Life in the World:
A Responsibility of Every Christian

101 To be a layperson is the natural condition and vocation of men and women, according to God's design as manifested in the relative autonomy God gave to creation. Every man and woman has been born in order to live in and build up the world. Fundamentally, humanity *is* the world, because God has established every aspect of creation to be at the service of humanity.

102 To be a layperson in the world means to be fully human, to embody the noble values of humanity, and to commit oneself to constructing a better society and a better world. Above all, this means struggling constantly for a freer, more fraternal, and more joyful humanity.

103 In embracing life in the world, young people recognize and value the relative autonomy of temporal things without ignoring their religious meaning and place. Christian faith helps to give both temporal and religious things their proper importance in the daily routine of family, work, study, and sociopolitical action. We believe that the God revealed in Jesus is a God of wisdom, whom we know better as we increase our knowledge of the world that God creates and sustains with infinite love. Furthermore, while it is true that science on its own cannot lead to belief in God, for the believer the sciences reveal God's greatness.

104 When young people embrace lay life as a Christian vocation, they find new depth in the central mysteries and symbols of the faith. Through lay life they fortify their faith, integrate it with science and modern culture, and discover the meaning of the world in

which they live. When this does not occur, secularization tends to displace the Christian vision of life and weaken young people's relationship with God. Then they fall little by little into a practical atheism that leads them to establish moral criteria according to their individual interests.

105   It is crucial that young Latinos, inspired and strengthened by the Christian faith, accept the challenges that the secular world presents to them. As Pope John Paul II said in his message to the youth of the world on World Youth Day 1993, in Denver, Colorado:

> Left to ourselves, we could never achieve the ends for which we have been created. Within us there is a promise which we find we are incapable of attaining. But the Son of God who came among us has given his personal assurance: "I am the way, and the truth, and the life" (John 14:6). As Saint Augustine so strikingly phrased it, Christ "wishes to create a place in which it is possible for all people to find true life." This "place" is his Body and his Spirit, in which the whole of human life, redeemed and forgiven, is renewed and made divine.[2]

The Evangelizing Mission
of the Church

✿ 6 ✿

The Evangelizing Mission of the Church

✿

The young, who have a special vocation to hope, should spread among their peers the message of light and life that is in Christ.

—National Conference of Catholic Bishops,
Heritage and Hope

1   The presence of Christianity in the Americas already spans five hundred years; the presence of Christianity on this earth, two thousand years. Recognition of these milestones and of the challenges and circumstances now confronting Christianity urges us to carry forward a "New Evangelization"—new in its fervor, its methods, and its expressions. In *Heritage and Hope,* a pastoral letter on the Fifth Centenary of Evangelization in the Americas, the Catholic bishops of the United States proposed that we launch this New Evangelization in two stages:

> In phase one, we call upon all to become increasingly aware of the need for being evangelized afresh, for bringing the light of Christ to our own lives and to those of our families and faith communities. During phase two, we urge reaching out to alienated Catholics, the unchurched, and society at large with the Good News.[1]

2   In this chapter, we reflect on the evangelizing mission of the church and on the role of young people in the New Evangelization. We also analyze the implications of the preferential options for the poor and the young on our evangelization efforts. Finally, we deal with two parish models: the passive parish and the missionary parish, and the place of Hispanic youth ministry in both of them.

The Church and Its Mission

The Church as Jesus' Legacy to the World

3   The mission of Jesus was to establish the Reign of God on earth—to communicate God's unconditional love, concern, and care for all people. Mark, at the beginning of his Gospel, mentions how Jesus proclaimed that the Reign of God had arrived: "'The time is fulfilled, and the kingdom of God has come near; repent, and believe in the good news'" (1:15).

4   Jesus taught people a new way of relating to God—as Father. Through his own unique relationship with God, Jesus passed on God's vision for and union with people. Through his own death and Resurrection, Jesus forever reconciled people with God. In other words, through his total identification with the message of salvation, Jesus proclaimed the Good News in his words, in his deeds, and in his own person.

5   Following his Resurrection, Jesus appeared to his disciples, commissioning them to teach, baptize, and make disciples in his name. The gift of the Holy Spirit at Pentecost not only gave the disciples a greater understanding of Jesus' identity, but it also transformed them into a true faith community—into the church. The experience of Pentecost really "founded" the church. It enlightened the disciples of their tasks on earth as "the church" and emboldened them to be courageous witnesses of the Risen Jesus. Foremost among the tasks given to the church were continuing Jesus' mission of building the Reign of God on earth and proclaiming the Good News to all nations—tasks which are almost synonymous with what we call *evangelization.*

Evangelization: Concepts and Goals

6   Before all else, to evangelize is to bear witness in a simple and direct way to the God revealed through Jesus Christ and the Holy Spirit. That is, to evangelize means to give testimony to the unconditional love of God for all humanity and to our calling to live eternally with God. At the center of all true evangelization efforts lies Jesus Christ, the Son of God, who was made human, died, and was resurrected. Jesus' life bore fruit in the salvation that he brought us as a merciful gift from God. Just as Jesus brought salvation into his world

through what he said, what he did, and who he was, we project salvation into our world through our words, actions, and being—through our love, self-giving to others, forgiveness, renunciation of sin, and service.

7 The evangelization of young people has three essential and complementary dimensions. First, Jesus, his message, and his mission must be presented to young people in ways that allow them to experience the saving presence of Jesus within the Christian community and to initiate a personal and communitarian relationship with him. Second, young people need to open themselves to the work of the Spirit and allow themselves to be converted in heart, mind, and in all of life, deciding to follow Jesus as disciples. Third, young people should accept as their own the task of continuing Jesus' mission, of extending the Reign of God on earth, actively working so that relations among persons and nations might be guided by justice, love, truth, freedom, and peace.

8 The *goal* of evangelization is not just to help people know and accept Jesus as a personal savior but also to help them see that the Gospel directly touches and confronts all dimensions of their life. Thus, evangelization should address young people's concrete life situations, thereby updating Jesus' message according to the needs of their personal, family, community, and social life in general.

9 Because social and economic problems so deeply affect everyone's life, it is impossible to dissociate God's plan for redemption from concrete situations of injustice and violence. Thus, evangelization is intimately linked to the promotion of human development and liberation, and the church should promote justice and peace as integral parts of the Gospel.

10 To carry the Gospel in a liberating and inspiring way, young Latinos need to have both the life God wants for them and the enthusiasm to continue Jesus' mission. Our country and our world need more young men and women who, moved by the Gospel, will pull down the idols of consumerism, power, and individualism and place God above all things and Jesus at the center of their life. These young people can carry the love of God to young people who have no family; to sick, suffering, or imprisoned people; to older people who lack companionship; and to children who need friends, role models, or peer tutors. Christian hope will be fed by the joy and dedication of such missionary-prophets, who denounce social

sin and generate hope for a culture of sharing and peace. In this way, Latino young people will participate in the evangelizing efforts of all Latinos, as indicated in the Segundo Encuentro Nacional Hispano de Pastoral:

> We understand evangelization to imply a continuous lifelong process in which a Christian makes an ever deepening effort to arrive at a personal and communal encounter with the messenger, Christ, and a total commitment to His message, the Gospel. Who does not live an attitude of daily conversion is not evangelized. Who lives it, personally and communally, proclaims the Gospel with the testimony of a life of service to one's neighbor, as well as by word and in other ways, for the transformation of the world.[2]

The Mission of Young People Today

11 Being a Christian young person today means having been called by Jesus to work in the vineyard of the Lord, in all the environments the modern-day vineyard encompasses: family, school, neighborhood, workplace, and so on. It means building an earthly world embodying the values of the Reign of God. God's will is revealed to young people through the situations in which they live. God calls young people to shape this world through their daily activities, to participate in the work of creation and redemption by filling their homes with joy, harmony, and support; by encouraging and sustaining their friends and *compañeros;* by serving their neighbors and other members of their community; and by constructing a culture of sharing and peace.

Receiving the Mission

12 The baptismal invitation that young people receive—to be workers in the vineyard of the Lord—also comes with the task of continuing Jesus' three roles in the world: priest, prophet, and servant-leader. Young people fulfill their priestly role and mission by offering up their daily lives to God and helping reconcile people to God and one another. Young people's offering up of their daily lives and joining of themselves with God and Jesus culminates in their participation in the Eucharist. Young people develop their prophetic role and mission by denouncing the absence of love, justice,

and peace in society and by proclaiming the Reign of God through the testimony of their personal and communitarian lives. Young people carry out their role and mission as servant-leaders by personally serving others' concrete needs.

13   In fulfilling their mission in the world, young people make real the salvation brought by Jesus, within the settings in which they live. It is not enough for young people just to pray, attend church, or meet in groups. Nor is it enough for them to settle for social activism based on their own efforts, forgetting the Spirit and the need to be vehicles for reconciliation with God and other persons. The arrival of the Reign of God is intimately linked to the struggle for love and justice. Commitment to this struggle is born and becomes real when young people truly center themselves and their life on Jesus.

Receiving Help for the Mission

14   In centering their own self and life toward building the Reign of God, young people should squarely face their life situations by critically analyzing the economic, social, political, and cultural conditions in which they live, including their values and problems, their concerns and hopes, their victories and failures. Those who aid young people in fulfilling their mission must be careful not to seal young people up in the church and isolate them from the world. Any separation between following Jesus in this world and taking concrete action to bring the Reign of God to this world is in no way legitimate. It is vital that young people accept responsibility for their part in the world's order and do what they can to transform reality by the light of Jesus' Gospel and the mind of the church.

15   The education of young people about social justice should begin with their own life situation. Hispanic young people should discover and analyze the injustices they suffer that are similar to those suffered by other ethnic groups: functional illiteracy, low levels of formal education, and high dropout rates; the imbalance that exists in wages, employment, and employment opportunities, which leaves nearly 30 percent of Hispanic children and young people below the poverty level, tens of thousands of parents without work, and many others dependent on public assistance; the lack of adequate available medical care; the disproportionate exposure to risk during war; and so on.[3]

16   These injustices place young Latinos at a strong disadvantage to young people of the dominant U.S. culture when competing for placement in higher education or the workplace. These injustices also give rise to complex social and cultural disorders, such as the high proportion of adolescent pregnancy and AIDS; the prevalence of gangs, gang violence, crime, drugs, drug addiction, and drug trafficking; and the frequency with which toxic waste sites are located in Latino neighborhoods—60 percent of Latinos live in contaminated areas.[4] Furthermore, these and similar realities make it extremely difficult for Latino young people to effectively prepare themselves to participate in the decision-making processes that affect their lives and the life of their community.

17   Young people's first reaction upon becoming fully aware of these and other problems will probably be anger. Youth ministers must not leave young people in a state of anger. Young people's discontent must be channeled toward positive action, focused on overcoming the principal challenges in our society, which include the following:

- the need for human solidarity based on the value of each human being and directed toward the construction of a culture of sharing and peace
- the need for dignified, productive, creative, and well-paying jobs that facilitate human development, family life, and the common good
- the need to find creative solutions to the exploitation and manipulation of workers, without relying on violent class struggle or on liberal capitalism's disregard for the common good and the new oppressions that it generates
- the need to have decent living conditions as the basis for autonomy and personal development
- the need to end the alienation and human oppression that result when we fail to recognize every person's vocation to be an "agent of history" and instead treat people as slaves of the economic, political, or ideological interests that dominate society

18   The search for God and the mission of building God's Reign in society will often be difficult for Hispanic young people because of all the human and religious challenges they face. In their journey, Hispanic young people generally welcome help and guidance from good shepherds who, following the style of Jesus, call, direct, heal, unite, and strengthen them. Therefore, those young people and

young adults who have encountered Jesus in the faith community, along with youth ministers and pastoral agents, should be effective bearers of the Good News to those who are facing difficulty in their journey toward God.

Latino Youth and the New Evangelization

Foreshadowings of the New Evangelization

19   The concept of a New Evangelization was proposed by Pope John Paul II at the Latin American Episcopal Conference (CELAM) in Haiti in 1983. The ideal of this New Evangelization is to help the church respond to the great challenges it must face as new situations emerge in Latin America and the world. "New" does not refer to the contents of the Gospel message; that message never changes; Christ is "the same yesterday, today, and forever" (Heb. 13:8). Rather, "new" refers to the attitude, style, strength, and planning—"the ardor, methods, and expression"—of this evangelization.[5] Many people have asked what the New Evangelization means: Do we need to change directions and do something different? Is it enough simply to redouble our efforts? Do we need to create new methods of evangelization? What does "new faith expressions" mean?

20   The New Evangelization really began almost thirty years ago as part of the renewal of the church following the Second Vatican Council. Since then, evangelizing efforts have been guided by the spirit of the *Pastoral Constitution on the Church in the Modern World* (*Gaudium et Spes*), the encyclical *Evangelii Nuntiandi*, the *Decree on the Church's Missionary Activity* (*Ad Gentes*), and others. The New Evangelization emphasizes the relationship among the Gospel, culture, and society; points to the vital mission of laypeople in the modern world; and promotes ecumenical relations between different Christian churches and dialog among different religions.

21   Latino people have established the foundations for this New Evangelization, guided by the meetings of CELAM in Medellín, Colombia (1968), and in Puebla, Mexico (1979). Latinos in the United States have begun to identify their pastoral needs, clarify a model of evangelization, and intensify pastoral efforts through National Encuentros and the *National Pastoral Plan for Hispanic Ministry*.

22   The concluding document of the Fourth Conference of Latin American Bishops in Santo Domingo in 1992, entitled "New Evangelization, Human Promotion, and Christian Culture," presents the spirit and concrete goals of this new missionary effort: a commitment to establish a new evangelizing strategy during the next few years through an overall plan of evangelization that has three priority lines of action:

1. *A New Evangelization,* to which all are called, emphasizing a pastoral vocation with a special role for laypeople, including young people. This New Evangelization must be achieved through continual education in the faith—through catechesis and the celebration of that faith in liturgy. And it must go beyond local and regional borders to create a missionary church.

2. *An integral human promotion* of the people as a whole, at the service of life and family, by means of a renewed and Gospel-based preferential option for the poor.

3. *An inculturated evangelization* that penetrates and becomes incarnate in diverse social settings—urban cultures and indigenous and African American cultures—through effective educational action and modern communication.[6]

Characteristics of the New Evangelization

23   The launching point of the New Evangelization lies in the certainty that in Christ there is an unequaled richness that we can always share. Regardless of the situation in which we find ourselves, we can always turn to Jesus. He offers his merciful love and fullness of life to anyone who accepts him as a source of life.

24   To speak of a New Evangelization implies that a previous evangelization has occurred. It does not mean that the first was invalid, but that new challenges and situations have arisen to which we, as Christians, urgently must respond.

25   The New Evangelization consists of offering the salvation brought by Jesus Christ in a new way that responds to today's world. This task requires, above all, inspiring young people who adhere personally to Jesus Christ and his church. Through these inspiring young people, the young men and women who have been baptized but live their Christianity without spirit will encounter in Jesus the faith that has been handed on to them but has not found meaningful expression in their life. Some young people complain that they find meaningless the faith they inherited from their par-

ents. To others, Jesus and his message were presented only weakly or superficially. Still others pass through adolescence without ever maturing in the faith that they learned as a child. The New Evangelization strives to reach all these young people.

26   The content of the New Evangelization is the same as for all evangelization: Jesus Christ, the Good News of the Father. Today, like yesterday and tomorrow, we must proclaim and present Jesus to young people. With words and deeds, Jesus announced that God is merciful to all of us, that God loves every man and woman with a boundless love, and that God desired to enter history through Jesus Christ, who died and rose again to free us from sin and all its consequences and to allow us to participate in divine life.

27   All things find their meaning in Christ. Christ breaks the narrow horizon in which secularism closes people. Life in Christ refuses to allow any temporal reality to become a supreme order to which human beings should subject themselves. Thus, life in Christ restores dignity to the daughters and sons of God.

The Evangelization Process

28   "There is no true evangelization if the name, the teaching, the life, the promises, the Kingdom, and the mystery of Jesus of Nazareth, the son of God are not proclaimed."[7] Jesus is the living evangelizer of his church. In announcing Jesus, we must do so in such a way that young people encounter him. This encounter should lead them to yearn to be his disciples, to recognize sin in their life, and to experience conversion through a profound experience of the grace of the Spirit received in baptism. Through this conversion experience, most young people will come to value and appreciate anew the sacrament of reconciliation, participate in the Eucharist, and practice their Christianity according to the model provided by Jesus.

29   The evangelization process will have renewing strength among young people if it remains faithful to the word of God. It will be embraced by young people if it is born of the Holy Spirit, who creates unity amid diversity, nourishes their gifts, and strengthens them in their ministries. Evangelization will bear fruit if the action of the Spirit is projected into young people's lives through the missionary commitment of the young people themselves. It will be effective if young people encounter in Jesus new light to help them solve their problems.

30   The New Evangelization arises in response to the problems of the American continents, where the separation of faith from life produces dramatic situations of injustice, social inequality, and violence. It demands commitment to the grand task of energizing Christians. The New Evangelization is not a re-evangelization that denies the truth of the first evangelization. Rather, it demands recognition of the rich and abundant Christian values that exist among the Hispanic people in order to deepen and complement those values while also seeking to correct previous deficiencies.

31   The evangelization process calls young people to change their lives and to be active agents of history. It makes real the hope of a new life. It provides a foundation for human promotion, the first step of building an authentic Christian culture. This evangelization must provide new vitality, a new Pentecost, in which the presence of the Holy Spirit draws forth a renewed people made up of free men and women who are aware of their dignity and are capable of forging a truly *human* history. This evangelization means carrying out actions, adopting attitudes, and using the means necessary to place the Gospel in active dialog with contemporary culture. It means trying constantly to inculturate the Gospel into the diverse cultural conditions of the American continents.

The Protagonists and the Goals of the New Evangelization

32   The protagonists of the New Evangelization are the members of the ecclesial community, each in his or her own mission—bishops, priests, deacons, religious, and laypeople; women and men; children and young people. All of us as members of the church have been called to evangelize through our personal vocations and God-given talents. The New Evangelization should be directed to every person and to the social influences that shape society.

33   The goal of this evangelization is to form mature persons and faith communities that are capable of responding fully to the situations in which we live. Our current era—marked by science, technology, and mass communications—brings with it new values that in themselves are seeds of the Word. But modern technology also creates new situations that tend to separate persons from God. Thus, evangelization must evangelize Catholics who themselves will become evangelizers of others as well as protagonists of human promotion and Christian culture.

Qualities of the New Evangelization

A New Ardor

34   Through his Spirit present in the church, Jesus Christ calls us to renew our apostolic enthusiasm and gives us strength to do so. In responding to this call, young people follow the radical example of Jesus Christ, the first evangelizer, animated by his Spirit acting in them. As this process moves forward, these young evangelizers gradually become sanctified, women and men of the Beatitudes.

35   The new ardor born of this identification with Jesus Christ presupposes solid faith, intense pastoral charity, and stubborn fidelity. Under the action of the Spirit, this commitment generates a *mística,* an invincible enthusiasm to announce the Good News. These qualities and *mística* lend credibility to young people's evangelizing action and make them capable of awakening the hearts of other young people so that they too can embrace the good news of salvation.

New Methods

36   The new situations in which young people live demand new paths of evangelization. These new paths should rely on the basic methods of every evangelization: personal testimony of young Christians, their presence in diverse human settings, and their confidence in the saving proclamation of Jesus and in the activity of the Holy Spirit.

37   But these basic methods are not enough. Evangelizers must use their imagination and creativity to extend the Gospel to all young people in the most convincing and educationally sound way. Because we live in a culture of images, we should use science and technology to communicate our message today. However, we must not rely on showy or superficial methods, but on methods that make the Good News reach the hearts of young people, the center of society, and the roots of culture itself.

New Expressions

38   Jesus Christ asks us to proclaim the Good News in a language that brings the unchangeable Gospel message closer to young people's lives today. From the unbounded treasure that is Christ, young people can find new expressions that help them evangelize in the settings in which they live, settings now deeply influenced by

urban, secular culture. Young people have the special vocation of inculturating the Gospel within the new forms of human culture now being born.

39   The New Evangelization has to become inculturated in the ways of being and living in young Latino cultures in the United States, bearing in mind the individual characteristics of each culture. The call to put special attention to the **inculturation** of the Gospel in the native and African American cultures of Latin America is also a call to reassess the value of the native and African roots of Latino people in the United States and to purify those cultural values that are contrary to the Gospel.

40   Thus, the New Evangelization will continue the Incarnation of Jesus, who, by becoming a human being, became fully inserted in his own culture, assuming its human and religious values and challenging those customs that opposed his Father's will. In the same way that Jesus urged the conversion of his people, the New Evangelization demands the pastoral conversion of the church. This conversion should be coherent with the teachings of the Second Vatican Council in such a way that the doctrine, personal and communitarian praxis, relationships of authority, and structures and dynamic forces contribute to the church becoming, each day with more clarity, an effective sign of the grace of God, a sacrament of salvation for all the children of God.

Principles and Actions for an Effective Evangelization

41   Most Latino young people have been evangelized to a limited extent. They urgently need to hear the Good News presented in a way that corresponds to their reality and to become connected and more deeply integrated with one another's lives and with the church. To aid an effective evangelization process among young Latinos, we as individual members of the church and the church as a collective body need to recognize and further principles and actions such as the following:

- presenting Jesus and his message in ways that young people find direct, intense, and meaningful
- facilitating young people's free and responsible commitment to Christ and his mission of salvation
- promoting a life of discipleship that demands a deeper loyalty and *entrega* ("surrender") to God

- offering catechetical formation that is simple, complete, and grounded in the Scriptures
- centering our faith on the power of Christ to give new life and on our commitment to love one another and to proclaim the Good News to others
- promoting a Christian vision of young people as active participants in history
- receiving, respecting, and valuing Latino young people in our church, so that they can be evangelized and taught the faith in ways consistent with their culture and their language
- confronting the secularism and consumerism that exclude Gospel values from young people's private and public lives

42   The call to recognize and further effective principles and actions is addressed not only to the hierarchical church and the adult community but also to the young people. All have something to offer, and together, all are called by Christ to share their gifts and serve those in need. Latino young people in the United States require the church's attention. At the same time, these young people are called to be the principal prophets among their peers and to be a force for renewal in the church.

43   Every young person who is a member of a youth group or a small community is there for a unique reason, but the end result—and perhaps the connecting factor—of everyone's reason calls them together to *be* the young church in a particular place and moment. Through the church community as a whole and through its members, people come to experience and know the loving God that Jesus proclaimed. The church community is the means by which Jesus remains incarnate in the world today. Thus, the church serves as a sign and an instrument of God's communion with humanity and of the unity of human beings among themselves. Therefore, *it is important that every youth group or small community have a significant relationship with the rest of the church community—with adults as well as with young people from other cultures.*

44   The church expresses and celebrates its identity primarily in the Eucharist, where members share in the body and blood of Christ, becoming continuously and increasingly united by the Spirit in order to be the Body of Christ, the church. As members of the Body of Christ, all Christians are called to continue Jesus' mission in and to the world. To the extent that the Christian community

fulfills this mission, it is a sign of the Reign of God among us. Therefore, *parish youth groups,* **small youth communities,** *and young leaders in apostolic movements should collaborate with priests in organizing eucharistic liturgies that are attractive and meaningful for young people.*

45   To be a sign of the Reign of God, all the members of the church—young and old—should be servants of those in need, performing corporal and spiritual works of mercy, healing, and reconciliation, and living out their commitment to life, love, justice, peace, holiness, truth, and so on. Because of our human limitations, weaknesses, and sins, we are a frail sign of the Reign of God; we require continuous nourishment and reconciliation as we journey toward God. Therefore, *all members of the church, but especially young people, should be alert in identifying and positively changing those things that oppose the Reign of God—whether those things are internal or external factors.*

Catholic Social Teachings and the New Evangelization

46   In order to have the necessary breadth to help young people renew all of creation, the New Evangelization should rely strongly on the social teachings of the church. Especially during the last hundred years, the Catholic church has identified the social problems most relevant at a particular time, illuminated those problems with the message of Jesus, and elaborated a body of teachings and guidelines for resolving those problems. Most of the teachings and guidelines also relate broadly to people's formation of conscience and struggle for social justice.

47   Latino young people, in working for social justice inspired by the Gospel, question the quality of life, the level of freedom, and the degree of peace that exist for them today. They challenge the unjust educational and working conditions they face, in order to build a future of hope in which social welfare and crime are not the only available or most compelling routes to survival. In the following list of selected church documents, we present the aspects of Catholic social teaching that we consider most relevant for providing a sound foundation for the evangelization of Latino young people:

- *Rerum Novarum* (*On the Condition of Labor,* by Pope Leo XIII, 1891) points out the problems caused by the new social and economic order of the late-nineteenth-century industrial era; among the problems are the oppression and exploitation of workers and the selfish accumulation of goods and resources. *Rerum Novarum* emphasizes the right to receive a just wage, hold a job that has dignity, form labor unions, and own private property.

- *Quadragesimo Anno* (*On Reconstructing the Social Order,* by Pope Pius XI, 1931) says that all economic activity should be guided by justice and charity, that national and international laws should balance personal interests and the common good, and that Christian alternatives to Marxism and unrestricted capitalism should be sought.

- *Mater et Magistra* (*On Christianity and Social Progress,* by Pope John XXIII, 1961) discusses social development and world interdependency, denouncing individual and social sin and the enormous difference between rich nations and poor nations. In *Mater et Magistra,* Pope John XXIII encourages worker participation in the management of companies, speaks of the right to collective bargaining to benefit industrial workers, and emphasizes the responsibility of Christians for the construction of a more just society.

- *Pacem in Terris* (*On Establishing Universal Peace in Truth, Justice, Charity, and Liberty,* by Pope John XXIII, 1963) maintains that peace among peoples should be founded on truth, justice, love, and freedom. The document contends that constructing a world of justice and peace requires recognizing the dignity, obligations, and rights of the human person. *Pacem in Terris* affirms democracy, the right to life, and the search for truth. It emphasizes freedom of initiative, freedom of expression, freedom of information, and freedom of worship, as well as the right to educate one's children and to relocate within one's country or move to another country.

- *Gaudium et Spes* (*Pastoral Constitution on the Church in the Modern World,* from the Second Vatican Council, 1965) expounds on the need to discern the **"signs of the times"** so that each generation can respond adequately to the questions of its age, on such issues and concerns as marriage, the family, cultural development, the economy, politics, and peace.

- *Populorum Progressio* (*On the Development of Peoples,* by Pope Paul VI, 1967) defines the meaning of development, focusing on an integral understanding of the human person, respect for all cultures, and the satisfaction of the religious, social, and economic needs of all people. The document suggests establishing an international fund to promote the development of all people.

- *Octagesima Adveniens* (*On the Eightieth Anniversary of "Rerum Novarum,"* by Pope Paul VI, 1971) addresses political power and the need to commit ourselves to take transformative action regarding social discrimination, the role of women in society and in the world, the role of the media in social communication, and the problems of urbanization and environmental degradation.

- *Justice in the World* (from the Synod of Bishops, Second General Assembly, 1972) speaks of justice as a "constitutive dimension of the preaching of the Gospel" (no. 6); and in a related message about evangelization, notes that "unless the Christian message of love and justice shows its effectiveness through action . . . , it will only with difficulty gain credibility with the [people] of our times" (no. 35). The document emphasizes the preferential option for the poor and the necessity of social reform in allowing all members of society to actively participate in economic, political, and cultural life.

- *Laborem Exercens* (*On Human Work,* by Pope John Paul II, 1981) articulates a spirituality of work, supports the rights of individual workers and of labor unions, emphasizes the supremacy of persons over things, and reaffirms the dignity of agricultural labor. The document also addresses the industrialized countries' practice of buying raw materials at the lowest possible prices and selling their products at the highest possible prices—a practice that commonly results in exploitation of Third World countries. However, in criticizing unrestrained capitalism, the document also states clearly that Catholic social teaching "diverges radically" from Marxism.

- *Sollicitudo Rei Socialis* (*On Social Concern,* by Pope John Paul II, 1987) calls urgently for universal solidarity in the distribution of goods and for the redirection of resources to alleviate the sufferings of the poorest countries and people. The document analyzes the enormous economic differences between the countries of the northern and southern hemispheres, and it urges humankind to respect the rights of all persons, to solve the problems of refugee populations, and to conceive of the human person in more than economic terms.

- *Centesimus Annus* (*On the Hundredth Anniversary of "Rerum Novarum,"* by Pope John Paul II, 1991) emphasizes that the teaching and the spreading of social doctrine are part of the evangelizing mission of the church. The church's social doctrine is an essential part of the Christian message; through its social doctrine, the church highlights, within the framework of the testimony of Christ the Savior, the meaning of daily work and the struggle for justice.

Fulfilling Preferential Options in Evangelization

48   The *National Pastoral Plan for Hispanic Ministry* makes a preferential option for poor people, young people, families, and women. These options are especially applicable in any youth ministry that serves large numbers of young men and women who live in poverty or in families facing strong tensions and challenges.

Giving Priority to the Poor

49   Among the foundations of Catholic faith is the conviction that human life reaches its completeness in the knowledge and love of the living God and in communion with others. Given this belief, we should promote the inalienable (not able to be given up or taken away) dignity of all people, regardless of race, professional status, or personal achievement. We must end the inappropriate use of resources and distribute power over those resources more evenly among earth's inhabitants.

50   Through his life—past and present—and through his Gospel, Jesus encourages his followers to seek the rule and justice of God before anything else. Jesus takes upon himself the cause of those who are discriminated against socially or religiously, attacks the use of religion to avoid the demands of charity and justice, reveals his presence among the poor, and calls "blessed" those who show mercy to the naked, the hungry, and the sick. In affirming that the poor are blessed and that the Reign of God is theirs, Jesus is not glorifying poverty, but rather praising the openness of the poor to God. Jesus also says that the poor will benefit in a special way from God's mercy and justice.

51   These are the outlines of the preferential option for the poor, an option that should seriously challenge every church community.

Young Latinos, as followers of Jesus and as part of the church, are called to accept the tasks and sacrifices that this option requires of them, to commit themselves in solidarity with those who suffer, and to confront the attitudes and customs that institutionalize injustice. This struggle must be renewed generation after generation, so that hope and promise may become tangible, living realities among people.

52   Evangelization gives moral priority to assuring justice and human rights for all. This implies that as individuals and as a nation, we are called to commit ourselves fully to the option for the poor. The call to evaluate our society and economy from the perspective of the poor comes from the commandment to love one's neighbor as oneself and from the urgent need to reclaim the rights of the marginalized and oppressed, to enable them to become active participants in the life of society. The U.S. bishops, in their pastoral letter *Economic Justice for All*, clarify what is meant by this reclamation of rights and enablement:

> The "option for the poor," therefore, is not an adversarial slogan that pits one group or class against another. Rather it states that the deprivation and powerlessness of the poor wounds the whole community. The extent of their suffering is a measure of how far we are from being a true community of persons. These wounds will be healed only by greater solidarity with the poor and among the poor themselves.[8]

53   Jesus teaches that the poor and the outcast deserve special attention, whatever their moral or personal situation, for although they are made in the image and likeness of God, that image is often at its most vulnerable, demoralized, and poverty-stricken. Therefore, Jesus loves the poor and the outcast and takes their defense, making them the first beneficiaries of the Good News. In its task of remaining faithful to the spirit of the Beatitudes, the church community is called to share its resources with the poor and the oppressed. All disciples of Christ and all Christian communities—including families, parishes, schools, dioceses, and other religious institutions—should sincerely reflect upon their lives, their attitudes, and their support for Hispanic young people, who are frequently poor and outcast in society.

Giving Priority to Hispanic Young People

54   The preferential option for young people has its roots in the fact that, by reason of their baptism, young people have their own place in the church. For a long time, the church has not given Hispanic young people their place. The church has shown a lack of effective pastoral concern for Hispanic young people, who seldom have been invited to participate in the life of the church community, fulfilling their mission and sharing their gifts.

55   Given their potential for living a deep faith and their openness to receiving the Good News and struggling for justice, Hispanic young people have a prophetic and transformative capability in society today. This potential may develop insofar as Hispanic young people are accepted in the church and receive appropriate care.

56   The adult church community should treat all young people justly and should responsibly support Hispanic young people as they work for renewal within the church and society. And in examining our support and the sincerity of our support, we must ask ourselves certain basic questions:

- Are Hispanic young people being invited to participate in parish decisions?
- Are the voices of Hispanic young people being heard in the church, and are they being listened to with respect?
- What proportion of material resources and pastoral personnel are dedicated to serving Hispanic young people?

57   Young people need the support of the adult community to confront the problems and injustices with which they live. Joint work involving adults and young people is the most effective way to provide this support. Furthermore, cooperative, collaborative efforts with adults will encourage young people to continue the tradition of joint work when they become adults.

58   The *National Pastoral Plan* emphasizes the necessity of encouraging and shaping Hispanic vocations for priestly and religious life. These vocations will be both stronger and more numerous if young people love Jesus, believe and commit themselves to his mission, and become aware of the pastoral needs of Hispanic people. To these ends, the Hispanic community needs priests and religious men and women who bear witness to the value of a life of poverty, chastity, and obedience in a society that values wealth, pleasure, and power. Hispanic people need compassionate priests who have a

solid and profound understanding of the sacred mysteries and of the urgency of promoting the social doctrine of the church. In the following passage from their first pastoral letter, *The Bishops Speak with the Virgin,* the Hispanic bishops of the United States sum up the significance of God and the Gospel made visible in human reality:

> The greatest strength of our people comes from the rediscovery of the Gospel that is our truth, our way and our life. The power of God in us is this:
> - His light illuminating the meaning of our life and the goal of our mission;
> - His love transforming our hearts of stone into human hearts;
> - His compassion moving us to action;
> - His hope encouraging us to continue struggling even when, humanly speaking, there is no hope;
> - His strength transforming our weaknesses and converting them into strengths for the good.[9]

The Passive Parish: A Challenge to Hispanic Youth Ministry

59 The parish is a vital center for people's faith-lives. Our bishops emphasize that the parish community should become a people of God who together share the mission of Christ. This emphasis requires a parish structure capable of sustaining community life and facilitating the community's primary mission, which is evangelization. Building such a structure represents a great challenge for parishes that are organized around "responsive" programs and services to the active community but that lack a focus on their mission toward unchurched people and nonparticipating or alienated church members.

60 Many parishes in the process of growth fall into bureaucratization and professionalization and concentrate on offering liturgical, educational, and social services to people who ask for them. Parish staff members tend to the needs of those who seek them out within the established parish department and schedule. Ministries and schedules of activities revolve around preparation for and cele-

bration of the sacraments. Parish work centers on activities that occur mainly on the church site. As a result, lay ministries are almost exclusively liturgical or educational.

61   These liturgical and educational services *are* vital to the church, but they do not make the church whole. They lack a missionary spirit that continues Jesus' project. Less than a third of U.S. parishes have active programs of evangelization;[10] thus, the majority of parishes follow a model of church different from the one proposed by Jesus. We call this dominant parish model the "passive" model because of its disposition to answer telephone calls, receive whoever comes in, and refer people to the services offered by the parish or other institutions in our society. In order to be evangelizers, our parishes need to overcome three challenges: pastoral nearsightedness, empty sacramentalism, and privatized and impersonal functionalism.

Pastoral Nearsightedness

62   In regard to young people, pastoral nearsightedness consists of serving only those young people who attend church and parish activities, while ignoring other young people—who tend to be the majority. Our church should heal itself of this infirmity and go out to search for the lost sheep, as Jesus indicated:

> "Which one of you, having a hundred sheep and losing one of them, does not leave the ninety-nine in the wilderness and go after the one that is lost until he finds it? When he has found it, he lays it on his shoulders and rejoices. And when he comes home, he calls together his friends and neighbors, saying to them, 'Rejoice with me, for I have found my sheep that was lost.'" (Luke 15:4–6)

63   Nearsighted parishes cannot fulfill their mission or respond to the pastoral needs of Hispanic young people. We live in a culture that constantly lures people away from God and encourages hedonism, paganism, and the acquisition of wealth, material goods, and power. If we want to evangelize, it is absurd to wait for young people to come to the parish; those who have not encountered God in their life do not generally go to church. We cannot be so nearsighted as to embrace only the young people who come to Mass on Sunday and resign ourselves to ministering to them alone. To continue

Jesus' mission, we must move from being a church that waits and responds to being a church that walks forward and seeks.

64   Hispanic young people become victims of pastoral nearsightedness when parishes settle for having a Hispanic youth group or a few Hispanic members in a youth group. In such parishes, all youth ministry revolves around these groups, and the majority of young people, who live outside the boundaries of parish life and need a more missionary evangelization, are not taken into consideration.

65   Furthermore, Hispanic young people who participate in the church are frequently ignored by the rest of the community or are invited to be involved only in the music group or in the cleaning and maintenance of church buildings. Many Hispanic young people feel belittled simply for being Hispanic, feared because others do not understand their culture, or rejected because they do not accept the customs and vision of adults. Many other young people, both Hispanic and non-Hispanic, feel that they are given consideration or status only as the church of the future. These realities generate alienation among young people, as expressed in the Tercer Encuentro Nacional Hispano de Pastoral:

> Youth are not merely the future of the Church but rather the young community of today's Church.
> Nonetheless, it is a frequent experience that they do not always feel this way but, instead, feel marginalized and overlooked.[11]

66   We must recognize the truth of young people's experiences—their feelings of marginalization—if pastoral activity among Hispanic young people is to take on the importance it requires. By living Christian lives today, young people can build a tomorrow in which evangelical values reign. In order to build such a future, however, young people need to be truly part of a living church community and its celebrations.

Empty Sacramentalism

67   In communal celebrations, especially in celebrations of sacraments, the passive parish tends to overemphasize ritual and sacrament and underemphasize evangelical practice. Young people's limited experience of the church keeps them from recognizing the connections and complementarity that exist between the word of God, the

sacraments, personal charisma, and the Christian witness that people give with their lives. As a result, many young people experience the sacraments as empty symbols, question the religious value and connection of the sacraments to daily life, and finally abandon the sacraments.

68   In order to understand the sacraments' symbolism, young people need to experience sacramental celebrations that bring the paschal mystery to life in their personal and communal lives. The sacraments are key moments for handing over to God the tensions, suffering, anxieties, and frustrations of life; for being filled with the transforming and liberating power of Christ; for uniting with the church community; and for gaining the strength to be faithful and courageous witnesses of the Good News. If, instead, the sacraments are seen only as obligatory actions without meaning, they become empty signs and symbols that neither lead to God nor generate new hope.

69   We must urgently overcome empty sacramentalism, because many young people see it in stark contrast to the vivid preaching of evangelical movements that emphasize the word of God as a source of life. We must rescue the richness of sacramental symbolism by connecting it with the Gospel and with the lives of young people. Discipleship with Jesus requires an evangelical life before, during, and after participation in the sacraments. Evangelization and catechesis should help young people understand the meaning of the sacraments so that the sacraments can be powerful occasions for conversion and new life.

Privatized and Impersonal Functionalism

70   Passive parishes can easily become furnishers of a privatized, functionalist religion, in which people concern themselves only with their own interests. Such parishes encourage a privatized relationship with God, which generates a cold spirit and superficiality in the church. Registration of members and collections take on great importance, people communicate through bulletins, and computers become more vital than human relations. Hispanic young people, meeting at the Tercer Encuentro, expressed this insensitivity as follows:

One perceives a "cold" Church, without fraternal love or a communitarian dimension, in great need of conversion and formation if it is to realize its evangelizing mission.[12]

71   Young people, with their vitality, joy, and fraternal spirit, have the potential to transform our church into a prophetic, evangelizing, and missionary community. Three hundred people united only by Sunday Eucharist do not make up a Christian community, nor do thirty young people in a youth group. Personal interaction, direct communication, and shared goals exist in a community. In a community, people know one another and support one another in their daily lives and in their faith journeys.

72   According to John Paul II, for parishes to be true Christian communities, they need to adapt their structures so that laypeople can participate in the pastoral responsibilities of the parish and create small ecclesial communities that facilitate their faith-lives.[13] Communicating the word of God through love and service is easily done in small ecclesial communities, and bearing witness to the Risen Jesus, alive and active in the world, is effective there as well.

73   The majority of Latino young people are not aware of the model of church put forth by Jesus. Only those who are active in ecclesial life and have been exposed to good pastoral ministry have experienced being part of a prophetic, communitarian, missionary, and evangelizing church. Those who go to church only out of obligation, tradition, or necessity have just a partial—and at times distorted—experience of the church and the faith.

The Missionary Parish: An Ideal Within Reach

74   In order for Hispanic young people to know, love, and follow Jesus, we need a church that is missionary, communitarian, and strongly evangelical. Faith is a gift from God, meant to be lived out in a community that goes out to communicate its faith to others. In his encyclical *Redemptoris Missio*, Pope John Paul II emphasized the Catholic church's missionary mandate as follows:

The Lord is always calling us to come out of ourselves and to share with others the goods we possess, starting with the most precious gift of all—our faith. The effectiveness of the

Church's organizations, movements, parishes and apostolic works must be measured in the light of this missionary imperative. Only by becoming missionary will the Christian community be able to overcome its internal divisions and tensions, and rediscover its unity and its strength of faith.[14]

75   Similarly, the *National Pastoral Plan for Hispanic Ministry* makes clear this desire of the Hispanic people for the Catholic church:

> To live and promote by means of a *Pastoral de Conjunto* a model of church that is: communitarian, evangelizing, and missionary; incarnate in the reality of the Hispanic people and open to the diversity of cultures; a promoter and example of justice; active in developing leadership through integral education; leaven for the kingdom of God in society.[15]

Together, these ideals from Pope John Paul II and the *National Pastoral Plan* outline the model of church we strive for. In the following sections, we examine various roles of this church—a community of people on a journey, an evangelizing community, a prophetic community, a community with a preferential option for the poor, and a community animated by a *pastoral de conjunto.*

A Community of People on a Journey

76   A church of the kind that Jesus calls us to build goes forth to announce the Good News throughout the whole parish territory, rather than restricting its evangelizing action to those people who go to parish facilities. As a community of people on a journey, the church acts out its missionary spirit, seeking out unchurched, marginalized, or alienated people with whom to share the Good News.

77   Far from draining or tiring the community, however, this evangelizing action renews the church and reinforces the faith with an enthusiasm and a motivation that are continually reborn. In addition, sacramental celebrations unify and revitalize members to go out to find those who live alienated from God, to imitate Jesus' disciples, who "went out and proclaimed the Good News everywhere, while the Lord worked with them and confirmed the message by the signs that accompanied it" (Mark 16:20). At the Tercer Encuentro, thousands of Hispanics demonstrated their awareness of the revitalizing power of evangelization with this pronouncement:

We believe that God is renewing his Church in the United States through the enthusiasm, missionary spirit, and prophetic voice of the Catholic Hispanic people.

We trust in prayer and spiritual strength, which give us faith, hope, simplicity, good will, and generosity so that, in the midst of frustration, we can yet accomplish our evangelizing mission and express through our songs the joy of having Christ in our hearts.[16]

An Evangelizing Community

78   The *National Pastoral Plan* calls us to evangelize through small ecclesial communities, where each person evangelizes and is evangelized by others through a process of communal reflection on the Good News and the evangelizing work of each member. Having a supportive, evangelizing community with which to share their life and apostolic experience encourages all members to sustain their Christian commitment and engage in the work of evangelization.

79   Young missionaries encounter God when they see the goodness, living testimony, idealism, hope, and needs—and even the sin, weakness, indifference, pain, and suffering—of the young people to whom they carry the Good News. In carrying the Good News to young people and receiving glimpses of God from them, missionaries experience Jesus' special love and constantly renew the church through the strength of their faith.

A Prophetic Community Sowing Seeds of Hope

80   Every parish community as a whole and any youth groups and small youth communities therein should re-examine how well they are living out the prophet Isaiah's idea of being a prophetic remnant in society. The role of prophetic remnant is not generally comfortable; it acts as salt to the bland indifference of a secularized society. But parish communities must heed Jesus' words about not losing their prophetic role, their "saltiness":

> "You are the salt of the earth; but if salt has lost its taste, how can its saltiness be restored? It is no longer good for anything, but is thrown out and trampled under foot." (Matt. 5:13)

81   The simple existence of missionary youth communities is a source of revitalization for our church, because these communities

demand a profound transformation of the church and see the involvement of young people as more than mere appearance for Sunday liturgy. Transformation means maintaining the essential while creating something radically new. Hispanic young people can make our church a youthful, prophetic, and missionary church. They can be a powerful breath of fresh air, sowing seeds of hope, living to be, rather than to have; to share, rather than to compete; to love and serve, rather than to center on self-interests; and to build peace and reconciliation, rather than to foster violence and ill will.

82   Pope John Paul II, in an apostolic exhortation to the laity, has directly called on young people to recover the best examples and teachings of their parents and teachers.[17] Recovering and applying these teachings can help young people shape a society that respects the dignity, freedom, and rights of all people and supports the growth of the ancient-yet-always-new treasure of the faith. In struggling for these values, young people can find joy and new strength for overcoming the egoism, hedonism, and desperation so present in modern society.

A Community Living Out a Preferential Option for the Poor

83   The church, following Jesus' example, should make clear its commitment to love and serve sick, disabled, poor, and hungry persons; immigrants and refugees; prison inmates; unemployed persons; elderly and isolated persons; abandoned children; and victims of war and violence. Making a preferential option for these people does not mean feeling a vague compassion for them or being condescending toward them. Instead, it means resolutely and firmly extending oneself for the sake of the common good—as seen from the perspective of poor and marginalized people.

84   The U.S. bishops, in their pastoral letter *Economic Justice for All,* indicate that the obligation to promote justice for all means that the poor put an urgent economic demand on the conscience of our nation. Christians—as individuals, as a church, and as a nation—are called to make a fundamental option for the poor by orienting social and economic activity toward the poor and by analyzing the results of such activity from their perspective. The demands of those who do not hold power and whose rights are denied should hold priority in society, so that justice may exist for all. The principal goal of commitment to poor people is to create

conditions in which they are able to exercise the power they need to share in and contribute to the common good. For this goal to become a reality, however, the more fortunate in church and society need to play an active and unselfish role; the U.S. bishops quote Pope Paul VI in this regard:

> "In teaching us charity, the Gospel instructs us in the preferential respect due the poor and the special situation they have in society: the more fortunate should renounce some of their rights, so as to place their goods more generously at the service of others."[18]

85   Serious, in-depth ministry to Hispanic young people—a group that is socioeconomically poor, relatively powerless, and culturally different from young people of the dominant culture—will never happen unless it becomes a priority. The church simply cannot allow Hispanic youth ministry to compete with other forms of ministry in a kind of "free-market" church, where the people with the money, power, and influence almost always decide things. Vigorous measures must be taken to develop Hispanic youth ministry. Otherwise, young Hispanic Catholics may not become the source of hope, strength, and renewal to which they have been called ever since their baptism.

A Community Animated by a *Pastoral de Conjunto*

86   The church has always emphasized its communion "with God, through Jesus Christ, and in the Holy Spirit." The characteristics of this communion—achieved by sharing the word of God, the sacraments, and common life—were highlighted by Pope John Paul II in his apostolic exhortation *Christifideles Laici:*

> [Ecclesial communion] is characterized by a *diversity* and a *complementarity* of vocations and states in life, of ministries, of charisms and responsibilities. Because of this diversity and complementarity every member of the lay faithful is seen *in relation to the whole body* and offers a *totally unique contribution* on behalf of the whole body.[19]

87   The Holy Spirit gives different power and gifts to each young person. These gifts complement one another in service to the community and do not represent levels of dignity or superiority. Youth

communities, like parishes and dioceses, need to discover the gifts of their members and discern how to best use them for the good of the community and its mission of evangelization.

88   Though their gifts and service take diverse forms, young people and adults alike participate in the ministry of Jesus, the Good Pastor who looks after his sheep and gives his life for them. Together, young people and adults form an ecclesial community that should work together in a *pastoral de conjunto,* in a "common ministry" where the work of all pastoral ministers is motivated by a shared vision and coordinated with a spirit of communion and coresponsibility for extending the Reign of God.

89   Underlying the concept of *pastoral de conjunto* is a way of being and understanding church. The *pastoral de conjunto* emphasizes unity of vision and mission within the ecclesial community while respecting the particular vocation and ministry of each member. Ideally, the spirit of *pastoral de conjunto* allows all pastoral ministers to feel part of one united church, a church that strives to fulfill its mission and not just to coordinate pastoral work or to formulate declarations, goals, and common objectives for ministry programs. Ministry with young Hispanics should be inspired by a spirit of *pastoral de conjunto,* so that this model becomes an integral part of youth ministry in all parts of our church. With this spirit, Hispanic youth ministry should collaborate closely with related ministries, such as liturgy, family ministry, catechesis, and social action.

90   Although there should exist Latino youth groups and small communities in which young Latinos can live out and express their faith, the spirit of *pastoral de conjunto* demands that these groups be open to sharing and collaborating with young people of other cultures. Only by uniting will young people carry sufficient influence in our church to effectively promote a culture of sharing and peace. The *National Pastoral Plan* summarizes this ideal in the following manner:

> These experiences help the Hispanic people to live the Church as communion. The *Pastoral de Conjunto* manifests that communion to which the Church is called in its fullest dimension. The Hispanic people wish to live this communion of the Church not only among themselves but also with the different cultures which make the Church universal here in the United States.[20]

The Journey
of Hispanic Youth Ministry

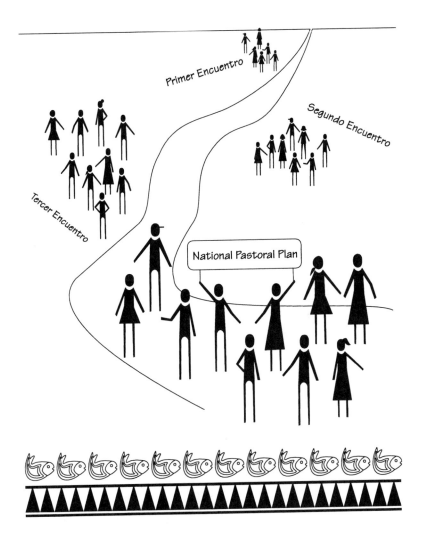

❧ 7 ❧

The Journey
of Hispanic Youth Ministry

❧

*W*e believe in the oneness of our goal, in our journeying together as a pilgrim Church, continuously led and
guided by God for the building of the Kingdom.
—Secretariat for Hispanic Affairs, *Prophetic Voices*

1   Hispanic youth ministry has only recently developed as an organized ministry in the United States, but as a form of pastoral action,
it has been present for at least twenty-five years. Hispanic youth
ministry assumes, or "takes ownership of," the reality of young Hispanics. From within that reality, Hispanic youth ministry helps
young people and young adults to know, love, and follow Jesus and
thus enables them to build the Reign of God around them.

2   Hispanic youth ministry has the following characteristics:
   • It is directed *toward* youth, making a preferential option for
     young people, because of their great numbers and their multiple
     pastoral needs.
   • It is accomplished *with* youth, because young people *are* the
     church, and they continually renew the church with their ongo-
     ing growth and action.
   • It springs *from* youth, as an offshoot of young people's personal
     experiences and complex realities.
   • It is often done *by* youth, because young people are the best evan-
     gelizers of other young people.
   • It expresses a positive stance *for* youth in that adult ministers and
     the community discern the needs of young people and act as in-
     tercessors between them, the church, and society.

Main Stages in Hispanic Youth Ministry

3   The journey taken by Hispanic youth ministry has varied among
places in the United States, depending on the Hispanic presence
and the local church's interest in ministering to Hispanic young
people. This section presents, in a broad way, the main stages of

Hispanic youth ministry, making reference to the Latin American and U.S. approaches that have most influenced it.

A Glance to the Past

4   In order to understand Hispanic youth ministry as a pastoral specialization, we must understand its development in both Latin America and the United States. In Latin America, prior to the 1960s, the directing of pastoral attention to young people was primarily in the hands of religious congregations and Catholic schools. For a long time, young people from the middle or upper classes received privileged attention and were evangelized in a way that rationalized and legitimized their privileges and limited their Christian horizon. Meanwhile, millions of young people from poor and marginalized families received sporadic or inconsistent pastoral attention, mostly from itinerant missionaries and from catechists with great zeal but little training. Their faith was fed primarily by a popular religiosity. There was clearly one ministry for the elite and a different ministry for the masses.

5   Despite the distinction in pastoral services among the different social classes, Catholic Youth Action was important in rural and urban areas among poor sectors of the population as well as the middle and upper classes. Centers for young people and parish youth groups could be found in various places. Some of these groups were pious organizations, others were social apostolate groups, and still others were clubs where young people could meet to socialize and reflect in a Christian environment.

6   In the United States, Catholic young people of European origin and those of the middle or upper classes were cared for in Catholic schools and universities. These same young people were also welcomed into and participated in the sports programs of the Catholic Youth Organization (CYO) and the Catholic Young Adult Club (CYAC). Catholic Youth Action was also important in the United States. Different types of parish youth groups existed. However, the immense majority of Hispanic young people grew up at the margins of these services, feeding their faith with devotional practices and family traditions.

Initiating the Journey

Primer Encuentro Nacional Hispano de Pastoral

7 The Hispanic people of the United States, young in their age and in their history as a distinct group, initiated a journey of self-recognition as a people of faith during the 1960s. This journey of self-recognition culminated with the Primer Encuentro Nacional Hispano de Pastoral in 1972, where for the first time, Catholic Hispanics of different national origins met as a new people being formed in the United States. Ever since, the Catholic church in the United States has officially recognized the Hispanic presence.

8 The Primer Encuentro encouraged the development of Hispanic leadership, the conscientization of Hispanic pastoral leaders about rights and responsibilities in the church, and the creation of regional and diocesan offices to promote Hispanic ministry. At that time, Hispanic youth ministry was seldom talked about.

9 Meanwhile, in Latin America, the church was becoming conscious of the injustice that prevailed there. This consciousness gave birth to the preferential option for the poor in 1968 at the Second General Latin American Episcopal Conference in Medellín, Colombia, and to the preferential option for youth in 1979 by the Latin American bishops at the Third General Latin American Episcopal Conference in Puebla, Mexico. Although these options have not achieved the needed emphasis and breadth, they did renew Latin American youth ministry by giving greater attention to poor young people and by introducing an overall vision from the perspective of poor and marginalized people.

Toward a Holistic Ministry

10 Change and renewal occurred in youth ministry throughout the 1970s. In the United States, ministry to young people under eighteen years of age was separated from ministry to young adults. The youth club model was left behind in favor of peer ministry.

11 Throughout the American continents, a more holistic pastoral ministry took shape by focusing on the following actions:
- taking into consideration the environment and the personal, social, and spiritual needs of young people
- inviting young people to share in the life, mission, and work of the community of faith

- developing programs about aspects of youth ministry, such as worship, creating community, advocacy, justice and service, guidance and healing, and enablement

Apostolic Movements

12   Apostolic movements that came from Spain and Latin America appeared in the United States in the late 1960s and in the 1970s. These lay organizations promote a better world by training leaders to offer strong evangelization experiences to Hispanic young people and young adults. Cursillos Juveniles (Short Courses for Youth), Encuentros de Promoción Juvenil (Encounters for Youth Promotion), and Jornadas de Vida Cristiana (Journeying in Christian Life) were the first and most popular apostolic movements among Hispanic youth.

13   Apostolic movements have been a vital force in Hispanic youth ministry due to their evangelization efforts, leadership training, and promotion of parish groups. Among Americans of European descent, the movements had less impact because they were reduced to retreat experiences like Teens Encounter Christ and Christian Awakening, or they were used merely to complement already existing pastoral efforts. In addition, movements for human rights, such as the Chicano movement and the United Farm Workers' movement, had more influence on Hispanic evangelization than on Euro-American evangelization.

Meeting as a People of Faith

Segundo Encuentro Nacional Hispano de Pastoral

14   In 1975, the National Secretariat for Hispanic Affairs convened the Segundo Encuentro Nacional Hispano de Pastoral (the actual meeting took place in 1977) and carried out a consultation process regarding the pastoral needs of Hispanic people. Three topics were identified as important: unity in pluralism, **integral education,** and social change. The participants in the Segundo Encuentro chose evangelization as the most urgent priority and emphasized its relationship to human rights, integral education, political responsibility, and unity in pluralism. Concern for youth of all ages was evident, as was stated in the proceedings of the Segundo Encuentro:

Since the present and future of the Church is in the hands of youth, we need for them a better formation and a greater participation in the leadership of our communities. Youth should be recognized and accepted as appropriate peer ministers.[1]

We approve and recommend the creation of a National Youth Task Force composed of members representing each of the six regions, elected by and from the youth participants of the Segundo Encuentro, in order to study and recommend to the episcopal conference the needs of Hispano youth in all that refers to evangelization.[2]

The Struggle for National Recognition

15   The period following the Segundo Encuentro forged great hope. Some dioceses hired personnel for Hispanic youth ministry and offered youth leadership formation programs. The National Hispanic Youth Committee was formed, and the Secretariat for Hispanic Affairs hired a person to coordinate the work of the National Hispanic Youth Committee. One report from the Secretariat for Hispanic Affairs stated:

My findings are that there is a thirst for cultural affirmation and leadership training among young Hispanics. They look to our church for answers.[3]

16   Thanks to the work of the National Hispanic Youth Committee, regional councils for Hispanic youth ministry were formed. Seven youth symposia were held in different regions in preparation for the Tercer Encuentro. Fifty young adults participated in each regional symposium and then repeated this experience in their own diocese. These efforts to share experiences at the regional symposia and to create national coordination led to the formation of diocesan Hispanic youth ministry teams, youth groups, and formation programs for leaders of Hispanic youth ministry. Despite the success of such efforts in promoting leadership, creating a network of support, and awakening many young people, a lack of funding terminated coordination at the national level after only one year.

17   Hard times followed. Neither the Secretariat for Hispanic Affairs nor the Department of Education (of the United States Catholic Conference), which was responsible for youth ministry, was able to attend to the needs of Hispanic youth. In addition, various

dioceses eliminated Hispanic youth ministry positions. In spite of this, Hispanic young people and young adults continued forming parish groups and participating in apostolic movements. And the National Hispanic Youth Committee expressed its statement of hope as follows:

> Recognizing that we are the salt and the light of the Church, we wish to live and be allowed to express our prophetic voice for the sake of Hispanic youth. We ask your support but most of all, your blessing so that we may give glory to Christ through his Church.[4]

Tercer Encuentro Nacional Hispano de Pastoral

18 In 1983, the National Council of Catholic Bishops (NCCB) issued a pastoral letter on Hispanic ministry titled *The Hispanic Presence: Challenge and Commitment* (*La Presencia Hispana: Esperanza y Compromiso*). In this letter, the bishops convened the Tercer Encuentro Nacional Hispano de Pastoral (1985) and called on Hispanics to raise their prophetic voices and to develop a national pastoral plan for Hispanic ministry.

19 Preparation for the Tercer Encuentro generated great enthusiasm and dedication. Hundreds of pastoral agents facilitated a process that included the identification and formation of leaders, an analysis of Hispanics' life reality in light of their faith, the sharing of life experiences, and prayer. The National Hispanic Youth Committee and the Hispanic diocesan youth ministry teams worked zealously to arrange for thousands of young people and young adults to participate in the Tercer Encuentro. Many dioceses reflected about youth and with youth, allowing young people to have profound experiences of evangelization and Christian leadership. These efforts assured the presence of youth in the regional and national meetings.

20 Young adults brought a fresh taste to the Tercer Encuentro and were a source of hope for the future of ministry among Hispanic young people and young adults. The Tercer Encuentro identified young people as one of the five central priorities for Hispanic pastoral action, along with evangelization, integral education, leadership formation, and social justice. A preferential option for young people and the poor was established during this encuentro. The **prophetic pastoral guidelines** stated these as follows:

- We, as Hispanic people, make a preferential option for and in solidarity with the poor and marginalized.
- We, as Hispanic people, make a preferential option for Hispanic youth so that they will participate at all levels of pastoral ministry.[5]

21   All of the prophetic pastoral guidelines identified in the Tercer Encuentro relate in a special way to young people and thus should be incorporated into Hispanic youth ministry. These guidelines give a priority to pastoral work with the family, the poor, and the marginalized; to missionary evangelization, leadership promotion, integral education, and promotion of justice; to valuing and promoting the role of women in the church, the family, and society; and to ministry in a style of *pastoral de conjunto.*

22   The socioreligious analysis of young people's reality, the strong commitment to missionary pastoral action, and the enthusiastic prophetic voices of youth at the Tercer Encuentro characterized the thrust of Hispanic youth ministry at that time. New parish groups and youth communities formed in the wake of the Tercer Encuentro, and more dioceses began to offer formation programs for Hispanic young people, young adults, and youth ministers.

Building for the Present and the Future

The *National Pastoral Plan for Hispanic Ministry*

23   The plan that the National Council of Catholic Bishops had called for in convening the Tercer Encuentro became a reality with the publication of the *National Pastoral Plan for Hispanic Ministry* in 1988. This plan organized the priorities and prophetic pastoral guidelines that were identified in the Tercer Encuentro into four dimensions of pastoral work: developing a *pastoral de conjunto,* supporting evangelization efforts, promoting a missionary option, and providing leadership formation. In addition to considering the poor and the young as priority groups of the church's missionary option, the *National Pastoral Plan* added families and women as priority groups to promote their participation in the church and to give special focus to them.

24   Although the *National Pastoral Plan* emphasized the preferential option for youth, the development of Hispanic youth ministry during the 1980s was slow and difficult due to a lack of ministers

and financial resources. In 1991, when the National Catholic Council for Hispanic Ministry was formed, nine national Hispanic ministry organizations existed, but Hispanic *youth* ministry had no organization to represent it.

A Glance at the Reality of Hispanic Youth Ministry in the United States

25   Throughout their history of successes and failures, struggles and challenges, Latino youth, young adults, and youth ministers have made use of every opportunity to increase their pastoral services. Ongoing efforts to know more about the reality of Hispanic youth ministry in the United States resulted in a survey carried out by Saint Mary's Press in 1991. Out of 151 dioceses that had offices for Hispanic ministry, 60 dioceses responded to the survey. These dioceses were of various sizes and levels of development in Hispanic ministry and were representative of all regions of the country. Relevant breakdowns of data are as follows:[6]

26   **On the diocesan level:** There were 51 dioceses (out of the 60 responding dioceses) that reported having diocesan personnel in charge of Hispanic youth. Of these 51 dioceses, 24 had personnel who specialized in Hispanic youth ministry. In 19 of the 51 dioceses, Hispanic youth were the responsibility of the office of Hispanic ministry. And in the remaining 8 dioceses, ministry to Hispanic youth was the responsibility of the diocesan director of youth ministry.

27   Forty-five dioceses reported holding *diocesan events* for Hispanic youth, including congresses, retreats, and workshops. Less common experiential offerings included vocation-discernment experiences, diocesan councils, and youth pilgrimages. Eighty percent of the regional activities occurred through the apostolic movements.

28   Thirty-six dioceses reported offering *leadership training programs* for youth leaders and adult advisers. These 36 dioceses disclosed the following information about program participation for the last five years:
- Ten dioceses offered programs whose length ranged from 130 to 350 hours; 1,300 youth leaders and 140 adult advisers attended these programs.

- Eight dioceses offered programs whose length ranged from 30 to 70 hours; 1,800 youth leaders and 316 adult advisers attended these programs.
- Eighteen dioceses offered short programs of less than 30 hours; 440 youth leaders and 98 adult advisers attended these programs.
- Thirty-one dioceses participated in regional programs.
- Twenty-two dioceses had no formation program, and only 3 of these 22 dioceses participated in regional formation programs.

29 **On the parish level:** A total of 1,290 parishes were reported as having Hispanic ministry programs. Of these 1,290 parishes, 738 provided services to Hispanic youth, and 256 had well-trained Hispanic pastoral agents.

30 **Apostolic youth movements:** Apostolic youth movements existed in 31 dioceses, and most of these dioceses included four or more different movements. Among the most common were Jóvenes para Cristo (Youth for Christ), Charismatic Renewal, Encuentros Juveniles (Youth Encounters), Encuentros de Promoción Juvenil (Encounters for Youth Promotion), Jornadas Juveniles (Youth Journeys), Cursillos Juveniles (Short Courses for Youth), Daughters of Mary, Hijos e Hijas del Movimiento Familiar Cristiano (Sons and Daughters of the Christian Family Movement), Pascua Juvenil (Youth Easter), Search, Catholic Youth Action, and Experiencia Cristo (Christ Experience).

31 The preceding information reveals the obvious need to initiate ministry to Latino youth and young adults in dioceses and parishes that need it and to improve its quality and scope in many places where it already exists. The need to multiply and improve leadership formation programs for Hispanic youth ministers and leaders of youth apostolic movements is also significant.

32 Some efforts have been made to produce bilingual documents that offer principles and structure for general youth ministry efforts. Works available in both English and Spanish include *The Challenge of Adolescent Catechesis: Maturing in Faith, A Vision of Youth Ministry,* and *Competency-Based Standards for the Coordinator of Youth Ministry.* Further work is needed, however, so that the reality and vision of *Hispanic* youth ministry can be expressed in official documents and implemented in our church.

33   Within the limits of the available resources, dedicated pastoral agents and leaders of Hispanic youth ministry continue working and struggling, looking for more-effective ways of evangelizing young people. They continue sowing the word of God in the barrios and in the countryside, organizing formation programs, preparing liturgies, holding retreats, and planning projects that will better serve Hispanic young people. Every day, more and more Hispanic youth and young adults become instruments of healing and reconciliation; they are prophetic voices and signs of a new day in the North American Catholic mosaic.

Principles and Elements in the Evangelization of Hispanic Young People

34   In the Gospels, Jesus identified himself as the Good Shepherd who came to save the lost sheep and gather those who are scattered. He personally tended to his disciples and taught them to live a life of service for others. He commissioned his Apostles to create a community of faith and to carry his Good News to the ends of the earth. Our ministry should be like Jesus' ministry, with an emphasis on *being* and *acting: being* Jesus alive among young Hispanics and *acting* out his saving love and deeds with them. The documents of the Third Latin American Episcopal Conference, held in Puebla, Mexico, speak of this mission:

> To introduce young people to the living Christ as the one and only Savior so that they will be evangelized and evangelize in turn; so that they, in loving response to Christ, will contribute to the integral liberation of the human being and society by leading a life of communion and participation [in the Church].[7]

Youth Ministry as the Church in Action

35   Youth ministry is the action of the church directed to help young people discover, follow, and announce the living Christ. This action focuses on both the present and the future, for youth are the young church of today and the hope of tomorrow—a hope that envisions faith being lived out intensely in the future, under new circum-

stances in society and under new forms of communion in our church. To achieve these ideals, Hispanic youth ministry must be an integral ministry that includes and ties together the various dimensions of pastoral work: human development, formation, and promotion; evangelization and catechesis; community life and communal action; spiritual growth and sacramental celebrations. It should also strive for incarnating the Gospel in the culture and for promoting unity, while celebrating diversity, among different cultures.

Evangelization as an Essential Task to Pastoral Ministry

36   The essential task of all pastoral ministry is evangelization: "Evangelizing is in fact the grace and vocation proper to the Church, her deepest identity. She exists in order to evangelize."[8] Hispanic youth ministry expresses the evangelizing mission of the church community in relation to its young people. The whole church has the responsibility of caring for and supporting the evangelization of youth. The preferential option for youth implies that all ministry efforts should take young people into account either by ministering directly to young people and young adults or by working indirectly to raise the consciousness of adults and orient them to work with, promote, or support youth.

37   Evangelization must be integral, or holistic, in order to respond to the concerns and anxieties of young people and young adults. It must also develop their ability to question and examine reality in light of the Gospels, as well as to examine the different religious visions and diverse sociopolitical ideologies to which they are exposed.

Pastoral Principles for Evangelization

38   When evangelizing young and young adult Hispanics, we propose fifteen pastoral principles that make up the backbone of the Prophets of Hope vision. According to these principles, the evangelization of Hispanic youth should help young people and young adults to do the following:

1. continue the process of conversion beyond their initial evangelization with a lifelong evangelizing catechesis
2. meet Christ in such a way that encounters with him carry liberation from the oppressions of personal and social sin

3. incarnate the Gospel in their personal experiences and in their concrete environment—with a broad and open vision toward all members of the church, the society, and the world

4. discover their personal, cultural, Christian, and Catholic identity

5. analyze with a critical, responsible, nonconformist, and rebellious spirit the false values of society

6. raise their consciousness regarding their personal responsibility to transform the realities of home, peer groups, school, and work; life in the barrio and life in the city; national, social, economic, and political structures; ecological systems; and international relations

7. renew the church and fulfill its mission of building a better world, enlightened and strengthened by the Holy Spirit

8. integrate their faith into their life, allowing the Gospel to inspire harmonious growth of the spiritual, intellectual, emotional, and social capabilities

9. acquire multidisciplinary human formation, incorporating basic knowledge on the human and social sciences, theology, spirituality, and pastoral work

10. be prophetic, announcing salvation in Jesus Christ and denouncing personal and social sin

11. be missionary, personally committed to continuing Jesus' mission, especially among young people

12. be messengers of love and Christian solidarity, especially among the poor and needy

13. be strugglers for justice and peace at home, in society, and in the world

14. be communal, fostering the formation of small ecclesial communities and permeating young people's lives with the Christian communitarian spirit

15. promote a common vision that leads to a *pastoral de conjunto*

39   Parents and the whole church community are responsible for encouraging their young people and young adults to know Jesus and to become his disciples. Youth ministers are often important evangelizers and models for young people. In addition, youth ministers are responsible for inspiring, preparing, and continually accompanying young people in their evangelizing mission. To encourage young people and young adults only occasionally, to

send them out to carry the Good News without adequate formation, or to abandon them in that mission would be a serious failure on the part of youth ministry.

Elements Essential for Evangelization in the Way of Jesus

40   Our church needs more young and young adult Hispanics with a strong missionary spirit to carry the Good News to their sisters and brothers in the settings where they live. We need to discover and promote the missionary vocations that exist among young Hispanics, whether those vocations are as laypersons, members of religious orders, or priests, and whether those vocations are for a certain period or for a lifetime. Jesus is calling many young people to continue his evangelizing mission. To evangelize in the way of Jesus, we need to demonstrate the same attitudes he had toward his Father, toward himself, and toward society.

41   **Authentic witness:** Today's young people tend to believe far more in experience than in doctrine, more in concrete events than in theory. The witness of Christian life is a fundamental and irreplaceable form of evangelization. Jesus is the most excellent witness, the model of how to give testimony on the presence of the Reign of God among us. With reason, Pope Paul VI noted:

> It is often said nowadays that the present century thirsts for authenticity. Especially in regard to young people it is said that they have a horror of the artificial or false and that they are searching above all for truth and honesty.[9]

42   Young evangelizers are witnesses and signs of the Risen Jesus when they demonstrate any of these characteristics:
- commitment to peace, justice, human rights, and human promotion
- profound involvement in the life of their people and an openness to universal brotherhood and sisterhood
- courage to stand up to corruption in political or economic power
- simple living, putting their goods at the service of the poor
- humility, openness to personal and communal examination of conscience to correct any anti-evangelical behavior that disfigures the face of Christ

43   **Love and service to brothers and sisters:** Jesus was love personified, especially for those who suffered most. He looked to

prayer and to the Scriptures for the strength and light necessary to share God's great love with all people, even to the point of giving up his life for us. Young evangelizers, like Jesus, appreciate all people and are always willing to share the love of God, especially with the neediest.

44   Authentic evangelizers always maintain an attitude of service in the way of the Teacher, making their service real and concrete through their attention to the daily needs of people. This attitude of service is fundamental, as Jesus himself indicated:

> "You know that among the Gentiles those whom they recognize as their rulers lord it over them, and their great ones are tyrants over them. But it is not so among you; but whoever wishes to become great among you must be your servant, and whoever wishes to be first among you must be slave of all." (Mark 10:42–45)

45   It is not enough just to say what Jesus said. Through a significant gesture in the Last Supper with his disciples, Jesus demonstrated the crucial importance—the essential nature—of an attitude of service:

> "So if I, your Lord and Teacher, have washed your feet, you also ought to wash one another's feet. For I have set you an example, that you also should do as I have done to you. Very truly, I tell you, servants are not greater than their master, nor are messengers greater than the one who sent them. If you know these things, you are blessed if you do them." (John 13:14–17)

46   Evangelizers serve young people by being understanding and warm, by encouraging dialog, by supporting them in the face of life's challenges and society's pressures, and by counseling them in the decisions they must make. Young people also experience the love and service of pastoral agents when the latter accompany them in their life journeying and share with them the joys, anxieties, and sufferings of life.

47   **A life of prayer:** As Jesus prayed, so every evangelizer must pray to discover God's will. In prayer, the Holy Spirit moves us toward conversion in our internal attitudes, strengthens us when we confront temptation, and purifies our interests. In prayer, young

people deepen and make their own the word of God received in preaching, study, and life experience. In prayer, they are filled with God and hear the voice of the Spirit.

48   Evangelizers, through prayer, find the resources and resolve to continue sharing God's life with others and to remain firm in their mission. Young evangelizers should give to prayer the time and silence necessary to internalize the word of God. Evangelizers must help young people to see prayer as a daily action, an action from which Christian spirituality flows, rather than as a way to evade life and history. All Christians should view prayer and evangelization as complementary facets, because through prayer, Christians accomplish the following:

- They contemplate the sacramental dimension of life.
- They know that they are in the hands of God when they eat, study, or work, even though during such actions they may not reflect on that truth.
- They dedicate time to dialog with God.
- They hear the word of God in silence and allow it to echo in the depths of their heart and mind, so that their attitudes and life may continuously be converted.
- They celebrate their relationship with God in the sacraments, especially in the sacraments of reconciliation and the Eucharist, living intensely the liberating presence of God in such celebrations.

49   **Confidence, joy, and peace:** Jesus always trusted his Father and asked his disciples to trust that God would make fruitful the Good News that they sowed. As Jesus himself described:

> "The kingdom of God is as if someone would scatter seed on the ground, and would sleep and rise night and day, and the seed would sprout and grow, he does not know how." (Mark 4:26–27)

50   Trust in God is a fountain of enthusiasm and happiness, both of which are necessary to effectively communicate the Good News. In the face of the weariness, suffering, and frustration that frequently accompany the work of evangelization, joy and peace are vital gifts that keep alive the efforts of the evangelizer.

51   Only through an integral, conscienticizing, and communal evangelization will it be possible to achieve the ideal proposed in the vision of Prophets of Hope. This ideal was identified by the

pastoral agents who, in solidarity with Latino youth, planned this series:

> We, the Hispanic youth of the United States, having found Jesus and being aware of our cultural identity, accept the commitment that his message presents. Transformed by his Gospel, we choose to become agents to change society, incarnating in our own life and in the world the values of the Reign of God: justice, love, life, freedom, truth, and peace. We challenge our brothers and sisters from Alaska to the Rio Grande and from Puerto Rico to Hawaii, to become different. We challenge them to take the risk for Jesus' cause in the building of a better world for ourselves and for our children.[10]

Models of Organization
in Hispanic Youth Ministry

Models of Organization
in Hispanic Youth Ministry

The Church has so much to talk about with youth, and youth have so much to share with the Church. This mutual dialogue, by taking place with great cordiality, clarity and courage, will provide a favorable setting for the meeting and exchange between generations, and will be a source of richness and youthfulness for the Church and civil society.

—John Paul II, *Christifideles Laici*

1   For effective evangelization with Hispanic young people, the church needs to provide communitarian spaces in which young people and young adults can grow as Christians, develop as persons, and intensely live their faith. The church itself needs specific models of organization and pastoral ministry, models that will carry evangelization to the settings in which young people live and that will actively incorporate young people into the life of the church. The lives of young people are so active, and are filled with so many challenges and crossroads, that only creative, diverse, and versatile pastoral ministries will be able to keep pace with young people.

2   In order to promote the carrying out of all pastoral action with a spirit of *pastoral de conjunto,* we explain in the first section of this chapter what the concept of *pastoral de conjunto* involves. We then present three models for Hispanic youth ministry—parish youth groups, apostolic movements, and small youth communities—and follow up by examining the kinds of communitarian spaces needed by all Hispanic young people and young adults, regardless of any organizational membership. Finally, we address how the diverse environments and realities of Hispanic young people and young adults necessitate certain specialized pastoral ministries.

Hispanic Youth Ministry and *Pastoral de Conjunto*

3   As the contents of this book indicate, the challenges that pastoral agents and young adult leaders face are both many and complex.

However, rather than discourage people, these challenges should motivate them to more effective action. *"A Dios rogando y con el palo dando"* ("praying hard and working harder") is a common proverb among Hispanic people who are confronting tasks that seem beyond their abilities. This proverb can be a source of inspiration for pastoral agents and other members of the ecclesial community.

The Meaning and Practice of *Pastoral de Conjunto*

4   In the glossary of this book, *pastoral de conjunto* is defined as the action of all pastoral agents, ministers, and committed Christians— each in their own specific ministry—animated and directed by a common vision and coordinated in a spirit of communion and coresponsibility. In other words, *pastoral de conjunto* is the harmonious coordination of all the elements, ministries, and structures of the church in their work of bringing about the Reign of God. The following points specify and expand on the meaning of each of these concepts.

5   *Pastoral de conjunto* is action. Just as evangelization is carried out by evangelizing, so pastoral work is carried out by "pastoring." Neither becomes a reality simply by planning activities while sitting in offices or on pastoral committees. Planning is necessary, but in itself does not constitute the whole of pastoral work; therefore, it should not occupy a disproportionate amount of time, personnel, or resources. In practice, people have concrete opportunities to live out and own their belief in Jesus and to keep planning connected to the real life of people.

6   *Pastoral de conjunto* is carried out by all pastoral agents, ministers, and committed Christians—each in their own specific ministry. All who contribute to the mission of the church fulfill the specific ministry to which they are called by God. No particular role or charism (that is, "gift") fosters a spirit of *pastoral de conjunto* more than any other role or charism. Just as people's gifts and talents differ, so do people's expressions of *pastoral de conjunto.*

7   *Pastoral de conjunto* is animated and directed by a common vision. The *pastoral de conjunto* vision is infused with the Reign of God and holds Jesus as the model to follow. It means creating con-

ditions in which people with distinct charisms, ministries, spiritualities, personalities, and pastoral projects can focus on the Reign of God. In practice, it means considering young people's reality and working with young people and all committed Christians to advance the Reign of God. *Pastoral de conjunto* does not mean being "regimented" by a uniform vision of reality or a single form of pastoral work.

8   **Pastoral de conjunto is coordinated in a spirit of communion and coresponsibility.** The spirit of communion exists in people's action as members of the Body of Christ, members whose functions differ but who are united by one faith, one baptism, and one God. The spirit of coresponsibility arises from this communion and from people's vocation to collaborate in the creative and redemptive work of God. This whole "spirit" requires that people work in community and not in isolation or competition. Coordination of a *pastoral de conjunto* demands a process of reflection and interaction, so that all those involved in the pastoral ministry of the church foster a sense of a common mission. In Hispanic youth ministry, this means to work together—especially with the rest of youth ministry and with Hispanic ministry.

Revitalizing the Church Through the Actions of Its Young People

9   By carrying out its evangelizing work with a *pastoral de conjunto,* the church can find renewal and revitalization through its young people. Given the slightest encouragement by or integration into the church community, evangelized young people tend to create a communitarian spirit wherever and whenever they can. Young people also find creative ways of responding to their world, generally involve themselves with the needy, and work well within a poor but dynamic church that does not need great economic resources or ecclesial power to fulfill its mission.

10   When young people are not well integrated into or given encouragement by their church, the church and its vitality usually decline. With young people out of the picture, adults tend to focus on or idealize the past. In analyzing the present, adults often become overwhelmed or frustrated by the magnitude of the problems they face. In contrast, young people tend to look toward the future and

devote their energy and vision to creating something different. They infect adults with their youthful and adventurous spirit. Young people do not focus permanently on inactive ecclesial models or outdated pastoral methods, but rather are anxious to create more participatory pastoral projects. Young people take interest in finding new ways to express and celebrate their faith; they love to challenge adults to change. As a result, young people who feel that the church is theirs—that they are the church—are an active and challenging force within the church.

11   On the other hand, a young community that does not consider the wisdom, experience, abilities, and knowledge of its adult generation has a hard time maturing and is seldom effective in its service to the world. Older generations give stability to young people, provide them with spiritual and organizational orientation, help them understand the world, and share with them their experiences and expertise. In accomplishing these tasks, adults furnish young people with a necessary link to Catholic tradition, a source of continuity, and a challenge for growth.

Models of Organization for Hispanic Youth Ministry

12   The *National Pastoral Plan for Hispanic Ministry* emphasizes the value of small groups, apostolic movements, and small ecclesial communities for evangelization, because in these environments it is easy to communicate the personal love of Jesus and make the church feel like a home and not like a place. The discussions in this section are dedicated to examining these three models of pastoral ministry.

13   The following chart, which compares a youth group and a small youth community, emphasizes the differences between them with two intentions. The first intention is to help pastoral agents and youth leaders analyze their present groups and, based on that analysis, decide whether they want their groups to move in the direction of a youth group or a small youth community. The second intention is to assist young people who are in youth groups and apostolic movements and who want to form small communities. The chart enables these young people to identify the characteristics of a small community already present in their group and then to prioritize the areas in which they can start working for transformation into a small youth community.

Characteristic	Youth Group	Small Youth Community
Size	May be any size—from 8 to 120 young people, for example.	Typically fluctuates between 8 and 15 adolescents or 8 and 30 young adults.
Stability of membership	Membership fluctuates constantly.	Membership remains stable.
Relationship of members	Everyone belongs as an individual; one's absence frequently goes unnoticed.	All members interrelate; a person's absence is noted and the person sought for.
Group focus	Determined by the sociological needs of the group.	Determined by each young person's needs and the community's mission.
Leadership	Requires flexibility, creativity, and ability to change styles according to the needs of the group.	Requires maturity and a leadership style based on **animation** and participatory coordination.
Handling of conflicts	Leaders often spend much time and energy in solving internal group problems.	Members often focus together on each member's life and on the challenges of pastoral action.
Activities	May consist of a mix of activities, or may focus on a single activity such as talks or prayer.	Maintains a balance of activities, always including dialog, reflection, prayer, study, and community service.
Role of adults	Possible without adult accompaniment and counseling.	Requires adult accompaniment and counsel.
Type of commitment	Not all members are committed.	All members are committed.
Level of sharing	Focused on the group's meeting days.	Members share their lives, even outside of the meetings.

14   It is important to note that some Hispanic youth groups in parishes, and some leadership teams in apostolic movements, have more characteristics of a small youth community than of a youth group. The spirit of a small community sometimes exists in large youth groups, especially among people who have been steady members of a youth group for several years.

15   The vision of the Prophets of Hope series promotes small youth communities as an ideal for Hispanic youth ministry. This does not mean that youth groups and apostolic movements do not have a place in the life of young Hispanics or the church. Hispanic youth ministry needs these three models of organization in order to successfully evangelize Hispanic young people. Each model responds to different needs, fulfills distinct functions, operates best under particular conditions, and attracts young people with different personalities, spiritual needs, vocations, and levels of human and faith development.

16   Small communities may be formed with young people who have been active in a youth group or an apostolic movement, as well as with young people who have never participated in any church youth organization. Also, it is possible to transform a youth group into several small communities or to create a small community with the core group or leadership team in an apostolic movement or youth group. These transformations can be achieved little by little, starting with the most easily adopted dimensions of the life of a small community and gradually maturing to live out more complicated aspects of a small community.

Youth Groups

17   The existence of youth groups is vital for the evangelization of Latino young people. Through youth groups formed in all places—parishes, dioceses, homes, neighborhoods—Latino young people encounter Christ and a communitarian environment that helps them in their human development and socialization process.

18   In some parishes, the existence of Latino youth groups is seen as a blessing. In other parishes, such groups are prohibited or find their work made difficult, either because some people believe there should be a single, nonethnic youth group for the whole parish or because Latino young people are looked down on or feared. In many cases, young people are "allowed" to have a group in the par-

ish, but often without being able to use the parish facilities and re-sources. This means that the pastor recognizes the youth group as a parish group but does not provide any pastoral assistance to it. In such cases, young people provide their own leadership, seek their own resources, organize themselves, and try to grow as Christians the best way they can.

19   Many young prophets exist in these groups—young people who courageously seek to bring their peers and friends into the group, who make strong efforts to maintain the other members' interest in the activities of the group, and who seek the contribution of adults, through conferences and workshops, in bringing topics of interest to the whole group. However, because of a lack of appropriate pastoral support, these groups tend to dismantle when they face conflicts, especially internal conflicts. Sometimes the groups dismantle spiritually rather than physically, becoming just social clubs without a purposeful Christian spirit or mission.

Different Youth Groups Incorporating Hispanic Young People

20   Young people with different languages and cultures are best brought together by first ministering to each in their own language and culture and encouraging their unity through a *pastoral de conjunto*. Only after young people have gained some maturity, self-confidence, and appreciation for their own culture and religious expression will they be able to encounter the religious expressions of other cultures with a mature attitude. All too often, Hispanic young people are forced to listen to religious messages or expressions that they cannot understand or relate to their own lives.

21   There are three basic models for ministry with Hispanic young people in parish youth groups: Hispanic youth groups, youth groups of European origin, and multicultural–multiracial youth groups. Each model offers advantages and disadvantages and is appropriate for different circumstances.

22   **Hispanic youth groups:** Hispanic youth groups frequently include young people from fourteen to twenty-five years of age. Sometimes the majority are adolescents; at other times the majority are young adults. Generally, Spanish is spoken in these groups, but young people who do not speak Spanish well and prefer to express themselves in English also attend these groups. Everybody

seeks the warmth and joy that characterize the Hispanic communitarian spirit. These groups have the following advantages for effectively evangelizing Hispanic young people:

- The young people receive the word of God and reflect on it from within their own sociocultural reality, expressing themselves in the language they speak best.
- The group reinforces the young people's cultural, social, and personal identity, which helps them know, value, and evangelize their culture.
- The young people's parents can also participate in events, especially in traditional cultural celebrations.
- The younger members find guidance in the group's young adult members, who bring leadership and a certain maturity to the group.

23   The principal challenges that Hispanic youth groups face are the following:

- relating to young people from other cultures
- offering diverse opportunities for reflection, opportunities that are appropriate to the various ages and maturity levels of the group's members
- overcoming the tendency to form separate groups of Hispanics from different countries of origin

24   **Euro-American youth groups:** The essential characteristics of youth groups of Euro-American origin are that English is spoken in them. Usually, the majority of the members are middle-class young people of northern European ancestry. Generally, these groups serve young people between the ages of fourteen and eighteen. When this type of youth group incorporates Hispanics, it facilitates the evangelization of Hispanic young people by doing the following:

- encouraging members to accept Hispanics as brothers and sisters
- sponsoring special events and complementary activities that help young Hispanics explore the relationship between their faith, traditional Hispanic culture, and modern culture
- sponsoring opportunities for mutual enrichment between young people of both cultures

25   The principal challenges in this type of group are as follows:

- achieving a true unity and a fraternal spirit between young people of different cultures by coming to know, respect, and positively value both cultures

- integrating young people who speak only Spanish or who do not feel at home in this type of group because of cultural, social, or economic factors
- adopting processes, methods, and activities that allow Hispanic members to have profound religious experiences and embody the Gospel message in their lives
- achieving collaboration on the part of Hispanic parents, especially those who do not speak English well

26   **Multicultural–multiracial youth groups:** In large cities, one often finds youth groups made up of young people from several distinct racial and ethnic groups. In some parishes, youth under eighteen years of age make up 40 percent of the parish community. And in some dioceses, young people from multiethnic communities represent more than half of Catholic youth. Youth ministry in these communities is vital, and the challenges are great. Among these challenges, the following stand out:

- Hispanic young people must receive ministry in keeping with their cultural characteristics; at the same time, marginalizing them from other ethnic groups should be avoided.
- When there is not sufficient leadership to minister to each of the different groups in their own language, it is very difficult to evangelize young people and to help the youth group mature.
- Often, there are not enough role models or pastoral agents who know how to work with persons from different cultures and who can give stability to groups that represent a variety of cultures.

27   The solutions to these challenges are only beginning to become apparent. Some dioceses have formation and training programs in which pastoral agents, adult advisers, and young leaders learn how to attend to the specific needs of Hispanic young people, while promoting a multicultural youth community. Some multicultural parishes and dioceses have formed youth councils that represent various cultures. Others have multiethnic teams that reinforce the values and gifts of each culture and seek creative ways to meet the pastoral needs of *all* youth.

Multiple Youth Groups in a Single Parish

28   The presence of several different youth groups in a single parish multiplies the opportunities for evangelizing young people. The existence of various groups, either of Hispanic or of other ethnic

origin, is not necessarily a sign of division. Churches minister to groups of children according to their age, and churches also form different adult groups according to their focus—for instance, scriptural study, prayer, or social action. In the same way, churches can minister more effectively to young people by having different groups that meet different needs. With only one group, parishes usually cannot minister to the specific needs of many of their young people.

29   It is inaccurate to think that the youth community is united simply because a single parish group exists. A parish's young people may be divided because they cannot find any way to participate meaningfully in the church. The parish that has only one youth group generally fails to attend to the needs of the immense majority of its young people. It would be marvelous if every parish faced the challenge of trying to sustain unity among multiple groups and communities of young people!

30   The concept of having multiple youth groups within a single parish does not refer only to having different groups for young people of different languages and cultures, but also of different ages, interests, and levels of understanding of the faith. Examples of particular groups include the following:
- groups for charismatic prayer, social action, and Bible study
- groups for male and female adolescents
- groups for different neighborhoods or geographic sectors
- groups that can only meet on specific days of the week
- groups for young people just beginning their faith journey
- groups for those with a strong commitment as church

31   Evangelization efforts must not ignore the diversity of young people, abandon them, impose a false unity on them, or keep them divided. Ecclesial communion is strongest when all young people receive pastoral attention, each person and group has a clear identity, and all have opportunities to develop their talents and contribute to the common good. In such a context, the existence of different youth groups signifies great richness and the opportunity for mutual evangelization among all young people.

Elements for Consideration in Youth Group Ministry

32   The following areas examined briefly here simply indicate some important elements to consider in any group ministry with Hispanic young people:

33   **Variations in the size and makeup of the group:** Hispanic groups tend to vary in size according to young people's migrational patterns or work schedules and according to the quality of leadership available. Many young people attend a group only for short periods. This uncertain attendance, or even uncertain membership, leads to instability in the group and complicates the task of providing ongoing evangelization to the more stable members. In such cases, it is important to identify and give consideration to the reasons for some members' sporadic attendance. The activities of a group can be reorganized so that all members feel welcome whenever they can come, while the more stable members can successfully deepen their faith.

34   **Excessively large groups:** Very large groups run the risk of confusing "amassing people" with "unifying people." Unifying people means drawing individuals together while respecting their unique value and personhood. Amassing people means lumping individuals together for the sake of efficiency, and often results in depersonalizing them. Treating a group of people as a single unit, or addressing only a group's commonalities, generally fails to satisfy the pastoral needs of the majority of individuals. Forming various small groups within a large group can provide more personal attention to the members. The small groups can organize joint reflections and liturgies in which all can participate.

35   **The goals of the youth group:** A periodic review of the goals, spirit, substance, and methodology of a group's activities can help the group determine whether it provides its members with enough opportunities for experiencing a profound encounter with Jesus or whether it simply offers entertainment and fun. When the latter occurs, ministry is impoverished and encourages a superficial Christianity that no one feels called to or committed to. It is especially important to avoid orienting group activities simply to provide a good time for young people or to collect funds for further activities.

Levels of Organization in the Youth Group

36   To contribute to implementing the Reign of God in society, youth groups must be organized to bring about a communitarian, evangelizing, and missionary church. All youth groups should have three levels of pastoral focus and organization:

37   **The core leadership group:** The core leadership group is traditionally formed by three or four young people elected by the group members to facilitate the group activities for a certain period of time. Frequently, the core leaders are organized following a civic organization model—president, vice-president, secretary, treasurer, and committee chairpersons. Other times, these positions are defined in relationship to the functions fulfilled by the leaders, such as coordination, animation, finances, public relations, and secretarial work.

38   Regardless of the model of organization, youth ministry leadership should follow Jesus' model, fostering in the group a clear understanding and vision of its mission and a maturing process of young people's Christian life, so that they can play an active role in the church. In order to accomplish these functions as effective Christian leaders, it is important that young people participate in leadership training and formation.

39   **The parish youth group:** The parish youth group is formed by all the young people who attend the group regularly and consider themselves members. These young people need to receive pastoral attention for their own needs, but they should also have a spirit of mission and service to the rest of the young people in the parish.

40   **The young people of the parish:** The parish's young people as a whole constitute the largest group. Generally, for each young person who participates in the youth group, there are hundreds that live at the margins of ecclesial life. Many require some initial evangelization, and the majority need to be invited and accompanied personally in order to participate in church activities. A good proportion of the parish youth group activities should be directed toward them.

Apostolic Movements

41   Apostolic youth movements are ecclesial organizations whose well-defined structure allows them to serve a large number of young people. This structure also gives apostolic movements a fair amount of internal stability. These movements have as a goal the evangelization of young people through one or several intense experiences of church or prayer. Almost all apostolic movements also concentrate on forming young leaders.

42   For young people in general and Hispanic young people in particular, the evangelizing potential of apostolic movements is greater than that of parish youth groups. Parishes often lack well-trained adult leaders for youth ministry, parish youth groups tend to be less personal than apostolic movements, and parish structures or personnel sometimes marginalize young people or openly reject them. Furthermore, the characteristics of apostolic movements in themselves tend to strongly attract young Hispanics.

Characteristics of Apostolic Movements

43   Apostolic movements usually offer young people an environment in which they find the acceptance, warmth, security, inter-personal relationships, and understanding that they do not find in society and often fail to find in parishes as well. Especially given the present conditions in society—cultural conflict, relativism of values, and pluralism of religious viewpoints—apostolic movements offer a valid alternative that attracts and motivates Hispanic young people. Furthermore, young people who participate in an apostolic movement typically get the feeling that through the movement, the church *seeks them out* to offer them a new life and *needs them* to carry Christ to other young people.

44   The effectiveness of the apostolic movements rests on their organization and *mística*. Generally speaking, these movements encourage young people's Christian development because they offer three important levels of participation:

45   **A strong experience of evangelization:** Thousands of young Hispanics meaningfully and deeply encounter Jesus in retreats or congresses organized by apostolic movements. These experiences have a powerful impact on the lives of young people, especially young people who have received only limited evangelization, have never had a positive experience of church, or who have left the church entirely. As a result, every year many young people begin the process of active participation in the church through the apostolic movements.

46   **Human and Christian growth:** Following their powerful evangelization experience, young people who continue participating in apostolic movements often find an opportunity there to join a group of peers, discover the meaning of Christian community, and receive direction and support for deepening their faith.

47   **Leadership formation:** Identifying, forming, and supporting new leaders are important aspects of nearly every apostolic movement. Some movements strive to provide their leadership with a holistic formation, but others focus only on spirituality and the activities of the movement itself.

48   An apostolic movement's *mística* is at once both a source and a consequence of the qualities that give stability to the movement and that generate within it a strong vitality and continual growth. An apostolic movement's *mística* expresses itself through the following:

- an active method of evangelization and invitation
- the creation of a strong sense of belonging to the movement and, as a member of the movement, belonging to the church
- a spirituality that attracts young people
- well-defined processes that interest, motivate, and commit young people to become evangelizers
- adult advisers who sustain the spirit of the movement and give security and direction to young people
- schools and formation programs for leaders
- powerful evangelization experiences that are facilitated through retreats (with small groups) and congresses (with large numbers of young people)
- structures that transcend the confines of local parishes and provide connections at diocesan, national, and even international levels
- processes, projects, and experiences that encourage the Christian growth of leaders, provide mutual support among young people from diverse areas, and create a larger sense of church

49   Unfortunately, the same characteristics that make an apostolic movement so attractive and help provide an experience of Christian community can also make the movement become almost a sect within the church. This occurs when young people enclose themselves within the movement, fail to acknowledge or respect other experiences of church, concern themselves more with gaining new followers than with evangelization, proselytize young people from parish groups or other movements, and refuse to work with a spirit of *pastoral de conjunto*.

Effective Evangelization in an Apostolic Movement

50   Successful evangelizing action by apostolic movements grows out of good follow-up to the strong experiences of evangelization that apostolic movements provide. This follow-up may occur through "cells" or small communities within the movement itself or through the work of parish groups. The pastoral action of movements is weakened when they lack ongoing processes of evangelization, because leaders then limit themselves to providing powerful but short-term evangelization experiences. Such a limited focus furthers apostolic movements' tendency to abandon those who lack a vocation and abilities for leadership. These individuals often end up frustrated, and the movements lose any potential they might have had to truly evangelize their surrounding culture and its social structure.

51   In addition, it is crucial that the evangelization promoted by apostolic movements encourage young people to fulfill their social, ecclesial, and political responsibilities. Through this practical connection to the "real world," apostolic movements can avoid becoming an escape from reality and can promote a dynamic faith incarnated in the sociocultural context in which young people live. Leaders of apostolic movements should enter into a process of pastoral-theological reflection at least every three years. This periodic reflection is necessary for leaders to update their understanding of the reality in which they work, deepen their knowledge of Jesus and the church, and revise the focus, substance, and process of their evangelization. Through accomplishing these tasks, leaders can avoid stagnating in an outdated vision and methodology.

52   Diocesan and parish directors of youth ministry and leaders of apostolic movements would benefit from meeting with one another to exchange ideas and promote pastoral coordination. Together, they could analyze the pastoral needs of young people and search for ways to support and complement one another in their evangelical tasks.

Specialized Pastoral Ministries

53   Youth ministry must respond to the challenges faced by Hispanic youth and young adults in the diverse environments in which they live. This need for contextualized or "situational" ministry demands a series of pastoral specialties. Outstanding among these specialized

pastoral ministries are student ministry, campesino ministry (ministry with Hispanic farmworkers), and ministry with young people facing crisis situations.

Student Ministry

54   Student ministry happens in three types of settings: Catholic high schools, Catholic colleges and universities, and the Newman Centers at public colleges and universities. Public high school students that seek pastoral attention look for it in their parishes.

55   Ministry in Catholic schools and universities has its own independent status. Educational institutions have a special role in the integral evangelization of young people, because these institutions can combine evangelization with young people's human and social formation. In addition, these institutions are able to accompany young people in their process of maturation, in their relationship with Christ, and in their experience of a church that promotes a culture led by the values of the Reign of God.

56   Catholic schools have a special responsibility to their Hispanic students. According to the National Catholic Educational Association (NCEA), all Catholic schools should educate with a multicultural focus rather than an assimilationist focus, and they should respect and promote Hispanic culture and identity. Schools are to be sensitive to Hispanic values and *idiosincrasia*, and not impose norms and values that are specific to the dominant culture. School personnel are challenged to adopt attitudes that favor inculturation by providing ways for Hispanic young people to relate the Catholic faith to their culture and by providing liturgical experiences that allow Hispanic young people to live out and express their faith. The NCEA urges all educators to treat Hispanic young people with warmth and personal attention and to promote Hispanic leadership in churches and schools.

57   Facing the small number of Hispanic students in Catholic schools, the NCEA recognizes that Catholic schools need to open their doors more fully to Hispanics in order to help young Hispanics overcome inequality of opportunity and racial discrimination.

58   Although only a small number of Hispanic young people enter universities, it is important that Catholic universities actively open their doors to promote Hispanic people's access to higher education. Once in a university setting, Hispanics should be offered

attention that takes into account their culture, their needs, and their unique expression of faith. For instance, Newman Centers at public colleges and universities need to be diligent in identifying, seeking out, and ministering to Hispanic students.

59   University ministry should concentrate on the following tasks:
- being an evangelizing presence that brings students together to live their faith as members of the church and the university community
- focusing on students' ethical responsibility to promote life and truth
- offering opportunities for reflection on the relationship of faith to science, culture, technological development, social justice, and intellectual responsibility
- promoting student involvement in processes of social change, so that students can lend their support and solidarity to popular organizations, social movements, and political bodies that serve the community and are in agreement with the Gospels and Catholic social teaching
- raising young professionals' awareness of their responsibility to lessen the distance between intellectuals (or technical experts) and the general population

Through all these activities, Hispanic college students can perceive their professional life as a way of living out Christian love. This ethical orientation should include constant sensitivity to the social, political, economic, cultural, and religious problems they and other Hispanics face.

Campesino Ministry

60   Campesino ministry occurs in two different settings: that of migrant farmworkers and that of established communities of farmworkers. In both cases, evangelization should accompany Hispanic young people in their personal growth and communitarian development, emphasizing young Hispanics' personal dignity and the value of their Hispanic, Catholic, and campesino identities. These aspects of their identity form the crucial foundation for their relationship with Jesus and with other persons, as well as for their conscientization regarding their rights and responsibilities. Upon this foundation, young people can build the security they need to express their thoughts and feelings and to struggle for a more just society.

61   Young people from campesino families tend to be less divided by age-groups than young people from urban areas, because campesino adolescents, young adults, and adults share the same work. This shared work experience may make young people's faith sharing easier in intergenerational groups, but it should not hinder the coming together of only young people to reflect on issues related specifically to their age and level of maturity. The following themes are especially relevant for young campesinos:

- their experience of the divine work of creation and their experience of farmworkers' cocreative role in caring for the land, planting, and harvesting
- the consequences of industrialization: the division of labor as farmworkers specialize in specific tasks, the serious effects of pesticide use, the breakdown of ecological balance, and the rupture of farmworkers' direct relationship with plants and the land
- their lack of confidence in themselves and the feeling of isolation that exists among migrant farmworkers and in small communities isolated from one another
- their feelings of powerlessness in the face of unjust working conditions and abusive employers or *contratistas* (hiring contractors)
- the need to develop a sense of solidarity with other farmers and farmworkers, especially with young migrants who enter a given area only during periods of heavy agricultural activity

62   Pastoral work with young migrant campesinos presents specific issues that should not be forgotten. A large number of young people migrate every harvest season between Mexico and the United States; many others migrate continuously within the United States, following the agricultural cycle. As a result, young people in both groups experience great instability. The resulting insecurity in family life, economic situation, and work and housing opportunities strongly affects their lives.

63   Young migrant farmworkers need evangelization projects that reach out to the migrant camps, ranches, and rural towns they visit. These evangelization efforts should accommodate agricultural work hours and be organized in short time spans that correspond to the short time migrants usually spend in any one place.

64   In addition to a focus on the themes mentioned previously, which are relevant in all campesino ministry, migrant young people need the following:

- the creation of a network of human and pastoral support that extends throughout migrant young people's migratory route, preferably formed by the stable youth groups and communities of parishes along that route
- the formation of a faith community among the young migrants themselves, supported by adults, so that the young people directly experience the pilgrim church as the People of God
- evangelization through popular religious practices that can be sustained as the young people migrate
- an awareness of the consequences of their migrant way of life on the continuity and nature of people's personal development and on the stability of their family life

Ministry with Young People Facing Crisis Situations

65 Evangelization among Hispanic young people who live in situations of drug addiction, alcoholism, gang violence, delinquency, sexual promiscuity, sexual abuse, and street vagrancy requires special dedication. Successful evangelization among such young people also requires a special evangelical focus and process. The arrival of the Good News in these young people's lives should literally mean a new life for them.

66 First, we must offer at-risk young people communitarian spaces that help them avoid the problems and situations mentioned. Second, we need to give support to young people who suffer pain and emotional imbalance because they live in homes where these problems exist. Our support can help young people avoid succumbing to destructive pressures and can even help young people become evangelizing influences in their families. Third, we must give special attention to young people who have fallen into self-destructive behavior. These young people need a new vision of life in order to change their lives, reintegrate themselves productively into society, and work to improve their world.

67 Young people who live in crisis situations have a special need for the warmth and security that only mature persons can provide. Mass evangelization, youth groups without responsible adult advisers, and peer ministry among young people fail to overcome the problems or situations that young people face. Furthermore, confronting crisis situations requires serious and constant work by a team of persons actively struggling for transformation through the following means:

- offering direct, personal attention to young people's families
- encouraging strong political action at the local level
- promoting better education and a better environment in secondary schools
- finding sources of work for young people
- offering professional services for psychological consultation, both for young people and for adults
- organizing projects and actions dedicated to social change

68   Pastoral ministry with young people facing crisis situations often implies establishing youth centers where young people can find new life and the support and direction needed to become evangelizers and agents for change. Those who live in crisis situations cannot fulfill themselves as persons or become effective agents for change if they lack horizons of hope to replace their fear or avoidance of reality. Only within a context of hope and action can workshops on drugs, sexual promiscuity, and violence make a difference. These workshops can raise young people's awareness and help them see these problems from a Christian perspective. However, young people also need supervised practice in order to be empowered to overcome crisis situations and problems.

Communitarian Spaces and Christian Growth

69   All Christian young people have been called to follow Jesus and live according to the Gospel, but not all Christian young people have been called to live in a small community, join a youth group, or participate in an apostolic movement. Therefore, it is important that the church provide young people with "communitarian spaces," lively spaces in which young people can feel at home, grow as persons, meet Jesus, socialize in a Christian setting, and find support for living out their mission. Communitarian spaces are not events or short programs, nor are they places of refuge that isolate young people from the world. Rather, communitarian spaces provide places to explore how Gospel values and Christian faith can be woven into all areas of life. Communitarian spaces prevent young people from seeing their faith-life as something belonging only within church structures or found in specific religious programs.

70   Young people want to see consistency between what the church preaches and how it acts, between the church's testimony and the church's concrete involvement with them. Young people

want the church to offer a healthy environment in which to share life, an environment that helps them find meaning in life, supports their human formation, and encourages them to take an ethical stance in confronting life's complexities. Young people yearn for the church to offer them a message of salvation in the face of a threatening world, and they seek a setting in which they can reflect together and find solidarity in confronting the challenges they face. A church that cares about young people provides communitarian spaces, and communitarian spaces like youth clubs, educational programs, family gatherings, and youth centers help supply an integrated approach to lived Christian faith.

Youth Clubs

71   Young people's fulfilling use of free time always bears good fruit and usually provides a form of education for adult life. Unfortunately, thousands of young people do not know how to use their free time in fulfilling ways, nor do they have an adequate place to do so. Youth clubs, especially in poor neighborhoods and small towns, greatly attract young people. These clubs offer young people the chance to socialize and organize activities within their economic means. Three kinds of clubs stand out in importance:

- **Social clubs** offer opportunities for healthy recreation, an environment in which young people can form friendships and discuss their ideals without being ridiculed, and a means to organize parties, trips to the countryside, and cultural or tourist excursions.
- **Art clubs** encourage young people to develop their gifts for poetry, drama, music, dance, drawing, or painting.
- **Sports clubs** offer recreational opportunities in an environment of camaraderie and fun for participants and spectators alike.

72   Youth clubs provide excellent ways to reinforce young people's Christian identity and values. However, it is important not to reduce pastoral work to establishing clubs, or to use clubs only to collect money.

Family *Convivencias*

73   Communication and understanding between parents and children are very important to the development of young people. Youth ministry can facilitate both by providing diverse types of family *convivencias,* in which parents and young people dialog about topics of common interest, such as the following:

- aspects related to the development of young people and their psychological, emotional, social, and religious dimensions
- cultural tensions that affect the family in general and young people in particular, including the conflict between traditional Hispanic culture and the dominant U.S. culture and the tensions young people experience in facing pop culture
- values formation in the midst of cultural tensions and conflicting messages that young people receive from society
- the transition that parents need to make from being educators of children to being friends and fellow travelers of young people and young adults

74   These intergenerational *convivencias* should be carefully planned and carried out by well-trained persons. Among the models that have been effective in the Hispanic community, three stand out:

75   **The forum model:** In the forum model, many young people and their parents gather at a meeting place that is usually large and has several smaller rooms in addition to an auditorium. Workshops in the forum model typically include these seven steps:

1. welcoming and icebreaking activities, in which both parents and young people participate
2. separate forums for parents and young people, though each group reflects on the same theme
3. exchange of conclusions from each group
4. identification—by everyone together—of the similarities and differences in each group's conclusions
5. dialog between the two groups regarding the differences, explaining the reasons for each group's position *without* arguing about it
6. separate reflection in each group on the other group's position, enlightened by the perspective of the other group
7. celebration of the experience with a liturgy and social gathering

76   **The roundtable model:** Roundtables (conferences in which people meet around a table to discuss a topic) of twelve to sixteen people are formed, with each table including roughly equal numbers of adults and young people, and men and women. All the roundtables discuss the same topic. It is best that parents and their own young people participate at different tables, so that no one

feels inhibited about speaking openly and so that both generations receive the other's ideas without preconditions. After the round-table session, parents are encouraged to speak in private with their children regarding the theme chosen. The roundtables should avoid falling into discussions that carry authoritarian, rebellious, accusatory, or moralizing overtones; none of these contribute to improved communication or mutual understanding.

77   **The family model:** Parents and their young people are brought together *as families* for interpersonal dialog. The family members discuss one or several topics introduced by a moderator, who usually participates in a family discussion only when specific questions or disputes arise. Otherwise, the moderator simply listens to various discussions and passes out reflection or exercise material at appropriate times. This model works well only with families already accustomed to dialog; the objective is to deepen the dialog and relationships already present between parents and their children.

78   Organized family outings and traditional cultural and liturgical celebrations are also appropriate settings for nurturing family relationships, especially when the events are organized by young people. Also important are special invitations to young people to participate in adult church conventions, pilgrimages, processions, missions, service projects, and other activities organized by adults. At times it is difficult to motivate young people to participate, but when they do, they fill these events with joy and find their faith strengthened and their horizons broadened.

Youth Centers, or *Casas del Joven*

79   Youth centers, or *casas del joven* (youth homes), are open houses where young people can find a stable environment, healthy relaxation, and adults disposed to support young people, encourage them, provide guidance, and dialog with them. Youth centers are places where any young person searching for Jesus can fit in and where efforts at human formation, evangelization, catechesis, and ministry training can be organized. At youth centers, various groups and youth communities can congregate, celebrate their faith together, and advance in their Christian formation.

80   Youth centers are a visible and effective sign of Christian hope for young people. The effectiveness of these centers depends on the

pastoral agents and adult advisers who facilitate young people's efforts to form community, experience the life of the church, and plan, organize, and direct their own activities. Activities desirable for young people to plan and direct on their own include youth get-togethers, intergenerational dialogs, formation programs, youth liturgies, missionary efforts, political and social action projects, individual counseling, and pastoral orientation.

Small Youth Communities: A Model for Pastoral Action

81   Jesus began his ministry by forming a small community of disciples. He inspired and formed these disciples so that when he was gone, they would continue his mission. Though Jesus preached to the multitudes and challenged all people, he paid special attention to forming his disciples for a whole new way of life. Jesus himself never became independent of this community. He went out to proclaim the Good News in the streets and public areas, but always returned to his small community. When Jesus appeared after his Resurrection, it was to this small community of his followers: to the women at the tomb, to the disciples on the road to Emmaus, and to the Apostles in the upper room or fishing at the lake. This fact is significant. Jesus revealed himself as the Risen One to his small community in order to strengthen their faith and send them out to continue his mission of planting the Reign of God everywhere.

82   The disciples dedicated themselves to announcing the Gospel and forming small communities made up of new followers of Jesus. This was the first model of the church, appearing almost two thousand years ago. These communities were not dedicated just to making their own members feel good about themselves. Rather, they were communities dedicated to others, to doing good for all persons, presenting Jesus to those who did not know him, and instructing the new disciples. For them, the focus of every action was to launch a new vision of human beings and the world, a vision reflecting the teachings of Jesus. So when these first communities formed, they committed themselves to the teachings of the Apostles, the breaking of bread, shared prayer, and the continuation of Jesus' mission.

83   Throughout the history of the church, believers have created small communities and tried to live according to Jesus' model. Since the Second Vatican Council, these efforts have received a new impetus. In many places, small communities modeled on Jesus' example have become the basis of the church's organizational and ecclesial life.

84   In the United States, the number of small ecclesial communities grows every day. Because small communities are a model of church consistent with Jesus' example, and because they are potentially able to provide Catholics with the support they need to live out their faith and fulfill their mission as Christians in the world, the Hispanic community has chosen to try to make this model of church a reality. The *National Pastoral Plan for Hispanic Ministry* indicates that small communities are a privileged site for the evangelization of Hispanics and a source of renovation for the ecclesial community, both at the parish and diocesan levels. Therefore, the Prophets of Hope model proposes forming small communities of young people and promotes evangelizing Hispanic youth via such communities.

Constitutive Elements of a Small Community

85   The goal of small ecclesial communities lies in facilitating their members' commitment to living out the Gospel and, with the same spirit as the first Christian communities, carrying the Good News to others. To achieve this goal, small communities try to maintain a balance between different practices appropriate to a community of Jesus' disciples. These practices include the following:

- **sharing life**, with its ups and downs, sadness and joy, failures and successes, in such a way that the members of the community accept, care for, and love one another as sons and daughters of God
- **sharing prayer**, with both spontaneous and structured prayers of petition, thanksgiving, praise, and forgiveness, all leading to the culminating act of thanksgiving—the celebration of the Eucharist
- **sharing faith**, reflecting together on the Scriptures, and mutually edifying one another by retelling their experiences of God's action in their personal lives and among the people of faith
- **evangelizing and serving others**, not only within the community but, above all, beyond it: bearing witness to Christian life in all settings of daily life and engaging in concrete missionary efforts

to carry Jesus to persons who have not found him or have moved away from his love

- **deepening in faith** through study of the Scriptures and church teachings
- **relating faith to life,** trying to discover God's presence or absence in the social, economic, cultural, and political worlds, striving to identify the signs of the times through which God calls the community members to personal conversion and to transform the world so that love, justice, and peace might reign

86   Together, these practices—carried out every day, not just on the days the small group meets—constitute the life of a true small ecclesial community. Certainly, not all small communities follow the same pattern: each chooses the element or elements that it wishes to emphasize, according to its members' vocations and needs. Some small communities emphasize prayer, missionary evangelization, Bible study, or faith reflection. Others revolve around members' ministry, need for a support group, or desire for Christian formation for action.

87   A parish should be a community of many small communities: adult groups, intergenerational groups, and youth groups for young people of various ages. A small community (whether its made up of adults, young people, or both) has achieved maturity when its members

- have a profound relationship of solidarity, mutual support, and shared life
- know that all participate equally in a shared and valuable effort in which all have the same mission and level of commitment
- are aware that a small community's energy to fulfill its mission is born of a spirit of personalization and communion, pluralism and unity, growth in mutual responsibility, sense of belonging to the group, and affirmation of the group's shared identity and values
- are well rooted in reality, that is, well acquainted or well attached to a place where they or their ancestors have lived for a long time; confront the problems and challenges they encounter in their efforts to extend the Reign of God; engage in transformative action in the various dimensions of their personal and social lives; and establish action priorities as a community that are consistent with the Christian ideal

- act together on the basis of minimal structure and maximal mutual effort, taking advantage of the gifts of *all* the members, developing their talents, and coordinating their ministries

Small Youth Communities

88   Small communities have multiplied among Hispanics in the United States. Young adults are involved in intergenerational communities, and small *youth* communities of adolescents and of young adults have begun to appear. Although most small communities are naturally intergenerational, forming small *youth* communities is very important. Young people enjoy the spirit of these communities in which they can live out and strengthen their faith with others of their age and life circumstances.

89   The primary function of small youth communities is to nourish the faith-lives of young people and guide them to become salt, light, and leavening for the world in which they live. In this way, they can become signs of the presence of the Reign of God among youth. Small youth communities are stable groups in which young men and women can have deep interpersonal relationships and feel mutually responsible for the well-being of all. The members of a small community do not reduce their relationship to group meetings, but rather share their daily lives with a Christian spirit and mutually support one another in becoming faithful followers of Jesus. Communities are open to new members who seek shared life in community, prayerful encounters with God, help in reflecting on their life, and support in fulfilling their mission.

90   There are small communities of preadolescents, adolescents, and young adults. Each type of community corresponds to the specific characteristics and needs of its members' developmental stage. These communities center themselves on Jesus and his project of the Reign of God, so that young people may be missionaries in their own world. Small communities favor a model of pastoral ministry with young people.

91   Parishes that have used this model of pastoral ministry for years now have young adult communities that were formed when the members were preadolescents or adolescents. These communities of young adults usually have a maturity level comparable to that of adult communities. When the young adults marry, they often

form communities for young couples or join already-established adult communities.

92   It is vital for various youth communities to relate to one another and to communities of people of all ages. Through this interaction, all groups are edified and become models of Christian and ecclesial life for one another. In small youth communities that have interaction with adults, young people enrich the total community with their perspective and spontaneity, broaden their own vision, and mature in the faith. Young people involved in small communities should also meet together and share their experiences as church members with young people involved in parish youth groups and apostolic movements. Retreats, gatherings, weekend encuentros, and joint projects are all appropriate means for facilitating this kind of interchange.

Formal and Informal Aspects in the Life of a Small Youth Community

93   Life in a small youth community is rich and invigorating. Many dynamics and opportunities for growth are at work as young Christians participate actively in the mission of the church through their engagement with the world. For the community to bear the best fruit possible, it must include structured opportunities for formation and pastoral action and encourage constant Christian practice in its members' daily lives.

94   The formal or structured aspects of the life of a small community include the following:
- reflection on reality in light of the Gospel
- study of and deepening encounters with the Scriptures, especially the Christian Testament
- participation in opportunities for human and moral formation
- study of church Tradition
- reflection on the meaning of sacramental life
- joint planning, implementation, and evaluation of pastoral programs

95   The informal or more spontaneous aspects of the life of a small community include the following:
- prayer and spiritual growth
- discernment of personal vocation, especially its communitarian dimension; seeking God's will for one's life, especially during moments of decision and challenge

- communication, social relationships, and mutual support among members
- strengthening of faith through personal testimony and mutual sharing of religious and apostolic experiences
- development of the gifts and abilities needed to sustain the life of the community and grow as Christian leaders

Ecclesial Character of Small Communities

96 Small communities can provide young people with a more complete experience of church than parish groups or apostolic movements can, because small communities follow more closely the model of a community of disciples. Furthermore, small communities see themselves as a cell of the universal church and stay focused on the church's mission, both in their daily informal experiences and in specific projects and actions. Small youth communities are a sign of hope for the parish and diocesan levels of the church to the extent that they maintain their ecclesial character and promote an authentic sense of membership in the wider church. Small youth communities maintain this ecclesial character through the following:

- intimate communion with God and profound union with their brothers and sisters of the community and the entire church
- continuous education in the faith, education that responds to the questions and concerns of daily life and also keeps alive the spirit of the Gospel
- a clear Catholic identity, achieved through study and faith reflection, communion with the church, participation in the Eucharist, collaboration in ecclesial ministries, and participation in the pastoral work of the parish and diocese
- profound union between faith and life, achieved by analyzing and critically judging experiences in light of the Gospel, making a conscious choice to follow Jesus faithfully, sustaining hope even in times of difficulty, discovering the Christian meaning of life, sharing possessions with a spirit of universal sisterhood and brotherhood, and keeping a special solidarity with the poor and oppressed
- a common spirit that moves each member and the group as a whole to action, sustains the life of the community, and allows it to mature by collaborating in the formation of new small communities

- active participation in the evangelizing mission of the church, in which young people are guided by a strong and sincere missionary spirit, the social teachings of the church, and a serious commitment to provide a Christian presence in society and to be agents of social change

Youth Ministry in Small Communities

97   In chapter 6, we reflected on the ideal of a "missionary parish" and on the challenges presented by "passive" parishes that are focused on providing services only to those who worship there. Small youth communities can be effective instruments for facilitating the transition from one model to the other. This shift can be achieved by forming small communities when establishing a new Hispanic youth ministry in a parish or by helping young people transform a current parish youth group into a series of small communities. However it occurs, the passive parish needs to change its institutional organization and its pastoral focus so that small communities can really be the basis of parish life. The change from a pastoral strategy of reception to one of communion and participation in small communities has five stages. We enumerate some indicators of these stages below:

Point of Departure:
The Parish Is a Passive Provider of Services

98   The following are two characteristics of a parish that focuses only on providing services to active members:
- Full-time employees of the parish stipulate how all activities and responsibilities of the parish are to be organized and carried out.
- Young people of the parish are invited to help the priest or other parish employees in their work.

Stage 1:
The Parish Forms a Pastoral Council

99   In stage 1, the parish forms a pastoral council to promote parishioner involvement in parish decisions:
- A pastoral council is formed, with or without representation of young people. This council influences the decision-making process regarding parish activities.

- Priests and other full-time employees discuss parish affairs with the pastoral council.
- Training of the pastoral council focuses on its responsibilities as an advisory body.
- The whole congregation is invited to choose the members of the pastoral council. However, young people are sometimes excluded from this process.

Stage 2:
The Parish Awakens

100   In stage 2, parish members begin to take a more active role in parish life:
- More parishioners, generally older adults, participate actively in the responsibilities of the parish, but they are seen as "helpers" of priests and parish employees.
- Various people try to conscienticize parish members regarding the mission of laypeople in the church.
- Home visits are carried out to invite members and potential members to participate in church activities.

Stage 3:
The Parishioners Embrace Their Commitments

101   In stage 3, the parishioners begin to embrace their baptismal commitments:
- Various groups of people commit themselves to parish responsibilities beyond the walls of the church, such as catechesis in homes, premarital formation experiences, and marriage encounters.
- Young people of the parish organize a committee for youth ministry and begin to carry out evangelization activities.
- Bible study groups form in homes.
- A welcome ministry is formed to greet new members and visiting worshipers; visits to people who are sick, aged, or incarcerated occur more regularly.
- A catechumenate program begins for those interested in converting to the Catholic church.
- Training programs are offered for community ministries, especially liturgy, catechesis, and Bible study leadership.

Stage 4:
Small Communities Are Formed

102   In stage 4, parishioners of various ages decide to form small faith communities:

- Christians in a given neighborhood meet periodically in someone's home to share Bible readings, prayer, and reflection.
- Parents form communities to help them educate their children in the faith.
- Young people form small communities of their own age-group. Through these communities, they strive to become agents of change in society and to present Jesus to other young people of the neighborhood.
- Community members as individuals and small communities as a whole begin to participate in civil and political activities that promote social justice and a better world.
- Communities meet on Sunday to celebrate the Eucharist, being sure that new members are also invited to participate in liturgical ministries.

Stage 5:
Small Communities Take Action to Transform the World

103   In stage 5, the small communities take an active role in trying to transform the world:

- Small communities unite to improve people's living conditions through concrete actions at the local level to combat injustice, improve schools, eradicate violence, minister to adolescents, or take wider political action for more-just laws.
- Small communities send representatives to the pastoral council. The council seeks to help all members of the parish community fulfill their mission as Christians in the world and in the church.
- Youth communities are recognized and valued as much as adult and intergenerational communities. As a result, the parish becomes more vibrant and vigorous.
- The parish takes responsibility for its evangelizing mission and for incorporating new Catholics and returning Catholics into the small communities.
- The parish organizes opportunities for human and religious formation, spiritual growth, and pastoral-theological reflection for members of the small communities.

• The communities take responsibility for obtaining sufficient financial resources to meet the needs of the parish.

104   The bishops of the United States, in their pastoral letter *The Hispanic Presence: Challenge and Commitment*, say the following:

> Hispanics in the Americas have made few contributions to the Church more significant than the *comunidades eclesiales de base* (Basic Ecclesial Communities). The small community has appeared on the scene as a ray of hope in dealing with dehumanizing situations that can destroy people and weaken faith. . . . Since these communities are of proven benefit to the Church . . . , we highly encourage their development.[1]

------- ❧ **Final Reflection** ❧ -------

A New Dawn in Hispanic Youth Ministry

1   Chapter 21 of the Gospel of John describes Jesus' third appearance to his disciples following his Resurrection. Through symbolic language, John's Gospel speaks of the model of church and the Christian leadership established by Jesus. Reflecting on this chapter from John's Gospel should offer many insights to people involved in youth ministry.

Leadership in the Manner of Jesus

2   One day, John's Gospel tells us, Peter was on the beach with some of the companions whom Jesus had called to be disciples—fishers of people. Peter said to the other disciples, "I am going fishing." The disciples followed Peter, who was the leader of the group, and said to him, "We will go with you." Though the Risen Jesus had already appeared twice to the disciples, they had not taken up being fishermen of the Reign of God; instead, they had returned to their old roles as ordinary fishermen.

3   The disciples, who would become the pillars of the church, got into the boat, which symbolizes the church. It was night, and the light of faith was missing. The disciples fished for hours but caught nothing. Without Jesus, their church and their efforts were sterile. The disciples were weary and frustrated. Then, at dawn, something extraordinary happened:

> Just after daybreak, Jesus stood on the beach; but the disciples did not know that it was Jesus. Jesus said to them, "Children, you have no fish, have you?" They answered him, "No." He said to them, "Cast the net to the right side of the boat, and you will find some." So they cast it, and now they were not able to haul it in because there were so many fish. (John 21:4–6)

4   This knowledgeable and patient group of people had long worked in vain. Now they succeeded, on the advice of a man who called out to them from the shore but whom they did not recognize. Why did they listen to him? This unknown man had taken an interest in them, had initiated a dialog by asking them about the fruits of their labor, and had treated them as friends. The disciples, for their part, told him honestly about their failure. So the unknown man joined with them in solidarity, made their search his own as well, and told them that to be successful they needed to change the direction of their efforts. Perhaps without much enthusiasm and with many doubts, they decided to pay attention because he seemed confident, they saw no self-interest in his suggestion, and their continued efforts had not succeeded.

5   As leaders in Hispanic youth ministry, we must ask what this passage tells us about our own style of leadership:

- What happens when we lose sight of our mission as fishers of people and instead go after material rewards or prestige?
- Do we, as leaders, need to consider new possibilities for our pastoral action? Do we listen to others' advice?
- Are we fishing where the majority of young people spend their life?
- Does our leadership focus attention on ourselves, or do we focus on facilitating the pastoral mission of the young people involved?
- Do we show a sincere interest in young people's experiences as they engage in pastoral work? Do we take their search to heart?
- What motivates the advice we give to young people on how they can fulfill their missions and be effective in their work?

Discipleship in the Manner of the First Followers

6   When he saw the great quantity of fish, the Apostle John exclaimed, "It is the Lord!" The disciples had seen a new light, given to them by their teacher, even though they did not recognize him. It was the fruits of the disciples' labor that led John to recognize Jesus in the unknown man, and John's exclamation made the rest of the group realize that Jesus was present.

7   Earlier, the boat full of followers—symbolizing the church—was passing through a time of darkness. In facing Jesus' absence, the

disciples had returned to their normal occupations and were discouraged by the barrenness of that work.

8   Encountering and paying attention to Jesus changed the whole picture. The fruits of the disciples' labor filled the disciples with hope and optimism and gave them a new yearning to encounter Jesus once again. Peter literally could not contain himself; he forgot about the fish, jumped out of the boat, and went the last hundred yards through the sea to greet the master. The other disciples took the boat to shore and went to meet Jesus too. Alerted by John's exclamation, Peter led the way back to Jesus.

9   As disciples of Jesus, we must ask what this passage tells us about our ability to follow, recognize, and respond to Jesus in a selfless way:

- Do we recognize Jesus when other people show him to us?
- Do we find new energy and motivation in seeing the fruits of our work?
- When we encounter Jesus, do we communicate our experience to others?
- How often do we try to do our work while relying only on our own strength?
- Do we know how to recognize Jesus' voice when he asks us to change the direction of our life and ministry?
- Do we dedicate time to encountering Jesus and sharing our desires, frustrations, and successes with him?

Fellowship and Community in Jesus' Type of Church

10   When the disciples returned to the beach, they found a fire lit and fish and bread on the coals. Jesus was there, making breakfast.

> Jesus said to them, "Bring some of the fish that you have just caught." So Simon Peter went aboard and hauled the net ashore, full of large fish, a hundred fifty-three of them; and though there were so many, the net was not torn. Jesus said to them, "Come and have breakfast." Now none of the disciples dared to ask him, "Who are you?" because they knew it was the Lord. Jesus came and took the bread and gave it to them, and did the same with the fish. (John 21:10–13)

11   Jesus did not await his disciples with the typical tools of an administrator or teacher: books, procedure manuals, or organizational charts. He awaited them with different tools, the life-giving tools of a servant: a fire, bread, and fish. What lesson was Jesus giving to his disciples? Perhaps to some this whole scene seems useless. Why waste time cooking? Why didn't Jesus take the time to explain to Peter and the other disciples how to administer the church, hold a council, organize a committee, determine policy, defend the faith, and resolve the doctrinal problems they would confront?

12   But Jesus was not wasting time. He was showing his followers the type of church that he wanted them to become—a community in which each person would share what he or she had. The strength of the church community lies in the sharing of its mission and its bread.

13   Earlier in John's Gospel, Jesus had proclaimed:

> "I am the living bread that came down from heaven. Whoever eats of this bread will live forever; and the bread that I will give for the life of the world is my flesh." (6:51)

The disciples had heard, believed, and recognized Jesus as the Messiah; walked with him, embraced his vision, and shared bread with him. After Jesus' death and Resurrection, the disciples could neither see him nor share time with him like they could before. They had to discover and relate to the Risen Jesus, whom they recognized through their faith and the fruits of a search that he joined in. On the beach, Jesus met the disciples under the appearance of some unknown man walking at dawn, who told them how to fish and offered them bread.

14   The one hundred fifty-three fish have a special meaning. They symbolize the one hundred fifty-three nations known by the Jews in Jesus' day. The net full of fish represented all the nations of the world—that all belonged to God.

15   As members of the church community, we must ask what this passage tells us about the fellowship and reception we show toward Jesus in all the forms that he appears to us:
- How does Jesus meet us today?
- Do we recognize Jesus in the bread of the Eucharist?
- Do we recognize Jesus in whatever "unknown persons" we encounter in life?

- With what attitudes and missionary spirit do we approach young people of other cultures?
- Do the needs of our own people cause us to lose sight of the universal dimension of the church?

Pastorship for Jesus' Life Project

16   Jesus and his disciples shared their breakfast and talked awhile. Surely the disciples felt both glad to be with the Master and uncomfortable before the mystery of the Risen Jesus. In this situation, Jesus initiated a very important conversation with Peter about his role as leader of the rest of the disciples:

> "Simon son of John, do you love me more than these?" [Peter] said to him, "Yes, Lord; you know that I love you." Jesus said to him, "Feed my lambs." A second time he said to him, "Simon son of John, do you love me?" He said to him, "Yes, Lord; you know that I love you." Jesus said to him, "Tend my sheep." He said to him the third time, "Simon son of John, do you love me?" Peter felt hurt because he said to him the third time, "Do you love me?" And he said to him, "Lord, you know everything; you know that I love you." Jesus said to him, "Feed my sheep." (John 21:15–17)

17   Today if we were to interview a candidate for the papacy, for a ministerial position in the church, or for a position as coordinator of an ecclesial group, surely we would ask a good number and variety of questions. But for Jesus, only one question was important: "Simon son of John, do you love me?" Once again, Jesus was unique and surprising. Today, many people would find serious obstacles to Peter's becoming pope after he denied Jesus three times just days before Jesus' death. By questioning Peter three times and then three times affirming Peter in his mission, Jesus indicated to all people that although he knows our weaknesses, he trusts in our love and chooses us to continue his mission.

18   In his dialog with Peter, just as in his Last Supper address to his disciples, Jesus made clear the heart and source of his life's project: "Do you love me? . . . Feed my lambs. Tend my sheep. . . . Love one another as I have loved you." Love lies at the heart of

every true Christian project. For all Christian leaders, love must be the most important thing, their motivation in ministry and their reason for being.

19   After affirming Peter in his mission for the third time, Jesus solemnly indicated to Peter that Peter was going to die a prophet's death—giving glory to God with the witness of his faith, and being abused by those who rejected his invitation to a new kind of life. As Jesus demonstrated with his life and in this chapter from John's Gospel, the task of every Christian leader involves fulfilling three roles: servant-leader, pastor, and prophet.

20   Finally, Jesus said to Peter, "Follow me." Peter went with him, and John followed them.

> When Peter saw [John], he said to Jesus, "Lord, what about him?" Jesus said to him, "If it is my will that he remain until I come, what is that to you? Follow me!" (21:21–22)

With this last instruction, Jesus gave to Peter, as leader of his church, another clue about how he was to carry out his mission: follow the Master's mission and teachings, and allow others to follow as they are called.

21   As pastoral workers in Jesus' life project, we must ask what this passage tells us about the pastorship we show toward others—and toward ourselves:

- What motivates us in our pastoral work?
- Are we aware that loving Jesus means caring for our sisters and brothers in imitation of Jesus, the Good Shepherd?
- To what extent is our leadership focused on pastoring young people?
- How authentic is our own faith witness?
- How courageous and dedicated are we in taking on our prophetic task of promoting Latino young people?
- Do we follow Jesus in our daily life and in all our actions?
- How often do we focus on checking out what others are doing instead of looking at the quality of our own pastoral work?

22   This account about the church, the mission of Christian leaders, and interaction among members of the Christian community is a challenge to all baptized people, but especially to the young leaders of this generation, who have to navigate the new waters of a new age. Christian leaders have the task of rediscovering the model of

church that Jesus revealed through his actions and teachings. They have to analyze, in light of the story from John's Gospel, the style of leadership that Jesus wants in his church. They must propose new models of organization and leadership to facilitate the following of Jesus.

A Look Back, A Look Ahead

23   This first volume of Prophets of Hope has presented a general view of the reality of Hispanic young people and a broad view of Hispanic youth ministry, as seen from a ministerial perspective. The preceding reflection on the Gospel of John helps us see clearly that pastoral action must be carried out by loving Jesus and following his model as fisher and pastor—casting a net where young people are, caring for them as shepherds care for their sheep, and serving and nourishing them as disciples. Only with Jesus and with disciples that are his witnesses and followers will we keep alive our experience of the Reign of God and our hope of spreading that Reign throughout the world.

24   In the second volume of Prophets of Hope, we examine young people's human formation and personal development. We also present Jesus as a brother, savior, and prophet of the Reign of God. This presentation allows us to better know and communicate to others the person of Jesus—a fascinating and mysterious human being who, two thousand years after becoming incarnate in human history, is still Good News and is still capable of inspiring great deeds and sacrifices. By knowing Jesus—the man who challenges us to love unconditionally and to overcome the barriers of race, age, sex, or ability—young people will be able to experience the God who offers us resurrection and eternal life. Young people will encounter Jesus as the Way, the Truth, and the Life; find the deepest meaning of their existence; and prepare themselves to exercise leadership in society and in the church. The rest of the second volume focuses on the process of evangelization and on specific steps in offering young Hispanics an integral evangelization.

25   Together, the two volumes of Prophets of Hope will help carry out the New Evangelization that must respond to the challenges and questions confronting young people today. As the Latin Amer-

ican bishops said at the Fourth General Latin American Episcopal Conference:

> The new evangelization is something operational and dynamic. It is first and foremost a call to conversion . . . and to the hope that rests on God's promises. Its unshakable certainty derives from Christ's resurrection, which is the primary proclamation and the root of all evangelization, the foundation for all human advancement, and the principle of all genuine Christian culture.[1]

❧ Notes and Resources ❧

Chapter 1:
Hispanic Young People and
Their Process of Maturation

Notes

Epigraph: John Paul II, "Santa Misa con los jóvenes," in *Segunda visita pastoral a México* (México, DF: Conferencia del Episcopado Mexicano [CEM], 1990), no. 170.

1. Paul VI, "On Christian Joy," in United States Catholic Conference (USCC), *A Vision of Youth Ministry* (Washington, DC: USCC, 1986), 25.

2. Secretariat for Hispanic Affairs, USCC, *Prophetic Voices: The Document on the Process of the III Encuentro Nacional Hispano de Pastoral* (Washington, DC: USCC, 1986), 12.

3. John Eagleson and Philip Scharper, eds., *Puebla and Beyond* (Maryknoll, NY: Orbis Books, 1979), no. 1168; originally published as *Puebla: La evangelización en el presente y en el futuro de América Latina*, by Consejo Episcopal Latinoamericano (CELAM) (Washington, DC: National Conference of Catholic Bishops [NCCB], 1979).

4. NCCB Secretariat of the Committee for the Church in Latin America, *Santo Domingo Conclusions: New Evangelization, Human Development, Christian Culture* (Washington, DC: USCC, 1993), nos. 114–115; original Spanish-language text copyright © 1992 by CELAM.

Additional Resources

Bagley, Ron, ed. *Young Adult Ministry: A Book of Readings.* Naugatuck, CT: Youth Ministry Resource Network, Center for Youth Ministry Development, 1987.

Fromm, Erich. *The Art of Loving.* New York: Harper and Row, 1956.

Galilea, Segundo. *El alba de nuestra espiritualidad.* Madrid, España: Narcea, 1986.

———. *El camino de la espiritualidad.* Bogotá, Colombia: Ediciones Paulinas, 1987.

———. *La inserción en la vida de Jesús y en la misión.* Bogotá, Colombia: Ediciones Paulinas, 1989.

Instituto Internacional de Teología a Distancia (IITD). *Los jóvenes.* Curso de formación catequética. Madrid, España: IITD, 1984.

John Paul II. *Familiaris Consortio.* Washington, DC: USCC, 1981.

Mejía, Alejandro. *El misterio de la existencia.* 3d ed. México, DF: Editorial Progreso, 1989.

Sánchez García, Urbano. *La opción del cristiano.* Vol. 3. Colección Síntesis. Madrid, España: Sociedad de Educación Atenas, 1986.

Shelton, Charles M. *Adolescent Spirituality: Pastoral Ministry for High School and College Youth.* Chicago: Loyola University Press, 1983.

USCC. *Human Sexuality: A Catholic Perspective for Education and Lifelong Learning.* Washington, DC: USCC, 1991.

———. *The Sexual Challenge: Growing Up Christian.* Washington, DC: USCC, 1990.

Vidal, Marciano. *Moral fundamental.* 6th ed. Moral de actitudes, vol. 1. Madrid, España: Covarrubias, 1990.

———. *Moral de la persona.* 6th ed. Moral de actitudes, vol. 2. Madrid, España: Covarrubias, 1990.

Whitehead, Evelyn Eaton, and James D. Whitehead. *A Sense of Sexuality.* New York: Doubleday, 1989.

Chapter 2:
Human Relationships and Hispanic Young People

Notes

Epigraph: CELAM, *Pastoral juvenil: Sí a la civilización del amor,* 2d ed. (México, DF: CEM, Comisión Episcopal Mexicana de Pastoral Juvenil, 1989), 97.

1. NCCB, *The Hispanic Presence: Challenge and Commitment* (Washington, DC: USCC, 1984), 21.

2. Frank and Renee Schick, *Statistical Handbook on U.S. Hispanics* (Phoenix, AZ: Oryx Press, 1991), 197.

3. U.S. Bureau of the Census, *The Hispanic Population in the United States: March 1991* (Washington, DC: U.S. Government Printing Office, 1991), 18.

4. Mary Rose McGeady, "Disconnected Kids: An American Tragedy," *America* 164 (15 June 1991): 642.

5. Joy G. Dryfoos, *Adolescents at Risk: Prevalence and Prevention* (New York: Oxford University Press, 1990), 54–57.

6. Robert Fiala and Gary LaFree, "Cross-National Determinants of Child Homicide," *American Sociological Review* 53 (June 1988): 433.

7. Robert E. Emery, "Family Violence," *American Psychologist* 44 (February 1989): 321.

8. Dryfoos, *Adolescents at Risk*, 22–23.

9. Gelasia Márquez, "Educating in Love: Toward Sex Education Within Family Structure, 1984–1988," Office of Catholic Education, Diocese of Brooklyn, typescript, 10–11.

10. John Paul II, *Familiaris Consortio* (Washington, DC: USCC, 1982), no. 51.

Additional Resources

Boff, Leonardo. *The Maternal Face of God: The Feminine and Its Religious Expression*. New York: Harper and Row, 1987.

CEM. *Directorio nacional de pastoral familiar*. 2d ed. México, DF: CEM, 1989.

Márquez, Gelasia. "One Response to the United States Bishops' Pastoral Letter on Hispanic Ministry: The Hispanic Family Ministry." Family Life Ministry for the Hispanic Community, Diocese of Brooklyn, 1985, typescript.

————. "Who Am I? The Identity Disorder and Its Importance as a Diagnostic Category Within the Hispanic Community." Fordham University, n.d., typescript.

Ortega, Ray. "Amor en el Principio: A Youth Movement for Couples Going Steady," *Building Our Hope* 1 (Summer 1993): 1–4.

Sexualidad humana, módulo IV. México, DF: Centro Juvenil de Promoción Integral, n.d.

USCC. *Human Sexuality: A Catholic Perspective for Education and Lifelong Learning*. Washington, DC: USCC, 1991.

Urrabazo, Gloria. *Hispanic Families*. San Antonio, TX: Mexican American Cultural Center, 1989.

Urrabazo, Rosendo. *Machismo: Mexican American Male Self-Concept*. San Antonio, TX: Mexican American Cultural Center, 1985.

Chapter 3:
Hispanic Young People and Their Culture

Notes

Epigraph: Paul VI, *Evangelii Nuntiandi* (Washington, DC: USCC, 1975), no. 20.

1. Secretariat for Hispanic Affairs, USCC, *Prophetic Voices: The Document on the Process of the III Encuentro Nacional Hispano de Pastoral* (Washington, DC: USCC, 1986), 17.

2. Daughters of St. Paul, comps., *John Paul II in America* (Boston: St. Paul Books and Media, 1987), 156–157.

Additional Resources

Arbuckle, Gerald A. *Earthing the Gospel: An Inculturation Handbook for Pastoral Workers.* Maryknoll, NY: Orbis Books, 1990.

Beals, Ralph L., and Harry Hoijer. *An Introduction to Anthropology.* 3d ed. New York: Macmillan, 1965.

Deck, Allan F. *The Second Wave.* Mahwah, NJ: Paulist Press, 1989.

Ekstrom, Reynolds R. *Access Guide to Pop Culture.* New Rochelle, NY: Salesian Society/Don Bosco Multimedia, 1989.

IITD. *Los jóvenes.* Curso de formación catequética. Madrid, España: IITD, 1984.

McDonald, William. "Reports on the Investigation on the Pastoral Needs of Hispanic Youth." Research conducted for Saint Mary's Press, Winona, MN, 1987, typescript.

Southeast Regional Office for Hispanic Affairs (SEPI). *Joven inmigrante . . . deja tu huella.* Miami: SEPI, 1991.

———. *Joven siembra y evangeliza la cultura.* Miami: SEPI, 1992.

Warren, Michael. *Youth, Gospel, Liberation.* San Francisco: Harper and Row, 1989.

Chapter 4:
The Role of Hispanic Young People
in Social Transformation

Notes

Epigraph: Robert F. Sanchez, "Evangelization," in Secretariat for Hispanic Affairs, USCC, *Proceedings of the II Encuentro Nacional Hispano de Pastoral* (Washington, DC: USCC, 1978), 56.

1. USCC, *Brothers and Sisters to Us: U.S. Bishops' Pastoral Letter on Racism in Our Day* (Washington, DC: USCC, 1979), 10.

2. José Luis Rubio Cordón, "Iberoamérica, en la polarización internacional riqueza/pobreza," *Vida Nueva* 1.788 (4 May 1991): 23–30.

3. CELAM, Segunda Conferencia General del Episcopado Latinoamericano, *Medellín: La Iglesia en la actual transformación de América Latina a la luz del Concilio*, 4th ed. (Bogotá, Colombia: CELAM, 1968), chap. 2, no. 16.

4. NCCB, *Economic Justice for All* (Washington, DC: USCC, 1986), no. 16.

5. Secretariat for Hispanic Affairs, USCC, *Prophetic Voices: Document on the Process of the III Encuentro Nacional Hispano de Pastoral* (Washington, DC: USCC, 1986), 12.

6. John Paul II, *Christifideles Laici* (Washington, DC: USCC, 1988), no. 42.

Additional Resources

Arbuckle, Gerald A. *Earthing the Gospel: An Inculturation Handbook for Pastoral Workers.* Maryknoll, NY: Orbis Books, 1990.

Branch, Edward. "Racism in Our Day." In *Proceedings of the First National Youth Congress*, ed. Anita Marie Fusco. Washington, DC: National Federation for Catholic Youth Ministry (NFCYM), 1992.

Hayes-Bautista, David E., Werner O. Schink, and Jorge Chapa. *The Burden of Support: Young Latinos in an Aging Society.* Stanford, CA: Stanford University Press, 1988.

The Hispanic Policy Development Project. *Closing the Gap for U.S. Hispanic Youth: Public/Private Strategies.* Washington, DC, 1988.

John Paul II. *Centesimus Annus.* Washington, DC: USCC, 1991.

———. "To Build Peace, Respect Minorities." *Origins* 18 (29 December 1988): 467–469.

NCCB. *The Challenge of Peace: God's Promise and Our Response.* Washington, DC: USCC, 1983.

National Hispanic Leadership Conference (NHLC). *Hispanic Issues Are America's Issues.* Washington, DC: NHLC, 1988.

SEPI. *Joven, comunícate y grita la verdad!* Miami: SEPI, 1990.

———. *Joven hispano: Voz profética.* Miami: SEPI, 1991.

USCC. *Political Responsibility: Revitalizing American Democracy.* Washington, DC: USCC, 1991.

Warren, Michael. *Youth, Gospel, Liberation.* San Francisco: Harper and Row, 1989.

Chapter 5:
The Religious Reality of Hispanic Young People

Notes

Epigraph: NCCB, *The Hispanic Presence: Challenge and Commitment* (Washington, DC: USCC, 1984), 20.

1. John Eagleson and Philip Scharper, eds., *Puebla and Beyond* (Maryknoll, NY: Orbis Books, 1979), nos. 305–315; originally published as *Puebla: La evangelización en el presente y en el futuro de América Latina,* by CELAM (Washington, DC: NCCB, 1979).

2. John Paul II, "To the Youth of the World on the Occasion of the VIII World Youth Day—1993," in *A Year of Preparation: World Youth Day '93 Resource Manual* (Washington, DC: USCC, 1992), no. 3.

Additional Resources

Archdiocese of Los Angeles, Office of Religious Education. *Recursos para el proceso de preparación para la confirmación 1992.* Los Angeles: Office of Religious Education, Archdiocese of Los Angeles, 1992.

The Bishops Speak with the Virgin: A Pastoral Letter of the Hispanic Bishops of the U.S. New York: Maryknoll, 1981.

Boff, Leonardo. *The Maternal Face of God: The Feminine and Its Religious Expressions.* New York: Harper and Row, 1987.

———. *New Evangelization: Good News to the Poor.* Maryknoll, NY: Orbis Books, 1991.

Candelaria, Michael R. *Popular Religion and Liberation: The Dilemma of Liberation Theology.* Albany, NY: State University of New York Press, 1990.

Cervantes, Carmen María. "Roots and Wings of the Evangelization of Latino Youth." *Building Our Hope* 5 (Summer 1992): 8–9.

Codina, Víctor. "Sacramentales, sacramentos de los pobres." *La revista latinoamericana de teología.* Cochambamba, Bolivia: Universidad Católica Boliviana, n.d.

CELAM, Segunda Conferencia General del Episcopado Latinoamericano. *Medellín: La Iglesia en la actual transformación de América Latina a la luz del Concilio.* 4th ed. Bogotá, Colombia: CELAM, 1968.

———. *Pastoral juvenil: Sí a la civilización del amor.* 2d ed. México, DF: CEM, Comisión Episcopal Mexicana de Pastoral Juvenil, 1989.

Deck, Allan F. "Fundamentalism and the Hispanic Catholic." *America* (26 January 1985): 64–66.

———. "Proselytism and Hispanic Catholics: How Long Can We Cry Wolf?" *America* 159 (10 December 1988): 485–490.

———. *The Second Wave.* Mahwah, NJ: Paulist Press, 1989.

Díaz-Vilar, Juan. *Las sectas: Un desafío a la pastoral.* New York: Northeast Catholic Pastoral Center for Hispanics, 1985.

Editorial Advisory Board, Saint Mary's Press Project for Hispanic Youth Ministry. "Our Consultation Meeting: A Step Forward." *Building Our Hope* 2 (January 1989): 2–4.

Elizondo, Virgilio. *Christianity and Culture: An Introduction to Pastoral Theology and Ministry for the Bicultural Community.* Huntington, IN: Our Sunday Visitor, 1975.

———. *Galilean Journey: The Mexican-American Promise.* Maryknoll, NY: Orbis Books, 1983.

———. *Mestizaje: The Dialect of Cultural Birth and the Gospel.* Paris: Institute Catholique de Paris, 1978.

Estrada, Juan A. *La transformación de la religiosidad popular.* Salamanca, España: Ediciones Sígueme, 1986.

Fourez, Gérard. *Sacramentos y vida del hombre.* Santander, España: Sal Terrae, 1983.

Galilea, Segundo. *Religiosidad popular y pastoral hispano-americana.* New York: Northeast Catholic Pastoral Center for Hispanics, 1981.

González, Carlos Ignacio. *María, evangelizada y evangelizadora.* México, DF: CELAM, 1989.

González Dorado, Antonio. *Nuestra Señora de América.* Bogotá, Colombia: CELAM, 1986.

A Handbook on Guadalupe: Our Lady Patroness of the Americas. Kenosha, WI: Franciscan Marytown Press, 1974.

Huitrado-Rizo, Juan José. "The Expression of a People Coming to Life." *New Theology Review* (3 November 1990): 43–55.

John Paul II. "Santa Misa con los jóvenes." In *Segunda visita pastoral a México*. México, DF: CEM, 1990.

McDonald, William. "Reports on the Investigation on the Pastoral Needs of Hispanic Youth." Research conducted for Saint Mary's Press, Winona, MN, 1987, typescript.

NCCB. *National Pastoral Plan for Hispanic Ministry*. Washington, DC: USCC, 1988.

NCCB Secretariat of the Committee for the Church in Latin America. *Santo Domingo Conclusions: New Evangelization, Human Development, Christian Culture*. Washington, DC: USCC, 1993. Original Spanish-language text copyright © 1992 by CELAM.

Romero, C. Gilbert. *Hispanic Devotional Piety: Tracing the Biblical Roots*. Maryknoll, NY: Orbis Books, 1991.

Secretariat for Hispanic Affairs, USCC. *Proceedings of the II Encuentro Nacional Hispano de Pastoral*. Washington, DC: USCC, 1978.

Sosa, Juan J. "Religiosidad popular y sincretismo religioso: Santería y espiritismo." *Documentaciones Sureste* 4 (March 1983): 14–26.

USCC. *Prophetic Voices: The Document on the Process of the III Encuentro Nacional Hispano de Pastoral*. Washington, DC: USCC, 1986.

Chapter 6:
The Evangelizing Mission of the Church

Notes

Epigraph: NCCB, *Heritage and Hope: Evangelization in the United States* (Washington, DC: USCC, 1991), 41–42.

1. Ibid., 45.

2. Secretariat for Hispanic Affairs, USCC, *Proceedings of the II Encuentro Nacional Hispano de Pastoral* (Washington, DC: Secretariat for Hispanic Affairs, USCC, 1978), 68.

3. Ken Davis, "El esfuerzo por la justicia no tiene ni principio ni fin," *Voz Catequética* 3 (January 1991): 9.

4. Ibid., 5

5. NCCB Secretariat of the Committee for the Church in Latin America, *Santo Domingo Conclusions: New Evangelization, Human Development, Christian Culture* (Washington DC: USCC, 1993), no. 10; original Spanish-language text copyright © 1992 by CELAM.

6. Based on NCCB Secretariat of the Committee for the Church in Latin America, *Santo Domingo Conclusions: New Evangelization, Human Development, Christian Culture* (Washington DC: USCC, 1993), no. 302; original Spanish-language text copyright © 1992 by CELAM.

7. Paul VI, *Evangelii Nuntiandi* (Washington, DC: USCC, 1975), no. 22.

8. NCCB, *Economic Justice for All* (Washington, DC: USCC, 1986), no. 88.

9. *The Bishops Speak with the Virgin: A Pastoral Letter of the Hispanic Bishops of the U.S.* (New York: Maryknoll, 1981), 19.

10. David Byers, ed., *The Parish in Transition: Proceedings of a Conference on the American Catholic Parish* (Washington, DC: USCC, 1985), 3.

11. USCC, *Prophetic Voices: The Document on the Process of the III Encuentro Nacional Hispano de Pastoral* (Washington, DC: USCC, 1986), 11.

12. Ibid., 7.

13. John Paul II, *Christifideles Laici* (Washington, DC: USCC, 1988), no. 27.

14. John Paul II, *Redemptoris Missio* (Washington, DC: USCC, 1990), no. 49.

15. NCCB, *National Pastoral Plan for Hispanic Ministry* (Washington, DC: USCC, 1987), 8.

16. USCC, *Prophetic Voices,* 17–18.

17. John Paul II, *Christifideles Laici,* no. 46.

18. Paul VI, *Octogesima Adveniens,* quoted in NCCB, *Economic Justice for All,* no. 87.

19. John Paul II, *Christifideles Laici,* no. 20.

20. NCCB, *National Pastoral Plan for Hispanic Ministry,* no. 20.

Additional Resources

Castex, Pedro. "The Hispanic People and Youth Ministry." *Building Our Hope* 4 (Spring 1991): 8–12.

Cervantes, Carmen María. "Roots and Wings of the Evangelization of Latino Youth." *Building Our Hope* 5 (Summer 1992): 8–9.

Deck, Allan F. "Window of Opportunity: The Plan for Hispanic Ministry." *Origins* 19 (17 August 1989): 199.

Díaz-Vilar, Juan. *Parroquia comunidad misionera.* New York: Northeast Catholic Pastoral Center for Hispanics, 1983.

Fourez, Gérard. *Sacramentos y vida del hombre.* Santander, España: Sal Terrae, 1983.

Galilea, Segundo, and Juan Díaz-Vilar. *Servir como Jesús.* 2d ed. New York: Northeast Catholic Pastoral Center for Hispanics, 1986.

John Paul II. *Centesimus Annus.* Washington, DC: USCC, 1991.

———. *Laborem Exercens.* Washington, DC: USCC, 1981.

———. *Sollicitudo Rei Socialis.* Washington, DC: USCC, 1987.

John XXIII. *Mater et Magistra.* New York: Missionary Society of St. Paul the Apostle, 1961.

———. *Pacem in Terris.* Huntington, IN: Our Sunday Visitor, 1963.

Leo XIII. *Rerum Novarum.* New York: Paulist Press, 1931.

Paul VI. *Octagesima Adveniens.* Washington, DC: USCC, 1971.

———. *Populorum Progressio.* Washington, DC: USCC, 1967.

Pius XI. *Quadragesimo Anno.* Chicago: Outline Press, 1947.

Synod of Bishops, Second General Assembly. *Justice in the World.* Washington, DC: USCC, 1972.

Chapter 7:
The Journey of Hispanic Youth Ministry

Notes

Epigraph: Secretariat for Hispanic Affairs, USCC, *Prophetic Voices: The Document on the Process of the III Encuentro Nacional Hispano de Pastoral* (Washington, DC: USCC, 1986), 17.

1. Secretariat for Hispanic Affairs, USCC, *Proceedings of the II Encuentro Nacional Hispano de Pastoral* (Washington, DC: USCC, 1978), 71.

2. Ibid., 69.

3. Amelia M. Muñoz, "Hispanic Youth/Young Adult Evangelization Project: Final Report" (Secretariat for Hispanic Affairs, USCC, Washington, DC, 1984, photocopy).

4. Comité Nacional Hispano de Pastoral Juvenil, Memo to Archbishop Robert F. Sánchez, 5 April 1984 (Secretariat for Hispanic Affairs, USCC, Washington, DC, filed memorandum).

5. USCC, *Prophetic Voices*, 6.

6. Carmen María Cervantes, "Survey on Hispanic Youth Ministry in the United States," *Building Our Hope* 4 (Winter 1991): 7–9.

7. John Eagleson and Philip Scharper, eds., *Puebla and Beyond* (Maryknoll, NY: Orbis Books, 1979), no. 1166; originally published as *Puebla: La evangelización en el presente y en el futuro de América Latina*, by CELAM (Washington, DC: NCCB, 1979).

8. Paul VI, *Evangelii Nuntiandi* (Washington, DC: USCC, 1975), no. 14.

9. Ibid., no. 76.

10. Editorial Advisory Board, Saint Mary's Press Project for Hispanic Youth Ministry, "Our Consultation Meeting: A Step Forward," *Building Our Hope* 2 (January 1989): 3.

Additional Resources

Arroyo, Antonio M. Stevens. *Prophets Denied Honor: An Anthology on the Hispanic Church of the United States.* Maryknoll, NY: Orbis Books, 1980.

Bagley, Ron, ed. *Young Adult Ministry: A Book of Readings.* Naugatuck, CT: Youth Ministry Resource Network, Center for Youth Ministry Development, 1987.

CELAM. *La Iglesia en la actual transformación de América Latina a la luz del Concilio.* 4th ed. Bogotá, Colombia: CELAM, 1970.

Davis, Kenneth. "U.S. Hispanic Catholics: Trends and Recent Works," *Review for Religious* (Saint Louis, MO) (March–April 1991): 290–297.

Mexican American Cultural Center. *Fronteras: A History of the Latin American Church in the USA Since 1513.* San Antonio, TX: Mexican American Cultural Center, 1983.

NCCB. *The Hispanic Presence: Challenge and Commitment.* Washington, DC: USCC, 1984.

NFCYM. *The Challenge of Adolescent Cathechesis: Maturing in Faith.* Washington, DC: NFCYM, 1986.

————. *Competency-Based Standards for the Coordinator of Youth Ministry.* Washington, DC: NFCYM, 1990.

Office of Pastoral Research. *Church-Related Hispanic Youth in New York: An Exploratory Study.* New York: Office of Pastoral Research, 1983.

U.S. Catholic Historian. *Hispanic Catholics: Historical Explorations and Cultural Analysis.* Hanover, PA: U.S. Catholic Historical Society, 1989.

Warren, Michael, ed. *Readings and Resources in Youth Ministry.* Winona, MN: Saint Mary's Press, 1987.

Chapter 8:
Models of Organization in Hispanic Youth Ministry

Notes

Epigraph: John Paul II, *Christifideles Laici* (Washington, DC: USCC, 1988), no. 46.

1. NCCB, *The Hispanic Presence: Challenge and Commitment* (Washington, DC: USCC, 1984), 27.

Additional Resources

Ahumada, José E. "Inculturation Challenges Religious Education: Toward Faith Formation Programs Serving the Evangelization of Cultures." Master's thesis, Jesuit School of Theology, Berkeley, CA, 1991.

Archdiocese of Los Angeles, Office of Religious Education. *Recursos para el proceso de preparación para la confirmación 1992.* Los Angeles: Office of Religious Education, Archdiocese of Los Angeles, 1992.

Bagley, Ron, ed. *Young Adult Ministry: A Book of Readings.* Naugatuck, CT: Youth Ministry Resource Network, Center for Youth Ministry Development, 1987.

Bestard Comas, Joan. *El consejo pastoral parroquial: Cómo dinamizar una parroquia.* Madrid, España: Promoción Popular Cristiana, 1989.

Boff, Leonardo. *Eclesiogénesis: Las comunidades de base reinventan la iglesia.* Santander, España: Editorial Sal Terrae, 1980.

Bravo Pérez, Benjamín. *Cómo revitalizar la parroquia,* México, DF: Parroquia de Sta. Ma. Magdalena, 1985.

————. *Preparación a los procesos de conversión: Precatecumenado.* 10th ed. México, DF: Parroquia de Sta. Ma. Magdalena, 1992.

Centro Nacional Salesiano de Pastoral Juvenil. *El acompañamiento espiritual de los jóvenes.* Madrid, España: Editorial CCS, 1985.

————. *La animación, opción pedagógica y evangelizadora.* Madrid, España: Editorial CCS, 1990.

————. *Catequistas jóvenes.* Madrid, España: Editorial CCS, 1988.

————. *Tiempo de ocio creativo.* Madrid, España: Editorial CCS, 1990.

CELAM. *Pastoral juvenil: Sí a la civilización del amor.* 2d ed. México, DF: CEM, Comisión Episcopal Mexicana de Pastoral Juvenil, 1989.

Díaz-Vilar, Juan. *Parroquia comunidad misionera.* New York: Northeast Catholic Pastoral Center for Hispanics, 1983.

Ekstrom, Reynolds R., and John Roberto. *Access Guide to Evangelization.* New Rochelle, NY: Salesian Society/Don Bosco Multimedia, 1989.

Equipo de Consiliarios CVX Berchmans. *La iglesia: Catecumenado para universitarios—2.* Santander, España: Editorial Sal Terrae, 1983.

Johnson, Jeffrey. "Young Life Ministry: Room for Catholic Lay Ministers." In *Readings and Resources for Youth Ministry,* ed. Michael Warren. Winona, MN: Saint Mary's Press, 1987.

McDonald, William. "Reports on the Investigation on the Pastoral Needs of Hispanic Youth." Research conducted for Saint Mary's Press, Winona, MN, 1987, typescript.

Movilla, Secundino. *Catecumenando juvenil de confirmación.* 2d ed. Madrid, España: Editorial CCS, 1985.

NCCB. *The Parish in Transition.* Washington, DC: USCC, 1985.

Pablo, Valentín de. *Juventud, iglesia y comunidad.* Madrid, España: Promoción Popular Cristiana, 1985.

Sánchez García, Urbano. *La opción del cristiano.* Vol. 3. Colección Síntesis. Madrid, España: Sociedad de Educación Atenas, 1986.

Saravia, Javier. *Comunidades en camino.* México, DF: Centro de Reflexión Teológica, 1989.

Schineller, Peter. *National Survey on Hispanic Ministry.* Washington, DC: USCC, 1990.

Secretariat for Hispanic Affairs, USCC. *Proceedings of the II Encuentro Nacional Hispano de Pastoral.* Washington, DC: USCC, 1978.

USCC. *Prophetic Voices: The Document on the Process of the III Encuentro Nacional Hispano de Pastoral.* Washington, DC: USCC, 1986.

———. *A Vision of Youth Ministry.* Washington, DC: USCC, 1986.

"Vatican Report on Sects, Cults and New Religious Movements." *Origins* 16 (22 May 1986): 1–10.

Vecchi, Juan E. *Ambientes para la pastoral juvenil.* Madrid, España: Editorial CCS, 1991.

———. *Un proyecto de pastoral juvenil en la Iglesia de hoy.* Madrid, España: Editorial CCS, 1990.

———, and José M. Prellezo. *Proyecto educativo pastoral.* Madrid, España: Promoción Popular Cristiana, 1986.

Warren, Michael. *Faith, Culture, and the Worshiping Community.* Mahwah, NJ: Paulist Press, 1989.

———. *Youth, Gospel, Liberation.* San Francisco: Harper and Row, 1989.

———, ed. *Readings and Resources in Youth Ministry.* Winona, MN: Saint Mary's Press, 1987.

———, ed. *Source Book for Modern Catechetics.* Winona, MN: Saint Mary's Press, 1983.

Final Reflection

Notes

1. NCCB Secretariat of the Committee for the Church in Latin America, *Santo Domingo Conclusions: New Evangelization, Human Development, Christian Culture* (Washington DC: USCC, 1993), no. 24; original Spanish-language text copyright © 1992 by CELAM.

❦ Glossary ❦

Acculturation. A process that takes place when two or more cultures enter into direct contact; both the people involved and the cultures themselves are transformed, usually by adapting to or borrowing traits from one another, but without totally losing their own culture. *See also* **enculturation; endoculturation; inculturation; socialization.**

Acompañamiento, acompañante. Activities, attitudes, and the behaviors used by peers, leaders, ministers, and pastoral agents to guide, support, and motivate young people in their Christian journey. An *acompañante* is the person who fulfills this role.

Agentes de cambio. Literally, "agents of change." Persons who, consciously and intentionally, display a lifestyle and act concretely to produce a specific transformation in society or church.

Animation, *animadores*. Animation describes the role and attitude of a leader in a small ecclesial community, apostolic movement, youth group, parish program, or specific ecclesial activity. Animation involves motivating each person and the whole community, facilitating the community's prayer life, nurturing hospitality and mutual care among members, and sustaining the community in times of difficulty. This role extends to the whole life of the community; it is not limited to meetings. People who fulfill this role are called *animadores* (animators) and are different from coordinators, whose role is to facilitate the meetings of the community. *Animadores* need a certain charisma and appropriate training to succeed in their role.

Antagonism. Substantial or habitual opposition to a group of people, a principle, an ideology, or a political position that often leads to hostility between factions.

Anthropology, anthropological. The study of human beings—their origin; history; culture; physical characteristics; social, political, and economic dimensions; relationship with the divine; and so on.

Antivalues, disvalues. Concepts used in Latin American philosophy and in Spanish philosophy to identify values that are against God and the dignity of the human person.

Autonomy, autonomous. A person's capacity to assume responsibility for, and give direction to, his or her life. Autonomy does not imply separation or independence from one's broader community; rather, within a community, it implies respect for the self-direction and moral freedom of others, and a responsible interdependence.

Caciquismo, caciquista. Oppressive, abusive, and tyrannical system created by people in positions of power over others, particularly over those who are economically or politically dependent on powerful people. Hispanics in the United States, especially immigrant workers, most often suffer *caciquismo* under the *capataces* and *mayordomos* (forepersons or overseers) in agricultural and industrial work.

Cariño. An affectionate feeling characterized by tenderness, empathy, caring, and warmth.

Catechesis. An educational process by which people are instructed in the Christian faith according to the Catholic Tradition and are assisted in reflecting on their life in light of their faith in order to mature as Christians, become authentic disciples of Jesus, and live the Gospel.

Charisma. The gift of the Holy Spirit to be used for service to individuals and communities, in view of the formation of the Body of Christ and the building of the Reign of God.

Chemical dependency. An illness acquired by the intoxication of a person with a chemical substance. It has direct effects in disrupting the mental functioning, psychomotor performance, and social behavior of the person. *See also* **codependency.**

Christian discernment. A personal or communitarian process of reflection from a faith perspective to discover God's will, used when facing various life situations that require decision making.

Christology. The theological understanding, study, and interpretation of the person and mission of Jesus.

Cliques. Narrow, exclusive, and *closed* circles or groups of persons held together by common interests, views, or purposes.

Codependency. An unhealthy situation in which one person in a relationship suffers from a psychiatric illness, chemical dependency, or behavioral problems, and those close to the dependent person create defense mechanisms in order to survive in a dysfunctional relationship. *See also* **chemical dependency.**

Communitarian. A description meaning "related to a community." For Hispanics, a community is always formed by persons and not by individuals. The community is not a simple accumulation of individuals, but a reality that exists as a result of the interrelationships among its members. In Hispanic conceptual terms, a person cannot exist outside of a community, because it is the community that validates a person as a human being.

Compadres, comadres. People who form family-type social relationships in Hispanic culture by becoming godparents to people's children. The relationship between the godparents of a child and the child's parents is called *compadrazgo*. A *compadre* is a godfather; a *comadre* is a godmother. *Compadres* and *comadres* are members of the extended family.

Compañeros. People joined to mutually support and assist one another, to accompany one another in certain activities, or to journey together in a particular aspect of life. *Compañeros* differ from friends in that *compañeros* do not necessarily forge strong personal ties or share their whole lives with one another. And they differ from *acompañantes* in that *acompañantes* usually have a higher level of maturity and experience than the person they accompany in their journey of faith. Loyalty, understanding, respect, and interest in one another's well-being characterize *compañeros*.

Conscientization. The process by which people: (*a*) become critically aware of the cultural, social, economic, political, and religious aspects of their life, and (*b*) acquire a commitment to change those things that go against the dignity of the human person.

Consumerism. A viewpoint that considers individuals and communities as instruments of production and objects of consumption. Also, a strong tendency to always produce more, buy more, and have more.

Convivencia. In a general sense, sharing and celebrating life with other people. In pastoral ministry, events or meetings that build or strengthen friendship, understanding, and community among the participants.

Cooperaciones. Cooperative efforts by family members and friends who collect monetary aid, food, clothing, or other articles for someone facing an unexpected financial need.

Cultural dynamics. The patterns of development and change shown by cultures, including the forces that cause the development or change.

Defense mechanism. An intellectual or emotional reaction to a problem that allows people to avoid fully confronting the problem, especially if the problem threatens a fundamental belief or state of being.

Dueño de sí mismo. Literally, "owner of oneself," a concept that in English may have a business connotation. In Spanish, *dueño de sí mismo* corresponds to the psychological definition of freedom. The concept specifically encompasses self-knowledge, self-acceptance, and self-possession—three elements that form the foundation for a person's conscious and responsible exercise of freedom.

Ecumenical councils. Worldwide official gatherings of church leaders. In the Catholic church, meetings of the bishops, summoned by the pope, to deliberate and decide on doctrinal, moral, or pastoral matters and to provide direction to the church. The Second Vatican Council (1962–65) marked the beginning of an era of strong church renewal based on the Scriptures and on efforts to relate faith to modern culture.

Ecumenism. Efforts of various Christian churches to find unity among all Christians. From the perspective of the churches, ecumenism involves a constant renewal in order to be more faithful to their vocation; a conversion of heart to heal and avoid further divisions; common prayer for the unity of all Christians; better mutual knowledge and dialog among theologians and the faithful; collaboration in the various fields of social service; and an ecumenical formation of all members of the church, especially ordained ministers.

Encuentros Nacionales Hispanos de Pastoral. National meetings officially convened by the United States Catholic Conference of Bishops, at which leaders, participants, and pastoral agents gather, after conducting an organized process of pastoral needs assessment and theological reflection, to determine direction, coordination, and support for Hispanic ministry. There have been three Encuentros Nacionales to date—in 1971, 1976–77, and 1982–85. The Segundo (second) and Tercer (third) Encuentros encouraged active participation and pastoral-theological reflection by laypeople at the grassroots level, and encuentros at the diocesan, regional, and national level.

Enculturation. The process by which people acquire their culture, both at home and in society. *See also* **acculturation; endoculturation; inculturation; socialization.**

Endoculturation. The process by which people acquire their culture at home through sharing the values, beliefs, and traditions that are lived and taught in the family, especially by their parents. *See also* **acculturation; enculturation; inculturation; socialization.**

Euthanasia. The act or practice of putting to death incurable or terminally ill patients painlessly. Also called "mercy killing," euthanasia is rejected in traditional Judeo-Christian belief.

Evangelization. Implies a continuous, lifelong process of conversion by which a Christian makes an ever-deepening effort to establish a personal and communal relationship with Jesus and a commitment to live Jesus' message—the Gospel—and to continue his mission of bringing about the Reign of God. *See also* **New evangelization.**

Existential. The word existential has a down-to-earth meaning among Hispanics. To speak about the existence of a person is to refer to his or her whole life, particularly as related to the circumstances in which he or she lives.

Functionalist attitudes. Attitudes and behaviors that respond to a particular situation in a practical way without having as a frame of reference a worldview and a values system.

Fundamentalist. One who follows a movement emphasizing the literal interpretation of the Scriptures without considering the literary style, the historical context, and the intentions of the authors who wrote the Scriptures.

Hedonism. Doctrine that affirms that pleasure or happiness are the most important goods or goals in life.

Heterogeneous. Refers to something made up of a diversity of elements, such as groups made up of people with different characteristics.

Hispanic, Latino. These two terms are being used interchangeably in this book to refer to people originating from Caribbean countries, Latin America, and Spain, where the Spanish language and culture predominate, and their descendants in the United States, who may speak English or Spanish.

Holistic, integral. Terms that emphasize the totality of the human person and the interconnectedness of people's many dimensions—physical, psychological, religious, cultural, and so on.

Homogeneous. Refers to something composed of similar elements or to groups made up of people with similar characteristics.

Idiosincrasia. The psychological traits and culture embedded in the personality and "way of being" of a particular person or ethnic group.

Inculturation. The infusion of the Gospel within a culture to such an extent that the culture is reshaped and embraces Jesus' message and mission as its central guiding principle. *See also* **acculturation; enculturation; endoculturation; socialization.**

Indígenas. Indigenous or native people who lived in America before the arrival of Europeans; also, present-day descendants of the indigenous people who have not become *mestizos* in race or culture.

Integral education. Holistic education that includes the emotional, social, intellectual, spiritual, and skills domains at the personal level, and the cultural, economic, social, political, and religious areas at the structural level.

Mañanitas. Special serenades given at dawn for a loved person on his or her birthday or feast day (the day dedicated to his or her patron saint). Mexicans have a long-standing tradition of bringing *mañanitas* to the Virgin of Guadalupe on her feast day—usually around four o'clock in the morning—and following these serenades with a communitarian celebration and breakfast before going off to work.

Materialism. A theory that physical matter is the only or fundamental reality and that all beings, processes, and phenomena can be exclusively explained as manifestations or results of matter. Also refers to assigning an absolute value or a very high value to material progress.

Mestizaje. The intermingling between people from two different races or cultures that gives birth to a new people. Usually, the Hispanic culture in Latin America is identified as the "first *mestizaje*" and the Latino–North American culture in the United States as the "second *mestizaje*."

Mestizo, mestiza. These terms refer broadly to people whose parents or ancestors are from different racial groups. Used in a narrower, more specific sense, they refer to children of Spanish and *indígena* parents. *Mestizo* designates a male and *mestiza* designates a female. Used as an adjective, *mestizo* ("mixed") also describes the new people, and *mestiza* the new culture, formed from the intermingling of different races or cultures.

Ministry. Specific service to people and communities in response to a personal vocation on behalf of the church community, officially recognized and sponsored by the diocese or parish. *See also* **pastoral action; pastoral agents;** *pastoral de conjunto;* **pastoralists; pastoral planning; youth and young adult ministers.**

Mística. A set of ideals, attitudes, values, and feelings that enlighten and motivate individuals or groups in their faith journey, inspiring their response to God and producing a spirituality that animates their life and pastoral ministry.

Modern culture. In a strict sense, modern culture refers to the period between the eighteenth and twentieth centuries when the Industrial Revolution gave way to a new social, economic, and political order that affected all aspects of human life, especially through science, technology, democracy, capitalism, and secularization. In this book, modern culture is used in a broader sense to refer to the type of culture that has incorporated these elements as essential parts. *See also* **traditional culture.**

Moral relativism. A view affirming that ethical truths depend on the preferences of individuals and groups, negating the existence of objective and general norms of behavior based on Christian moral principles.

New evangelization. A call to conversion and hope that rests on God's promises and derives from Christ's Resurrection, which is the primary proclamation and the root of all evangelization, the foundation for all human advancement, and the principle of all genuine Christian cultures. It is likewise the effort to inculturate the Gospel in order to respond to the new situation people are facing as a result of the social and cultural changes of modernity.

Novios. Men and women who are in a love relationship that they expect will lead to marriage in the future. *Novios* are in a particular stage in a love relationship, a stage called *noviazgo. Noviazgo* includes two phases: going steady with a commitment not to date other people, and being *prometidos* (engaged persons), with a set date for marriage and practical preparations to establish a home.

Occultism. A belief in mysterious, spiritualist doctrines and practices to explain and control the supernatural phenomena of life.

Pastoral action. Organized ecclesial activity to facilitate and nurture the Christian growth of persons and communities, promoting their missionary action to foster the Reign of God. See also **ministry; pastoral agents;** *pastoral de conjunto;* **pastoralists; pastoral planning; youth and young adult ministers.**

Pastoral agents. Persons who, in responding to their vocation and as members of a church community, have a commitment to the mission of the church in the area of pastoral ministry.

Pastoral de conjunto. The action of all pastoral agents, ministers, and committed Christians—each in her or his own specific ministry—animated and directed by a common vision and coordinated in a spirit of communion and coresponsibility. Broadly, the harmonious coordination of all elements, ministries, and structures of the local and universal church in their work of bringing about the Reign of God.

Pastoralists. Persons with professional formation, practical skills, and experience in the field of pastoral ministry who are capable of doing pastoral planning, conducting pastoral-theological reflections, and elaborating theories for the development of pastoral ministry.

Pastoral planning. Effective organization of the church's action in fulfilling the mission of being leaven of the Reign of God in the world.

Pastoral-theological framework. Theological and pastoral guidelines originating from a specific vision and understanding of church. In this series, the framework is based on the Second Vatican Council's vision of church and on the pastoral guidelines of the *National Pastoral Plan for Hispanic Ministry.*

Person. In English, there is a frequent tendency to equate the words *person* and *personal* with the word *individual.* In the Hispanic philosophical framework, individual refers to the human characteristic of being a unique person; *individualista* (individualistic) refers to a human being in isolation, in himself or herself only. *Person* refers to the human being in himself or herself and in relationship with others.

Popular Catholicism. The set of Catholic beliefs and practices characteristic of the majority of Catholic persons in a particular culture. Hispanic popular Catholicism is usually influenced by either an *indígena* or African religious perspective and culture. Most forms of popular Catholicism are complex and diverse in their expressions and have different levels of coherence with official Catholicism.

Popular (pop) culture. Refers to the general culture of the United States when emphasizing that instead of being an expression of people's life, it is intentionally created for people's consumption. Pop culture is formed through the economic system and the mass media, which promote values that degrade the human person and nurture materialistic, superficial, and changeable attitudes toward others.

Popular religiosity. A set of religious beliefs, experiences, and celebrations that form the individual and collective consciousness with which a people perceive, feel, and live the mysteries of God. *See also* **religiosidad.**

Posadas. Nightly celebrations that precede Christmas and include a procession to nine different houses, asking for lodging for Mary and Joseph; reciting the rosary or other devotional prayers; the breaking of a piñata (a big papier maché figure filled with fruit, candy, and party favors); and food and organized games for children. People of all ages participate in *posadas.*

Positivism. A philosophical school of thinking based on the idea that knowledge of truth is based only on scientific description and explanation of measurable data.

Praxis. A Latin word that translates literally as "practice" or "action." Christian praxis involves people's discipleship and their critical reflection about their actions—all in light of the Gospel.

Prophetic pastoral guidelines. Pastoral-theological principles agreed on in the Tercer Encuentro Nacional Hispano de Pastoral to set the direction and spirit of Hispanic ministry.

Proselytism. The attempt to convert followers from one church or religious group to another, often through direct and aggressive attacks of their beliefs. *See also* **proselytizing sects.**

Proselytizing sects. Independent religious groups proclaiming that they are the only ones who will achieve salvation and whose methods to win followers are based on proselytism. *See also* **proselytism.**

Pseudoreligious groups. People united by some beliefs and rituals related to the transcendental dimension of life, but not necessarily to God as the source and goal of human beings.

Reality. A holistic concept that encompasses the life experience of a person, the concrete environment in which he or she lives, and the active influence of the economy, government, culture, religion, and educational institutions on the person.

Reign of God. Jesus' vision of God's primacy in people's hearts, minds, and actions; also, a state in which all personal relationships and social systems are guided by freedom, justice, peace, and God's love.

Religiosidad. A broad concept that includes the natural tendency of people toward the divine; their relationship with God and with the sacred world; the religious environment in which they live; and their concrete religious beliefs and experiences.

Religious syncretism. A process that integrates two or more religious systems with the aim of uniting their doctrines, rites, and experiences to harmonize them with the life and culture of the group.

Santería. The worship of African gods under the appearance of Catholic saints, resulting from the cultural and religious acculturation of the Caribbean people.

Satanism. An obsession with or affinity for evil, usually expressed in a cult of Satan, characterized by a parody of Christian rites and directed toward extreme cruelty or viciousness.

Secularism. A belief that rejects or is indifferent toward religion; considers the construction of history as a sole responsibility of the human being, without a place for God's intervention; is a threat to faith and culture; and promotes divorce between faith and life. *See also* **secularization.**

Secularization. A process linked to the development of science, technology, and urbanization maintaining that the material realities of nature and humanity are in themselves "good," that their laws should be respected, and that God respects the human freedom needed for self-realization. Secularism affirms the autonomy of science and art from religion, leads to sociocultural progress, and fosters the universalization of culture. The church views secularization as a process that challenges faith and presents serious pastoral problems. *See also* **secularism.**

Signs of the times. Different situations that characterize the reality of life in a particular place and time and that challenge Christians to discern God's will and act accordingly.

Small ecclesial communities. A way of being and living as church in which small groups of people have direct interpersonal relationships, share their faith with a constant spirit of prayer, unite with other small communities, participate in their local church, and are signs of Christ in the world.

Small youth communities. Small communities of young people and young adults.

Socialization. Process by which persons acquire their culture through society. *See also* **acculturation; enculturation; endoculturation; inculturation.**

Traditional culture. Refers to the culture of a population segment or a particular person characterized for having a worldview, values, and ways of economic production and socialization that were typical before the generalization of modern culture in Europe, North America, and more developed sectors of other countries. *See also* **modern culture.**

Voodoo. A religion derived from African ancestor worship and characterized by rites of appeasement and by communication with animistic deities through trances.

Youth and young adult ministers. Persons in a diocese or parish who are responsible for the pastoral care of youth and young adults. *See also* **ministry; pastoral action; pastoral agents;** *pastoral de conjunto;* **pastoralists; pastoral planning.**

❧ Index ❧

A

abuse, sexual, 35, 42, 54, 56, 225
acculturation, 81, 90, 263; historic waves of, 81–84; negative reactions to, 84–85; positive reactions to, 85–86; process of, 81–86
activities, planning of, 21
Ad Gentes (*Decree on the Church's Missionary Activity*, Pope Paul VI), 163
adolescence, concept of, 27
adolescents, 22–23; Hispanic, 14, 26–32
adulthood, young, 32–34
advertising, 80. *See also* mass media
affirmative action, 100
African Americans, 82, 83, 84, 100, 103, 106, 164, 168
agents, pastoral, 20
agents of change (*agentes de cambio*), 32, 34, 204, 236, 238, 263
agents of history, 85, 86, 162, 166
AIDS, 37, 68, 162
alcohol abuse, 54, 55, 63, 225
alienation, 20, 21, 59, 126–127, 151
Americanization, 82, 84–85, 90

animation, concept of, 14, 263
annexation, political, 82
anthropology, Christian, 263; responses to societal challenges, 150; three pillars of, 144–145
anticommunism, 144
antivalues, 25, 264
apostolic movements, 147, 196, 197, 226, 234; compared with youth groups, 210, 211, 212, 219; description of, 218–221; importance of follow-up in, 221; leadership training in, 220; origins of, 192; three levels of participation in, 219–220
armaments, expenditures on, 111–112
Asian Americans, 84, 100
assimilation, 84–85, 86, 90, 104
attitudes, sexual, 65–66
authority, respect for church, 129, 133

B

baptism, 129
basic ecclesial communities. *See* small communities
belonging, sense of, 125–126
biculturalism, 90–91

D

E

I

J

Y

❧ Permissions ❧

♦ Prophets of Hope ♦

Volume 2

Evangelization of Hispanic Young People

Contents

You may order this companion volume from your local religious bookstore or from Saint Mary's Press, 702 Terrace Heights, Winona, MN 55987-1320, USA, 1-800-533-8095